THE CULTURE OF VIOLENCE

THE CULTURE
OF VIOLENCE
Tragedy and history

Francis Barker

Manchester University Press

Published by Manchester University Press
Oxford Road, Manchester M13 9PL, UK

British Library Cataloguing-in-Publication Data
A catalogue record for this book is available from the British Library

ISBN 0-7190-3850-2 *hardback*
ISBN 0-7190-4116-3 *paperback*

Set in Scala
by Koinonia Ltd, Manchester
Printed in Great Britain
by Bell & Bain Ltd, Glasgow

To the memory of my brother Matthew

Beyond plight and time

1967–1987

Contents

PREFACE AND ACKNOWLEDGEMENTS   *page*   VIII

PART ONE   SIGNS OF INVASION

             1 The information of the absolute   3
             2 Nietzsche's cattle   93

PART TWO   VIOLENCE AND INTERPRETATION

             1 In the wars of Truth   121
             2 A wilderness of tigers   143

PART THREE   TRACES

             1 Tragedy and the ends of history   209

BIBLIOGRAPHY   235

INDEX   249

Preface and acknowledgements

Throughout the period of Western modernity, since the Enlightenment certainly, and arguably since the Renaissance, it has been customary to think of culture and violence as antithetical terms. This book takes another view. As it moves backwards and forwards between the problems of the historical interpretation of early modern culture, and the contemporary theoretical implications of those problems under conditions of modernity and postmodernity, the linking thematic of the volume is the contention that, contrary to post-Enlightenment humanist, liberal, and conservative theory, 'culture' does not necessarily stand in humane opposition to political power and social inequality, but may be profoundly in collusion with it, not the antidote to generalised violence, but one of its more seductive strategies. This may also be true of much recent 'critical theory'. Indeed, the overall aim of the book is not only to illuminate aspects of early modern culture, and to address imbrications of the 'cultural' text with the drives and the mechanisms of social and political power, but also to conduct a critique of some recent cultural theory for its insufficient attention to the part that culture plays in social domination, and the ways in which that complicity itself has tended either to be occluded or at best inadequately engaged.

The principal textual focus is Shakespeare (although Milton and Hobbes are also discussed in Part Two). Or rather, it is 'Shakespeare', a cultural formation which has come in recent years to be a site on which important debates have been conducted, theoretical ideas and interpretative strategies formulated and explored, and political positions marked out – not least those concerning the whole theoretical question of historicism and historicity. It is to an intervention in this field of questioning that the work here is devoted.

But if this is not – as ultimately it isn't – a book about Shakespeare, I should also say that its method is not empirical. In general, the work seeks to rise, in the manner of an anatomy, from the abstract to the concrete, beginning with textual readings and ending by addressing the conditionality of the present. But its process is not wholly linear. This book is composed of essays, written over a period of time and grouped in three semi-autonomous Parts. Each has its own integrity, as well as a role to play in fashioning the overall positions of the volume. Indeed, in making the book from essays – a strategy I have found both practical and enabling – an aim inheres in the form: my views are advanced on the particular pages below, but are also intended to be inscribed in the inductive and, I hope, dynamic structure of the inexplicit relations among the parts of the whole. In a similar way, I have preferred, especially in Part One, the situated use of a critical lexicon over formal introductions and definitions. Terms emerge, relatively uninflected at first (and doubtless with intended resonances which are not as yet apparent): eventually, I trust, they deepen their theoretical purchase somewhat. Things are not finalised at once; connections and contrasts are intended, and doubtless also unintended, among figures, ideas and arguments which are not immediately adjacent to each other. The book contains several elements of a reading of the ontology of tragedy (and, indeed, of 'theory'), but it is not a genetic study; 'violence' is a critical as well as a descriptive term; historicity is glimpsed in virtual effects and traces, but rarely 'in person'. And so on. The conceptual process is recursive, rather than sequential; the form synthetic and cumulative, rather than encyclopaedic.

In this and other ways, the design seeks to articulate something of the main underlying argument, as it rejects the filled time of positivism and historicism. It is my firm conviction, argued explicitly (and implicit in the shape of what follows) that just as historical temporality is not singular or monovalent, so strategies of understanding must involve themselves – howsoever I may have achieved this aim myself – in the complex parallaxes of movement among cultures and historical conjunctures, and in an intricate dialectic of theory and history.

To this end, the focus is finally widened, in Part Three, to raise the discussion of the particular forms of contemporary historicism and culturalism to another level of generality – that of the alleged postmodern 'condition' itself. Here a critique is required to be conducted as well by methods of parody, scorn and involution as by those of argument. Postmodernism, like all historicisms, has a single face, but wears two masks. One appears to stare into a future before whose advent it cannot but be at once curiously passive and egregiously triumphalist. Seeking the neutralisation of enemies, it bridges the abyss of the unknowability of times to come by a wishful quelling of conflict in quasi-philosophical proclamations of flat emptiness, underpinned by boastful – doubtless fearsome, but also somewhat anxious and defensive – threats and reminders of economic power and military supremacy. It declares the end of history, and a new world order. While the other mask appears to glimpse at a past which it agrees it cannot know but only – often anecdotally – re-represent; disabling itself in advance as a critical force. It isn't really any wonder that a new historicism and the end of history emerge, as it were, back to back. The effect of this conjunction is a radical flattening of time, a bracketing out of tragedy, and a deracination of the historicity of past, present and future alike. It is to some of the forms, implications and consequences of such an emergency that this book attends.

Versions of material now represented in these essays were given as lectures, addresses, conference papers, and seminars in the period 1986–92. I am grateful to the many people who have contributed to the development of the work, by comment, questioning and discussion. In particular, I would like to acknowledge the following colleagues, and in many cases friends, who were first kind enough to invite me to speak, and then to engage, and often transform, what I had to say: Marion Campbell and Stephanie Trigg, and David Bennet, of the Department of English, University of Melbourne; Howard Felperin, then of the School of English and Linguistics, Macquarie University; Neil Lazarus, Department of English, Brown University; Jonathan Sawday and Tony Crowley, Department of English, University of Southampton; Peter de Bolla and Tony Tanner, King's College, Cambridge; Tadeusz Rachwał, Institute of English and General Linguistics, University of Silesia; Gordon McMullan, then of Wadham College, Oxford; Jeremy Tambling, Ackbar Abbas, Jonathan Hall and Anthony Tatlow, of the Department of Comparative Literature, University of Hong Kong; Neil Forsythe and Peter Halter of the Section d'anglais, Faculté des Lettres, Université de Lausanne; David Lee Miller, Sharon O'Dair and Harold Weber, and Diane Roberts, of the Department of English, University of Alabama, Tuscaloosa; Michael Cahn, Philosophische Fakultät, University of Konstanz; Sérgio Luis Prado Bellei and José Roberto O'Shea, Department of Foreign Languages and Literatures, Federal University of Santa Catarina, Brazil.

I would like to thank my fellow members of the Early Modern Research Group at Essex – Jerry Brotton, Maurizio Calbi, Al Constantine, Tracey Hill, Paula Hutchings, John Joughin, Angelica Michelis and Stephen Speed – for the stimulating and critical discussions which helped formulate the ideas and strategies of this book, and for the steadfast comradeship which has also shaped it. They are in real senses co-authors.

In the academic year 1988–89 Tracey Hill acted as my research assistant on this and other projects. I want to acknowledge her friendship, her hard work then and since, and in particular her contribution to the bibliographical background of what I have written. She was also kind enough to comment on sections of the manuscript; and she made the index.

I am grateful to Lucien and Christiane Briot who lent me their flat in Geneva when I needed a place to work; I would also like to thank my sister Pax, and her husband Tim Clark for giving me a quiet space in Manchester.

Elizabeth Weall helped at various stages of the preparation of the manuscript. John Drakakis and Michael Schoenfeldt read it sympathetically and critically, and their comments contributed valuably to its development for publication. I am grateful to them, and to Anita Roy, my publisher at Manchester University Press, for her efforts on the book's behalf and for her advice and encouragement during its preparation.

I would like to offer my warm thanks to four close colleagues in the Department of Literature at Essex. Gordon Brotherston, Herbie Butterfield, Peter Hulme and Jonathan White all contributed significantly to the production of this book, discussing the work, reading chapters or passages of draft, and giving generously of their friendship.

Finally, I wish to thank my wife Marijn, whose support throughout has been immense.

Francis Barker
University of Essex

Part One

SIGNS OF INVASION

1

THE INFORMATION OF THE ABSOLUTE

Lear, the greatest of the mature tragedies, it is said, appears to begin on sovereign ground, secure in a seemingly untroubled first horizon. If so, the map which Lear uses to situate the partition of the realm among his daughters and their present or putative husbands is suitably formed. As a chart of sovereign possession, the language of its representation is appropriately shaped as a discourse not of domination but of pastoral idealism, the form of an almost numinously ideal terrain. To Goneril it offers 'shadowy forests ... with champains rich'd, /With plenteous rivers and wide-skirted meads' (I.i.62–4), while Regan and her 'hereditary ever' can expect 'this ample third of our fair kingdom, /No less in space, validity and pleasure, /Than that conferr'd on Goneril ...' (I.i.78–81). The benign fullness of sovereignty is immanent in the shady, rich'd, plenteous, wide, ample space, in the validity and the pleasure.

But the representation of the land is neither stable nor unequivocal in the text of *Lear*. It is important to trace the formations and mutations of the land as it is variously transacted. These cartographies disclose something important in the substrata of the representation of sovereign power with which I am concerned. In any case, the map itself is already a field of struggle. It simulates the land in the game of speaking love which Lear stages among his daughters. Despite the tranquil pastoral of Lear's language of the land, it is already the focus of power and danger, and the site of peculiarly powered or impotent linguistic performances, which both mask and disclose the desire to possess the land itself. The map, and the land it obliquely represents, are caught up in a process of the dynastic transmission of territory – this is usually not seen clearly enough – and in a forcefield of language and desire, as well as of possession: 'Let it be so; thy truth then be thy dower ...' (I. i. 107). In all, it is a completely structured discourse of property, like the play itself. If the land is a place of fulsomeness and abundance, it is at the same moment one of ideal emptiness, a depopulated landscape. No one lives or works in the country-side of Lear's map, and from the point of view of those for whom there is space and validity, emptiness of at least the appearance of those whose labour supports their pleasure may even be a definition of the ideal. A brutal contest for territorial acquisition and possession is secreted in the performance of discourses of love, but this is facilitated in turn by a deracination in representation of the land itself, figured as an unproductive place, a part of 'hereditary ever', and naturally not the site of an exploited agrarian economy. But then, whatever degree of screen idealism attempts to shield and mystify the materialism of landed propriety, the map – and the realm, this pecu-liarly empty sovereign plenitude – is immediately torn apart, and the tragic action, or what I shall call the 'event', is underway.

With this begins the exile of Kent, Cordelia and, in a sense, Lear himself. And with this the nature of – the representation of – the land also changes radically. The 'champains' of the first scene are replaced by a reduced, dangerous and in some ways almost unmarked land. Initially it is a place of urgent or displaced journeying between citadels, fashioning a structure of insiding and outsiding by which scenes are played at the gates of castles seen as strong interiors from without, as Lear and his diminishing train, and others, travel between the new seats of power. This is the landscape in which watches and traps are set and around whose edges, at the ports, surveillance mounted: for Edgar, for example, 'No port is free; no place, /That guard, and most unusual vigilance, /Does not attend my taking' (II. iii. 3–5). This is a torn land where dangerous power is abroad, al-though as yet in the form of armed patrols rather than in that of the subsequent armies which will contend across and for the realm. It is a bleak and comfortless place, to be travelled over rather than resided in, injected with a force which must be in turn evaded by those sought or threatened. And then, in a further declination from sovereign representation, within this imago of the land is formed the desolate landscape of the heath, readable as a kind of absolute outside, more or less beyond not only the citadels, but the signs of civility as such. Journeys are made to or from the heath, but it is not itself a place of journeying but of wandering and even stasis, that static endurance of suffering which is such a common feature of the symbols of limit virtue in the drama of the period. If the land outside the citadel can be traced by journey or flight, the heath is truly barren, threatening complete erasure or amorphousness. No less dangerous than the unmarked land of journeying, there is in a strange way not so much pursuit here, as 'mere' reduction. The vulnerability is more an absolute condition than a present threat; or it is this as well. And the population that has been absent so far is found in the substitutional form of the motley crew of the displaced who assemble there, in the distress, and in the empathy and congruence of an apparently popular idiom in the language of the heath, with signs of the dispossessed.

The realm is no longer centred; power has been invested in decentres: and the last movement is in any case out to the periphery, the margin. From the heath at last journeys are made to the final killing ground near Dover where, in a further mutation, the form of the land changes again, into the theatre of war. At the rim of the land, with its charged cliffs and a shore-line wandered by the blind and the mad of the old order – for the text has its historiography – the gathering of the dangers and dislocations so far, turns what was once a sovereign and ideal land into the scene of invasion, and the ground of battle. Sovereignty irredeemably violated, the reduced king is killed, in a kind of *de facto* pacification – of the realm and the text.

There is no sovereign plenitude in this mutable topography; and even the pacification is equivocal as a form of closure.

The form of the land is not exactly in the foreground of the habitual discussions of *Lear*. Indeed, it has to be a work almost of rewriting to bring the land, and the matter of the land, into focus. At best it is the subject of a double formation. This is not just a question of the text's oscillation between land as property and its symbolic value as realm, as metonym for the sovereign and component of its representation – and of the way in which saving equivocations between these are possible – but of another doubling as well. For in one sense *Lear* is about nothing but land, from the love-game at the beginning to the division of the spoils at the end, via, say, the problematics of Edmund's illegitimacy and the way in which that both empirical and metaphysical theme is imbricated with the tenure of the land: 'Well then, /Legitimate Edgar, I must have your land ...' (I. ii. 15–16). Yet at best it comes into focus and disappears again. Just as photographers will often manipulate what is called 'depth of field' in order to hide or diminish the significance of something which is unavoidable but undesirable in the subject they represent, so similar effects are achievable if not unavoidable in writing, and in *Lear* – and in its readings, certainly – there are faces in the foreground, as well as tiny figures in the middle and far distances of symbolic landscapes. But in *Lear's* outdoor portraiture, figures and faces are mostly brought into sharp relief against a background which blurs into insignificance. In the resulting pictures, which are fictions, pictorial and social (that is, historical), relations will have been established within the image and its context, and in the process meanings will have been articulated – and prevented – without the fact of their expression or suppression necessarily having been explicitly signalled.

At one level it is the political register of the text, including its incompleteness, which slips out of focus, present perhaps, but understated at best; even if in fact the political themes of the story can be stated quite simply. Gloucester's early fulmination against the 'ruinous disorders' of the present gives a very comprehensive account of perceived breakdown at every level of the political and social structure. If 'Love cools, friendship falls off', 'brothers divide' and the 'bond' is 'crack'd 'twixt son and father', no less is there 'in cities, mutinies; in countries, discord; in palaces, treason'. As 'the King falls from bias of nature ... We have seen the best of our time: machinations, hollowness, treachery, and all ruinous disorders follow us disquietly to our graves ... ' (I. ii. 103–14). 'Tis strange', he concludes, somewhat bathetically. Dissension in the royal house, a weakened and abdicated – if not in practice deposed – monarch, divided and unstable centres of power, all lay the country open to invasion, the figure which marks in various ways, and even in a subterranean fashion organises, each of the tragedies. Even if here the motive of the incursion is not, as the invading queen Cordelia claims, 'blown ambition' but that of restoring 'our ag'd father's right' (IV. iv. 23–8), instead of plentitude and integrity, nowhere, in *Lear*, is there any image of the wholeness and effectivity of the complete presence of the sovereign – in even this territorial sense – except perhaps in the very marginal trace of the ideal form of the initial map, or the language in which its signifiers are caught, and beyond that the desire that such a discourse of plenitude be sustainable. On the contrary, it is the story of a rapid deformation, and mutation of the land through patterns of tearing and emptiness, suffering and danger, which are *anything but* ideal accounts of sovereign territory sovereignly held, even if complex focusing of the depth of field serves to make the explicitness of the structure of this depredation indistinct.

To be sure, the foregrounding and backgrounding formation in *Lear* is not a merely cosmetic substitution of something blandly acceptable for something unacceptable – the depredations of what is sharply *in focus* are poignant enough, and much has been written about the violence, the despair, the misogyny, which the play either mobilises or represents. But whether it is thought of as tragic in the name of a kind of limit experience of suffering, or as the limit representation of such experience on the very borders of culture itself, or regarded as shading away into melodrama and histrionics, *Lear* nonetheless renders, in a certain way, an image of history. The role of the historical becomes symptomatic in the disturbed faces in the foreground, rather than being represented as it were 'in person'; and in that sense the text's performance of history is at least incomplete, foreshortened, if not actually mystified. Certainly the tradition has mainly tried to read the faces and the human forms. And this occlusion of the mutations of the form of the land as mutations of the representation of the sovereign territory (which is also a metaphor and a metonym of the king's sovereign, and therefore also palpably metaphorical, body – the tearing of the land *is* the tearing of this body), is probably what is at stake in this selective focus, even if it is also betrayed by and in the sharp, sometimes all too sharp, suffering of the play's 'individuals'.

In order to understand the quizzical viability of these figures in the foreground, it is necessary first to notice the interdependence of the land – its symbolism as realm and its invasion both empirical and metaphysical – with the various formations of identity and disidentity with which this text, and the tragedy more widely, are preoccupied. For if a story whose principal interest bears on the reading of a discourse that speaks of the land as – albeit equivocally – the site of the integrity of the realm, or about the politics of the representation of sovereignty and invasion, is not the story we familiarly read, either in Shakespeare or in the critical commentary on *Lear*, it is necessary to take into account instead another strategy of plenitude, another form – for it is only that – in which that sense of the ultimate transcendence of the play's project of sovereignty has been inscribed. It is the fullness attempted by the foregrounding of what has come to be called, in a deracination of the word, 'character'. Located in a grand symbolic framework which enables a supremely metaphysical discourse of man, nature, nothingness, suffering, error, redemption, and the rest, to be articulated, the hypostasisation of the individual has been, of course, a main support of discourses of mastery. And even quite radical appreciation of the tragedy, and of the figure of Lear in particular, has emphasised the pre-eminence of the play's treatment of individual integrity as the basis of its ethical and metaphysical explorations and assumptions, the centrepiece of its social and political doctrine.

One could argue that if we take the matter of character seriously, instead of a nobility exemplified in the endurance of suffering, what we find in fact in Lear – as is so often the case in this tradition – is a lack of self-knowledge feeding excesses of perplexed self-pity. It is certainly possible on occasion to have some sympathy with those who would silence him. But the foregrounded centrality – and the eponymous character of character – are undeniable. Indeed, under the forms of sovereignty, that it is Lear in *Lear* who is the focus and support of such a version of the centrality of the individual is not wholly unconnected with the way that kings – in some overt formal ways, and via a number of the subterranean conduits of the fabrication of sovereignty – are the types of characters: each offers to be that imaginary figure which in the unity of its presence, whether in cultural or political discourse, grounds the fixing of a conservative stability in the ideological formation and the social structure.

And yet, in *Lear*, rather than sovereign character, even as a literary figure, there is the insistence of figures not so much of full presence as equivocation. In, for example, the form of Kent in his internal exile in and from identity, and – to the extent that they share what is equivocal in 'him' – in the other residual figures of the play, the dispossessed of the text, is evinced a depredation rather than a plenitude of identity. Kent, consequent on the apparent rebellion and banishment which initiates his exile, survives through the history of the action disguised as another. His person-ality becomes question-able. Disguise is more than a convention here, it is a necessity and, paradoxically, a form of being, both more and less true than usual. He can only be what, as it were, he truly is, by not being himself. It is a condition of – to use one of those strange words whose meaning is identical with that of its opposite – dissimulation. Simulation and dissimulation are structural to *Lear's* representations, and especially to its thus damaged capacity to represent the authentic and the individual.

But it is important to see how the question of Kent turns not so much around being as a pure existential state, as on the possibility of a certain directness of speech; on the performability, in the event, of a discourse of truth about self and others. In disguise, self-definition becomes, of course, even more problematic than it normally is; perhaps doubly so if – this paradox or irony is persistent in Kent – it is one where a blunt plainness of speech is invoked as the definition itself. 'I can keep honest counsel', he says, 'ride, run, mar a curious tale in telling it, and deliver a plain message bluntly; that which ordinary men are fit for, I am qualified in, and the best of me is diligence' (I. iv. 32–5). But the tale Kent is telling is, in fact, a 'curious' one: an earl passing himself off as a serving-man nevertheless manages to sound the keynotes of plainness, service, diligence and ordinariness which even as it is not Kent who speaks, speaks the Kent that he always-already was. Those qualities of loyal service and plain speech – old-style qualities in the text's imaginary historiography – might be said to describe the 'real' Kent beneath the disguise, even if they served him ill in the emergency of Act I, and actually provoked his exile into the condition where now they must be once more asserted but are of necessity 'in disguise'. The problems of identity, in any case troublesome, are foregrounded in the exile which is truer than was the condition of the text's originary normality: 'If but as well I other accents borrow, /That can my speech defuse' he says,'my good intent /May carry through itself to that full issue /For which I raz'd my likeness.' (I. iv. 1–4) If a core of his 'real' self is suspended and prolonged in the project of his 'good intent', it is only on the basis of his *likeness* having been raz'd, of other accents borrowed, and on the condition of a *defused* speech. Defused, because at once deferred, disseminate and disarmed.

And yet this displacement is also ineluctable as a formation of identity. When urged at last by Cordelia to put off the false but true 'self', there is, along with a restatement of the paradox, a strange willingness to prolong this distance from himself: 'All my reports go with the modest truth, /No more nor clipp'd, but so .... /Yet to be known shortens my made intent /My boon I make it that you know me not' (IV. vii. 5–6, 9–10). Kent, rehearsing in now an undisguised voice, restates the plainness of the axiom of 'his' speech, but prolongs the disguised truth/identity further (although strangely without reason given – a lack of motivation in either the textual or the pseudo-psychological sense which may rather highlight the problematicity of identity than illuminate it): 'that you know me not' is the watchword of a voice that cannot be located easily. Who, after all, speaks?

But if there are perennial problems in the general *philosophy* of identity, and if – although this is less frequently acknowledged – the same problems perdure in the everyday life of identity (for if the alternative conception is one of ineffably pure being, are we not all in a sense disguised?), it is nonetheless worth focusing the fact that Kent's situation has a specific political contour: he has been banished, at several levels, by the King. Sent out from the sovereign presence, ordered beyond the symbolic frontier of the sovereign land, the realm, he is also displaced from his position in the sovereign order which defines identities – not exclusively, but not least – in terms of 'social' rank, with its attendant privileges and obligations. Not only is his current disguise in a sense enforced in the first place – significantly, the exile that necessitates it begins in the politics of the map and in his resistance to the division of the kingdom – but his encounters with the new powers in the land also turn on the paradoxes of the 'plain' speech of the identity of Kent-disguised. If in his blunt idiom there is something of the licensed fool, detached from the King that behaviour becomes vulnerable to the new powers, and loses its licence: the Kent whom Cornwall characterises as 'some fellow, /Who, having been prais'd for bluntness, doth affect /A saucy roughness' (II. ii. 92–4) gets short shrift. But at the same time power encounters a problem with him: Cornwall's perplexed 'What mean'st by this?' (II. ii. 105) is resonant in the context of Kent's turning over, as a kind of linguistic resistance, the paradoxes of a plain knave played off against a knave-like plainness: 'To go out of my dialect, which you discommend so much. I know, sir, I am no flatterer: he that beguil'd you in a plain accent was a plain knave; which for my part I will not be ... (II. ii. 105–9). Incomprehensible to a Cornwall – whose authority must then resort to violence: Kent is manacled in the stocks – these blunt paradoxes are an affront to that 'inauthentic' authority. Again, as much as on the content of what is duplicitously or ambiguously said, the matter turns on language or discourse in the conditional quality of its performable possibility as a feature of complex identity – if what I am describing can any longer be called identity at all – structured both by, and in distinction from, political authority. Identity is true when in allegiance; and yet dissembled in order to be in such a way true. If Kent is displaced in order to be *in place*, being in the proper place of allegiance to his master Lear means – in the actual, in the event of the play – being displaced. But being far from place and self in order to be in place and true not only to 'self' but to the bonds of authority and subordination, obligation and service of the old-order structure, one of whose principal bearers Kent is, then has important implications for the sovereignty of identity in the text. To emphasise again that what is represented here is not an *abstract* state of being, the conditions of possibility of performance are crucial. But 'old' identity – defined not least by those social and authority relations which are depicted as bonds of subordination, and not least to the sovereign – is *only* represented as performable – contrary, surely, to the expectations of the sovereign text – under conditions of displacement.

If Kent is first displaced, and then caught up in a problematic of impossible plain speaking, so too is Cordelia, if in almost a reverse situation. Where a glib plainness – lies – comes only too easily to her sisters, Cordelia can only plainly say *nothing* (even if this is 'plainly' said, in an aside ...). Hers is a saying – or a not-saying – which France links significantly both to history and, rather oddly in the diction of this speech but importantly nonetheless, to action: 'Is it but this? a tardiness in nature /Which often leaves the history unspoke /That it intends to do?' (I. i. 234–6). A history is something which must not simply be said, but done. And if it is represented as a consequence of her 'nature' – merely 'but this' – then that radically underestimates the degree to which the text otherwise problematises the performability of the speaking of plainness in history, as we have seen with Kent.

Whether the articulated silence of Cordelia's discourse is thought in the traditional terms of a modest diffidence or, as it has been more recently, in terms of complexity of access to, and disqualification from, empowered speech – or even as a kind of resistance by disengagement from the circuits of dominant speech –, it is probably importantly linked to the larger structure of Cordelia's relative absence from the action of the play. For there are different forms of displacement, each linked to the troubling of performable identity. Kent is displaced into place; although the place where he finds himself is not his place, he nonetheless remains inside 'history' (as the play 'does' it). While Cordelia, on the other hand, who also represents not only the moral charge of the old order but also something of its socio-political form (in as much as it is she who should – and in some senses does – best emblematise the old bonds of nature, in both familial and political registers of the sovereign), is displaced more or less altogether. Kent goes through events by not being 'himself'; or rather his identity is only preserved as an historical possibility by being obscured and disguised, and certainly it is represented as only able to speak itself in such obliquity. Cordelia's identity, however, is not so much put to the test of the historically actual as 'saved': her likeness is not raz'd by covering or disguise, she does not borrow accents or defuse her speech, but, on the contrary, finds her kind of 'integrity' in silence, and in, moreover, absence. Raz'd in another sense, Cordelia's identity is preserved by evacuation in large part from the play's event.

Rather than its dramatising resistance, it is perhaps indeed better to talk of the text as 'saving' *signs of* identity, if under very troubled forms and formations. Kent's language is not as much one of opposition as endurance or perdurance: the recklessness of his plainness is 'covered' by disguise and prosecuted through stoic persistence in his 'obscured course' (II. ii. 164) and in the *oblique* loyalty to that to which loyalty is for him a definition of identity, and in that, loyalty to what he 'really' is. But if Kent's strategy of resistance is a compromised one – not in a moral, but in a textual and ideological sense, in that it is preserved only by obliquity – so too, in a different but related way, is Cordelia's. Hers is another textual limit case of *Lear*'s 'old' represented in its actual breakdown, saved only by a virtual and displaced realisation. Unable to perform her identity as active history in the event of the drama, the text has to evacuate Cordelia from the 'action. That moral charge which she represents and carries, and the wider ideology of the play's absolute horizon of nostalgia for plenitude, can *only* be preserved by removing her from the tests of the play's representation of history. At the same time, the symbolic and ideological system of the play's pre-history can only be made to continue to function at the price of such abstraction and by an extremely 'literary' and wholly *undramatic* device. In this formal sense, of course, her 'saving' *is* performed, but by means of exile. Her 'history' is 'done,' but by not being done, by being done elsewhere; or rather done and not done, not in another positive place but in and by the *structure* of the displacement itself. To be sure, in neither the case of Kent nor in that of Cordelia is old identity, and all that goes with it, able to live unproblematically in the history of the event. The saving strategy of compromise even becomes structural to the formation of the text.

The play is emptily populated with people who are not themselves and who are displaced. That displacement is either represented or 'performed' (by the text rather than the character). On the heath in particular, however, the problematics of language and identity are extreme, and reach a textual limit form. If one axis of Kent's 'identity' is that of the figure who is – with the possible exception of Edgar – most deliberatively, articulately and simply at a distance from himself, he is emblematic here of a general formation or deformation which is sometimes more obscure or complex in others, but also arguably more radical. Certainly the disturbance in the speech of poor Tom, mad Lear and the Fool is, in different ways, profound.

The Fool, typically, both is and is not a special case, being as it were 'intrinsically' displaced and always-already unidentified. But he is also emblematic: his 'I would fain learn to lie' (I. iv. 174), where 'fain' puns on desire and dissimulation so that he dissembles even as he desires parodically to be able to lie, might almost be taken as a synoptic statement of the problematicity of the text's language of the self's articulation of the impossibility of its own identity. In general the discourse of the figures on the heath is characterised by an obliquity of speaking which considerably distorts 'normal' figurations of the syntax of self, and of self and others. It is not just that speaking to oneself of oneself as another, third, person, while knowing that other to be oneself, characterises the discourse of the heath; for although this might be thought contorted enough a mode of discourse, Lear, Cordelia and Kent, for example, all speak of themselves, and even address themselves as others, in the first scene of the play, under what must count as conditions of relative normalcy: 'What shall Cordelia speak?', Cordelia asks herself about her own problem of articulation, 'Love, and be silent' (I. i. 61). Rather, at the limit, it becomes a question of it being no longer entirely clear to the speaker, and often to the hearer, whether the other spoken of may not really be another rather than the self; or whether the self may not be that other. The discourse of the heath may thus consist in speaking of oneself as another where that other may be really other, or of speaking of, or to, another as the self that one no longer recognises oneself to be: on the heath, Lear in particular speaks both to others and of another as himself.

If to speak of oneself as another is to engage the premise of the identical nature of the self, (so that the desire of unity underpins the lament for a self which is not, and cannot be, itself), on the heath – that is, at the limit, so far as the play can represent it – discursive subject-positions and characters in the drama are unable to remain securely superimposed on each other. Certainly a reading of the literary figure of eponymous character as the model of selfhood becomes hard to sustain. And this is not simply a matter of mad delusion: Edgar knows full well that the fiend with a thousand noses he conjures for the blind Gloucester in IV.vi was himself disguised – although not as a fiend – disguised thus again in the re-telling. The question raised is of whether dissembling as disguise has not in a more fundamental sense introduced disguise into the very core of the identity which is thus – 'intrinsically' – dissembled, becoming thus unidentical as it were in its 'essence'. Or rather, if a full identity – present to itself in unconscious presence – is certainly the unspoken norm, there is in all these examples nonetheless the 'disguise' which instead sustains that presence in conditions of absence shaped not by psychological structure but 'social' dislocation.

Eventually out of these displacements of self and the discourses and practice of their fragmentation, as I have suggested elsewhere, comes historically a new subjection, as if the fall of the king has as its consequence the emergence of identity and not its shattering. But not, it seems, yet; and not here. The discourse of the heath is as yet one of the linguistic and cultural fragmentation itself, of the obliteration of stabilised languages of the self, even beneath the dissembling of which there might turn out to be the bedrock of, as one of the play's echoing keywords has it, 'Nothing'. The example of Edgar is again instructive. Fearing the total surveillance of the land, which makes his disidentity in disguise a compelled necessity and not, as it was once read, the symbol of an existential condition (and still less a consequence of the universal slippage of meaning from itself as more recent 'criticism' would hold), he understands the 'police' situation implicitly not only as a threat to his person, but as the prompt of its dissembling. If there is 'no place, /That guard, and most unusual vigilance, /Does not attend my taking', nonetheless 'Whiles I may 'scape, /I will preserve myself'. If escape is the condition of the preservation of the self, that preservation in turn entails escape. But the sequence is one first of the disguising of the Edgar who is 'bethought /To take the basest and most poorest shape /That ever penury, in contempt of man, /Brought near to beast', and then, both before and beyond the disguise as 'Poor Turlygod! poor Tom!', the ambiguous erasure of the primary identity thus apparently disguised: 'That's something yet: Edgar I nothing am.' (II. iii. 3–9, 20–1) The sense both that the 'I' that speaks is not Edgar, and that if it is Edgar it is – in the word which generally signals the text's language of reduction and erasure – nothing, is contained and confused in the transformation into Poor Tom; and something more fundamentally complex about the possibility of preserving identity under the conditions of the militarisation of the land is disclosed than the difficulties entailed simply by the mere fact of dressing up as a beggar. The potential authenticity of such experience of threatened, complex selfhood is, perhaps, not to be deprecated. But there is no reason to think that its validity has been authenticated by the brutal monism of sovereign domination.

In another sense, however, this is not so much the loss of identity as, indeed, its discovery; for after all, there is a 'subject' who utters this statement, and in one sense never is he more Edgar than when in this way and in these kinds of forms he denies the fact. Even in the 'mad' discourse of the heath, something at once more incisive and less amorphous than the total erasure of identity is at stake. It is rather a kind of dialectic by which there is *both* loss *and* discovery. Under the conditions extant, one is never more truly oneself than when speaking of oneself as not oneself, where the line between identity and dis-identity is not so much blurred as constantly rehearsed. Even Lear himself, who previously but slenderly knew himself, encounters on the heath a kind of irreducible core of being, which the text calls famously 'unaccommodated man' (III. iv. 104–6). On the heath, 'identity', in all the fragility – once displaced – of its constitution, is laid bare.

But it is also clear that the sovereign project of the text, in its investment in the integrity of selfhood, also discovers on the heath, rather than an aberrant extremity of condition, instead another kind of normality – at least, a dialectic between depredation and constitutive formation of identity. For it is capable of producing, in the figure of unaccommodation, a representation – possibly one which is proto-humanist – of self-standing autonomous identity, albeit, and perhaps significantly, one fashioned in conditions of formative immiseration. And one perhaps thus mystified in a genetic sense. Indeed, it would be wrong, in view of this side of the dialectic which insistently posits identity, in the face of displacement nonetheless, to rush to a romantic or postmodern conclusion that here outside the citadels and the signs is the space of non-identity, unaccommodated and 'anthropological' as the representation is: 'thou art the thing itself' (III. iv. 104). For neither the humanism that can only reveal itself in reduction, nor the celebration of otherwise formless disidentity will do: each truncates the negative dialectic by which identity is, but is not, itself, and by which it is only speakable as not itself, not in its own voice.

But, as such, this dialectic is powerfully spoken, not least – a certain political reading of the play must have it – in representations which can evoke the pathos that insists as the play calls into being what it sees as the madness and wretchedness of the insistent figure of dispossession which is the result of a sovereignty over the land that depends inherently on the unaccommodation of the people. And also in its anxiety: there is set loose in the text at this point a kind of anarcho-democracy in the discourse of the heath which summons up, as has often been remarked, resources from popular tradition to castigate the corruption of power and its institutional and executive forms and forces: 'The great image of Authority: /A dog's obey'd in office' (IV. vi. 156–7), 'Thorough tatter'd clothes small vices do appear; /Robes and furr'd gowns hide all' (IV. vi. 162–3), 'Plate sin with gold, /And the strong lance of justice breaks; /Arm it in rags, a pigmy's straw does pierce it.' (IV. vi. 163–5) The play calls up, and is haunted by, the imagined voices of the figures of the masterless, the displaced, the dangerously unfixed populace, which troublingly populated the anxious imagination of early modern power.

However, as in the wider structure of the tragic formation – the general form of which will be evoked below – this dialectic of dispossession from identity, and identity discovered in reduction to unaccommodation, is not 'even-handed'. The association of the reduction to a 'core' of humanity on the heath with the 'ordinary' dispossessed and with these thematics of injustice, corruption of power and oppression, is in fact an essentialisation of oppression: 'unaccommodated man is no more but such a poor, bare forked animal as thou art' (III. iv. 104–6). If irreducible identity is 'exposed', not only revealed but also made vulnerable, it is as the resource of 'compassion' that the dispossessed figure here; the reduction to a core of being provides an existential metaphysic, rather, ultimately, than the critique of a social or historical form.

Perhaps it would be better to remark that for the conservative ideology of the project of the text a kind of normality is indeed legitimated. For all that the heath is a special – normal – place, unaccommodation is by no means ultimately celebrated as a grounding value. Off the heath, identity without land is demonised.

It has been argued – I have myself argued – that at the time of Lear a newer sense of identity was historically emergent, and that this partially provides a dramatic and ideological resource. The compromise character of the Shakespearean text lies not least in the fact that it both admits and fends off this tendency to modernity. In Lear this is significant not least in the text's theorisation of 'natural' identity and the sexualised representation of such identity. Some time ago the contestation for concepts and languages of nature in the play became a topic for critical commentary. Edmund in particular was seen as promissorily Hobbesian, appropriating at any rate the old term 'Nature' to newer – modern – meanings, and in particular to a sense of identity and value independent of the framework of the older ideological symbology. Even if, as we have seen above, his first objective is the traditionally-coded one of land inheritance – 'and of my land, /Loyal and natural boy,' Gloucester says to him, 'I'll work the means /To make thee capable' (II. i. 82–4) – it is actually a new-style acquisitiveness: he is an *unpossessing* bastard' (II.i.66, emphasis added) as good as legitimate, prepared to pit intelligence and cunning against place, to reject the curiosity of nations and custom, and to avail himself not of nature moralised but of a naturalism that will attribute to, and equip man [sic] with, a liberating dynamism. If

nature is to be his goddess, the merest conventionalism of the apo-
strophe to a deity keeps this from being a thoroughly secular account
– it is in any case pagan, as not everything in the play is – of natural
capacities and drives entering for perhaps the first time a 'demystified', 'Machiavellian' world where appetitive naturalism and individual
advantage will *explicitly* supplant the supposedly traditional bonds,
hierarchies and value-symbology.

From within a certain moderately critical secularism, it is
doubtless possible to have some sympathy with Edmund: contemporary liberal opinion surely agrees, officially at least, with much
of what he has to say about illegitimacy; his invocation of a man-
centred dynamic is not antipathetic to many current assumptions,
and there certainly seems to be something engaged in the characterisation – if one wanted, as I do not, to invoke the authority of the
imagination of Shakespeare's sympathies. But it is impossible to
ignore the way in which the text produces the new forces and capacities as fearsome and dangerous. The play demonises the new claim to
identity which is not based on place but on – precisely – practice. It
characterises that practice of aggressive acquisition as one threatening, rather than transforming, the traditional order of social places
and landed property – 'Well then, /Legitimate Edgar, I must have
your land ... ' (I. ii. 15–16) – and then demonises it. And there are
enormously powerful symbolic and ideological resources available
for that demonisation.

Principally and in particular, the demonisation is done by the
play's sexualisation of the new, and a complementary mobilisation
and inscription of the resources of misogyny. The 'practical' counter-
part of Edmund's 'humanism' is the figuration of Goneril and Regan.
Although Edmund is hardly inactive in pursuing his self-defined
goals, he is nonetheless represented as reflecting conceptually more
fully on the legitimacy of his activity, whereas Goneril and Regan are
located rather in, as it were, the practice of his 'theory'. The language
becomes difficult here because of the transactions of the
problematics of the word 'nature': the monstrous women act
'naturally', that is to say, unnaturally. To fall away from the social,
familial and political roles defined by the erstwhile natural bonds of
kingship (which are of course anything but 'natural' in fact, although
they constitute the real, the social, that which counts as historical), is
to fall into the other nature, which can then be castigated by what is

still the overarching ideological framework of the play – however violated that is in what I am calling the event – with all the attributions of transgression coded in the language of bestiality, monstrosity, and even simply sex, which accrues to the wicked sisters. If sexuality is marked as such, it is, almost without exception, as a component of – and sometimes as a symptomatic clue to – the new, whereas it is missing from the older structures of power and identity as they are represented by the text. The language of Cordelia's betrothal and marriage to France, for example, is utterly without sexual charging, and in so far as can be judged from the brief and incomplete representation of the 'family' – with its significant displacement of the mother who is thus 'saved' from the text's misogyny, absolved of desire (but also of presence) – sexuality is something coded as extra-familial; and when it enters the arena of the familial it is as an alien and disruptive intrusion. Compared with the sexlessness of Cordelia, the competitive desire in love or pseudo-love of the father of a Goneril or a Regan is constructed to place desire on one side and love on the other of an ideological divide. This is then re-articulated later in the competition between the sisters for Edmund himself. And in these articulations another set of ideological equations is made: sexuality is in the nature of monstrous women, sexual women are monstrous; and the play's coding of sexuality is part of its demonisation of the new, and reciprocally associates the new with all that is fearsome in what it constructs as woman and beast, in beast-woman.

There is a piety in Edgar whose relative pallidity when he is not Poor Tom is representative of the old of the play. But pious or not, the vehemence of the terms in which he responds to the discovery of Goneril's murderous desire – 'O indistinguish'd space of woman's will! /A plot upon her virtuous husband's life, /And the exchange my brother!' (IV. vi. 268–70) – are to the point. If woman's will is an indistinguished space, it is a dangerous slippage from definition akin to the unmarking of the land of the heath consequent upon the demise of sovereign rule and inherent in the tearing of the map at the outset. As in the text's representation of identity in general, in this arena of its representation too, there is a tension between dynamics of fixity and those of erasure, which is both homologous with, and structural to, the text's wider dialectic between the project and the event, between projective coherence and sovereign control on the one hand, and disfigured and disfiguring interruption on the other. And at the same time a subterranean strand of the discourse speaks – in 'exchange' – of money rather than land-holding as a nexus of the new. Exchangable, rather than unnegotiable, value seeps into the materialism of the text, even as it resists that decathexis of its preferred higher symbolism. An anxious undercurrent in the text's acknowledgment of the emergent, historically these even risk an abstraction in the metaphors of both real and imagined transaction, an abstraction which would depart significantly from the real or imagined palpability of the power of definition by social 'place' grounded in territorial possession. In any case, woman's identity is thus also disidentity, within the traditional terms. Landlessness like that of the heath – indistinguished space –, if not dispossession, is represented as metaphorically intrinsic to women, in as much as for women to have possession is demonised by the play (as arguably in the larger society it largely was).

In something of a re-marking – if at another level – of the text's empty space of women, Albany speaks to and of Goneril in the following terms: 'See thyself, devil! /Proper deformity shows not in the fiend /So horrid as in woman ... ' (IV. ii. 59–61). If here is the demonising language which calls woman 'devil' and 'fiend', there is also a complex problematics of property and likeness. If there is something contradictory in 'proper deformity' – how can deformity be proper? – there is also the sense that her deformity is her own, a self-possession which is cognate with the free-standing identity the play recognises and fears, and with the implications for property in the more ordinary sense that are consonant with it. But also what is monstrous in her is that she is not what she is, but 'Thou changed and self-cover'd thing, for shame' (IV. ii. 62). Covered, and self-covered at that, he calls on her to be plain – 'Be-monster not thy feature' (IV. ii. 63) – in a sense resonant of the play's problematic of identity. But she isn't plain. She is self-made and also in that monstrous. These words all turn back on and undercut themselves as they admit a range of selfhoods (from identity through to property), and attempt simultaneously to ward them off. As a self which is in any case not itself, the affront offered in this by Goneril is itself monstrous, and attracts the violence it 'deserves' from the propriety of the text, in Albany's barely constrained will 'To let these hands obey my blood, / ... to dislocate and tear /Thy flesh and bones' (IV. ii. 64–6).

All that stops Albany from tearing her to pieces is a woman's shape – 'howe'er thou art a fiend, /A woman's shape doth shield thee' (IV. ii. 66–7) – but that 'shape', another covering, merely 'shields' her. It is and is not her 'herself'; woman, as identity, is proper deformity. As in the text's wider dialectic of fixity and erasure, identity is both proper and at the same time deformity.

Demonised sexuality – the only kind there is here – is a powerful symptomatic sign, in a range of textual displacements, of *Lear's* fascinated nomination of other forces than those of its sovereign project. It is not surprising that in Lear's account of the reduction to unaccommodation and displacement, copulation – the coupling of bodies, and more, of course – thrives. If there are traces of an emergent humanism in that notion of the irreducible core of being, it is not yet the sanitised incorporeality of subsequent ideological formations. On the contrary, it is as much at a distance from them as it is from the apparent sexlessness of the natural familial and political bonds of the play's opening symbology. Whether positive representation or symptomatic clue, sexuality is a cultural and political force in the text, and one associated both with what is allowed as challenging the master-discourse and with what is figured as the popular underside of the erstwhile sovereign rule of the king.

But, for all this, there is a sanitisation at work in the structure of the representation even of what is demonised. For Goneril and Regan, royal princesses, while they belong to the emergent in the play's 'historiography', come nonetheless from within the traditional landed class. This is true even of Edmund, in his way. The text has difficulty co-ordinating its class, gender and sexual anxieties. As vectors of textual force they are also a kind of substitute for an even deeper threat the play averts and wards off. For even in its demonisation the text prevents the perception that the real dispossessed, who are occluded from it, in 'screen' forms – and not merely the landless poor, but the systematically oppressed masses of both rural and urban economies – might not more than threaten but threaten to end the traditional structure of property and selfhood. There were – and are – those who even more than Edmund did not 'know their place'. Indeed, in important ways this whole question of the person, of identity or 'character' – especially when registered as self-knowledge –, is *both* a substitution for, a masking of, *and* an emanation from the politics of the representation of the sovereignty of the land, and consequently what counts in the text as history. The entire emphasis on character rather than historical force seeks to obscure the fact that what is actually at stake is a formation of historical power, and its crisis, by dramatising instead the existential universals of limit suffering, self-discovery and unaccommodated solidarity. But because the decline of that sovereignty is only symptomatically present in the foregrounding of character, it is doubly important to sharpen the focus of this latent Shakespearean dialectic, and in particular to see that, in the representations in question, non-identity with oneself is only – represented as – truer than one's true identity, more normal than normality, *if other conditions simultaneously hold*; if, that is, normality – and the powers both of the symbolic and ideological, as well as the material and institutional, force that constitutes and governs normality – is itself in question. The entire inner formation and the external legitimation – the sovereignty – of the normal, of 'economy', 'society', 'law', 'family', and the rest, must either be, or risk being, both historically challenged and, in that, discursively unsusceptible of representation, for this reassuring sense of the localisability of what is at issue in the very matter of the representation of the self to be possible in the first place.

The link between the crisis of – the representation of – identity and that of the forms of the ruling sovereignty – if not the general desire of sovereignty 'as such' – makes and depends on this equation in the substructures of the Shakespearean text.

In the event it takes a 'negative' form – for it is the depredations of the actual crisis, and the crisis of actuality, which are in fact dramatised. But the connection between the figure of invasion and that of disrupt, incomplete and impossible identity, is organisational of the wider discontinuities at work here. While they apparently take a culturalist form, questions of 'character', of identity and non-identity, have thus a strategic meaning: in tragedy, it appears, sovereignty must first be displaced, and the body of the land already and soon invaded. Certainly in *Lear*, no king, not even the mysteriously absent France – 'Something he left imperfect in the State, which imports so much fear and danger' (IV. iii. 3–5) – is equal to the old identity which can no longer be itself; still less can one match the dangerously new forms, which – seen from the point of view of the old – are landless, sexual and dispossessed. But even more signally, the interdependence of identity as fixed subjection and sovereign order – itself structurally located in and into the past by the text's most fundamental formational strategies – must have been forced to be represented as shattered in the demise of the sovereign representation of what then counts as tragedy.

To be sure, of the play's various disidentities, none is further from itself than that of the King. If in the first act there is already something risible in the discrepancy between the bluster of 'the Dragon and his wrath' (I. i. 121) and the evident injustice of his treatment of Cordelia and Kent, and in his misrecognition of Goneril and Regan, Lear's subsequent trajectory through the play and its outcome are still further from being credible dramatic representations of any theoretical or practical ideology of majesty, sacred, aesthetic or otherwise. What is thus actualised by the event of the play, is a reduction which, even if it trades on the subsequent ideological form of a potential humanisation in unaccommodation, remains a reduction nonetheless, and depends hardly at all, except as a lost horizon of the text, on performable majesty. It is, rather, a decathexis of the sovereign and the imaginative – without seductive charm – caught up in problematics of likeness and unlikeness, of representation, which, surely, the text – and the 'culture' more ambitious readings than this one would claim to address – can only find problematic.

Lear implausibly attempts to retain the cultural form of King – and even the political authority of that form – without the substantial institutional, instrumental, military, social and economic power of the crown, and without seeing how theoretically and practically doomed such a gesture has to be in the polity of the time which he takes still to be his. 'Only' to 'retain /The name and all th'addition to a king' (I. i. 134–5) while handing over – rather to his 'Beloved sons' (sons-in-law) than his daughters it is worth noting – 'the sway, / Revenue, execution of the rest' (I. i. 135–6) will not work. It is minatory of what from the point of view of the old is an apparently 'modern' form of being – loosened from the sovereign symbologies of the body and the blood – in which office and person, power and addition, name and execution, are at least conceptually separable. The project of the text fears such an eventuality. For if sovereignty is no more than office, and office can be held in principle by anyone, what in the short term stands in the way of the arriviste, if not the usurper, whether from within the traditional aristocracy, the rising mercantilist classes, or, still more unacceptable, the underclasses beneath? Such a conception of the disjuncture of office and person is insufficiently *grounded* in the symbologies by which the text naturalises monarchical rule, and dangerously offers too much to an emergent secularism and its functions and functionaries. But in any case the crisis is upon the text and the symbolic division of the regalia – 'This coronet part between you' (I. i. 138) – and the transmission of the power and revenue, while trying to retain the cultural and political authority, are clearly enough – even within the given, explicit, and historically undeciphered terms of the discourse – an absurdity. Rather than some full spectacle of sovereign power, which in any case we never see, there is instead the form of Gloucester's resonantly Foucauldian remark on the King's new situation: 'And the King gone to-night! prescrib'd his power! /Confin'd to exhibition!' (I. vii. 24–5) Exhibition rather than spectacle, confinement instead of the exercise of power: there is historical confusion here in that Lear has been reduced to mere display, and then confined in that condition. If there is – residual, according to the text's historiography – spectacle, then it is only in as much as the king has been made to become – in modern speech – a spectacle of himself.

The reduced spectacle of the reduced king is insistent. It is remarked, for example, in the words of the anonymous gentleman of Act IV: 'A sight most pitiful in the meanest wretch, /Past speaking of in a King!' (IV. vi. 201–2) This is a remark which is articulated, of course, against a background assumption of the normality of majesty, compared with which the '*sight*' of Lear in his reduction is one which defies representation, is 'past speaking of'. And even if the histrionics and self-pity – the tears and railing of Lear's 'madness' in the shock of reduction to humanity 'as such' – are, when they connect by an obscure identification in pathos with the wretchedness of the permanently dispossessed, evocative of an affect which accrues more to the spectacle of the sovereign reduction than to any – inevitably patronising – compassion for the oppressed 'themselves', nonetheless, in having become part of the discourse of the heath, Lear's identity and speech are problematised, and share the obscure lucidity of that discourse. As Edgar puts it – aside – 'O! matter and impertin-ency mix'd; /Reason in madness.' (IV. vi. 172–3) There is at least enough reason in Lear's language for him to be able to think that he can see this in his new condition: 'Infirmity doth still neglect all office /Whereto our health is bound'. There is, in other words, a deep disruption in any putative royal *presence*: 'we are not ourselves'. For 'When Nature, being oppress'd, commands the mind /To suffer with the body' (II. iv. 105–6) an equally fatal incision has been made in the attendant symbologies of nature and health, and of the apparently normative relations within those discursive constitutions of the mind and the body. Despite the invocation of 'Nature', it is now an alienated, 'secular' nature which commands, and commands a suffering in which 'Infirmity doth still neglect all *office*.' (II. iv. 103, emphasis added) 'Let me have surgeons', he screams later, 'I am cut to th'brains' (IV.vi.190–1). It hardly needs saying that this profound anatomical disruption and dismemberment is a reduction of the charged, artificial and 'political' body, and therefore of the sacred realm. So much for office without power.

Throughout, the spectacle of the reduced old man which humanist criticism tends to see alone, 'is' – in a sense of some complexity – the King, and it is the kingdom and kingship that is at stake. The reduction to humanity is indeed a reduction, rather than an alternative. Certainly the language of the king without power is in this way *involved* in the difficulty of the representation of identity. Thus, so much of the language of Lear's own self-registration is connected with difficulty of – precisely – *self*-perception, or rather, with self-misrecognition. Here it is particularly the representation – or better, the 'unrepresentation' – of the King that is the question. To Lear's poignant if histrionic questions 'Does any here know me? This is not Lear' and 'Who is it that can tell me who I am?', the Fool's reply is resonant: 'Lear's shadow.' (I. iv. 223, 227–8) The ambiguity here is important: the Fool's answer is a reply to two questions. To the question 'who can tell me who I am?' the answer is 'I, the Fool, your faithful shadow in these adversities'. But it is also a response to the implied question 'who am I?', to which the answer is 'Your shadow: you are reduced to no more than a shadow of your former self'. In each and either case, it is important to register the metaphor of the shadow as one of a representation which has the qualities both of reduced likeness and of unlikeness to what it represents. Throughout the representation of the king in his reduction, there is the insistence of a language of likeness and unlikeness, as when, for example, Lear compares his likeness to that of the true king on coin of the realm: 'No, they cannot touch me for coining; I am the king himself.' (IV. vi. 83–4) Contrary to the pathetically defiant assertion of continued kingship and substantial identity – 'the king *himself*' – there insists instead the disavowed suggestion that Lear is, rather, not just the criminal transgressor, the coiner who usurps the sovereign's power to authorise money, but the counterfeit image 'itself', the counterfeit likeness of the sovereign.

Chiding Lear's abjection from likeness, the Fool tells him ' ... now thou art an O without a figure.' (I. iv. 189–90) In reduction there is first the reversal, on which so much of this reach of the text depends, of the relative statuses of King and Fool – 'I am better than thou art now' – and then, beyond the reversal, the erasure of the king: 'I am a Fool, *thou art nothing*'. (I. iv. 190–1; emphasis added) But here again the reduction is not to humanity in the way traditionally seen as reduction to character, but rather one from character – the possibility of which had been guaranteed by erstwhile kingship – to character in the other more original sense of a figure of speech, or rather of writing. But then from that to nothing; the O being the character which, if its figure is removed, disappears. As does the King. And with this, by the way, it is also plain that the thematic of 'nothing' here, belongs not to a metaphysically existential register in the dialectic of the historical transformations of identity, but to another 'realm' of ciphered, *textual* space. It is a nothing on a ground that is first figured, but then uninscribed and – so much for the body of the king – disfigured.

Nothing is left but further pathetic assertion of kingship – 'I will die bravely, /Like a smug bridegroom ... I will be jovial: /Come, come; I am a king, masters, know you that?' (IV. vi. 195–7) – which then gives way to the admission of acknowledged ignorance (although this is celebrated by much humanist criticism as self-knowledge). For when it is possible for Lear at last to know 'himself' – 'I am a very foolish fond old man' – it is in the form of the recognition that he cannot know what he knows. Outward signs of identity, such as the clothing which, as semiosis, is usually thematised as radically am-biguous in Shakespeare, fail – 'all the skill I have /Remembers not these garments'; location is unrecognisable – 'I am mainly ignorant /

What place this is'; and 'to deal plainly' – as if this were possible, as Kent's condition suggests it isn't – 'I fear I am not in my perfect mind.' (IV. vii. 60, 66–7, 65–6, 62–3)

But ending is always a critical margin. If along with Lear has fallen an entire symbolic order – a *system* of inevitably political representation – the play does not, and from the point of view of the historicity of what I have been calling its project, cannot, leave things at that. At best there must be a figure of restoration, of the sovereign and the symbology, or, failing that, at least a filling of the vacuum. In the last evolution of the figure of Lear himself, we have *both* restoration and the invasion of the vacated 'place' of the King, a drive to closure even if it cannot be effectively a resolution of all that has been opened. The terms in which Albany pronounces the 'settlement' speech (V. iii. 295–303) are in this respect significant. Promising 'What comfort to this great decay may come /Shall be appli'd' and that 'for us, we will resign, /During the life of this old Majesty, /To him our absolute power' (V. iii. 296–9) would look, taken alone, very much like the figure of the restoration of the rightful monarch in particular, and of sovereign legitimacy in a wider sense. The forces both of foreign invasion and internal usurpation having been defeated, the commanding general restores the sovereign and rewards his most loyal supporters: 'All friends shall taste /The wages of their virtue' (V. iii. 301–2). If the suffering is not to be indelibly expunged, at least right is vindicated, and the *status quo ante* – no doubt strengthened by the afflictions it has undergone – is reinstated. Such would make the play the formal comedy that its structure sometimes seems to suggest it ought really to be, producing, despite the suffering wrought and represented, the political and discursive vindication of sovereignty, in the form of kingship in particular, as well as in that of the general sovereign order of the 'social' and even the 'real'. It is possible to find critics who advance this reading ...

Unfortunately for this happy point of view, the redemptive death of the King is neither the summation of – the – 'tragedy' nor the end of the play. Within a handful of lines Lear is dead. In another, more ordinary sense of the word, the text is unable to 'save' the king, or indeed Cordelia. They die, and the sovereign project can only sentimentally recuperate them. But if the restoration fails, the vacuum in power, indeed in sovereignty, can apparently still be filled. In a strange set of figurations, Albany turns first to Kent and Edgar: 'Friends of my /soul, you twain /Rule in this realm, and the gor'd state sustain.' (V. iii. 318–19) Precious little legal or blood right could legitimate an assumption of rule by Edgar or Kent, even if there is some moral or even 'poetic' justice in the idea. Nor has Albany been much noted before this for his friendship with either of them. But this is disidentical, textual prevarication. Neither Kent's prediction of the final loyalty of his own imminent death – 'I have a journey, sir, shortly to go; /My master calls me, I must not say no' (V. iii. 320–1) – nor Edgar's conviction that 'we that are young /Shall never see so much, nor live so long' (V. iii. 324–5), is a speech of confident accession to a restored throne, and with it a vindicated sovereignty. In short, there is behind these feints towards first restoration and then moral succession, a real power. It doubtless overstates the political clarity of the text to call it a *coup d'état*, but the text needs *this* 'invasion'. Its 'person' is, of course, Albany, who invades the space left by Kingship. Already before Lear's actual death Albany is speaking, as if habitually, in the royal plural, and that alone might give cause to Edgar's suspicion that he will not be anything like as long for this world as Lear and the rest of the elders had been. Albany's assumption of power – if not explicitly opportunist, it is certainly pragmatic – is no more 'grounded' than in the fact that he alone of the aristocratic principals remains; and at the head, moreover, of a victorious British army. Improbable as that victory of the tumultuous and divided indigenes over the foreign invader is, it has to do. Closure must be. For after all, in what passes for 'culture' *someone* has authoritatively to speak.

In the achievement of this inadequate closure, there is a quality which, even if it has been prepared for by the text, cannot but appear arbitrary. Among the principals, Albany has been dramatically the least prominent, and this in turn serves to feed the way in which he is 'morally' less involved in, and contaminated by, the event of the play, and the actions and desires of what I have been calling the new powers. His various regretful comments on the course of events, and in particular his denunciation of Goneril cited already, contribute to the effect of keeping him 'clean' for the eventual assumption of power. But by the same token, the closure of the project, the sovereign master-discourse of the text, is shown to need, or to have to resort to, this kind of device in order to fend off the representation of 'settlement' as otherwise achieved in the installation of forces which the text has represented as usurpatory of the very sovereignty it seeks to cherish. This would be closure by conquest, either from within or outside the sacred realm of ideological legitimacy. Or, as the language of the time indeed had it, in another still darker sense which the play seeks to avert, 'invasion'.

That Albany's assumption is an effect of power there should be no doubt: at the level of the drive to closure of the project, it is the re-making of rule and the re-marking of the land as sovereign territory that is attempted and at stake. The very structure, the formation of tragedy, here insists. The relatively 'backgrounded' character of Albany both conceals and at the same time deploys the compromised character of the representation of power on which the text is – historically – constrained to 'settle'. Like the simultaneous disfiguration and 'saving' of the value – if not in the event always the form – of identity, here a 'fundamental' dynamic of the projective saving of the sovereign land is engaged – not least because of the imbricated dependence of the former on the integrity of the latter.

What, at the level of the project, are desirable Shakespearean forma-tions of identity, are equal in turn to the representation of sovereign characters, and to signs not of the critical differential of representa-tion but to identity as the full and the present, as the sign and the substance of presence. This non-difference – the ideal of the sover-eign is its substance and its figure – is, in turn, the equivalent of peace in the silent equations of the text's ideological construction. And that, of course, is a strategy of domination. In as much as peace is inconceivable to the Shakespearean project without the ('closure' of) settlement of rule, the commitment to identity is thus a commit-ment to stasis, to domination.

For this reason the figure of invasion can symbolise a very total crisis. But it can also play a part in a curious dissipation of tragic consequence. There is something both violate and protective in the focusing, invasive of the sovereign and at the same time drawing back from the sharpest devastation, not just of the Kentish battleground, but of the sovereign symbology itself. The figure of invasion can instead act as a kind of lightning-conductor drawing off as displaced charge the form and even the 'real-historical' substance of the crisis. In *Lear* it seems to offer restitution in as much as Cordelia is the figurehead of the French incursion and at least its official purpose that of restoring Lear to the throne in particular, and of relegitimating the old order in general. But perhaps more importantly than this, it acts as a screen for the impossibility of that effect. Instead it becomes the focus of the event so that the defeat of the invasion can count as 'victory' even though it is nothing like the original or originary 'problem', in the sense neither that it was this with which the tragic action began, nor that this 'solution' could be said to bridge the affective, symbological or ideological gap between what I have been calling the event and the 'deep structure' of the project's representation of – and totalised 'desire' for – sovereignty 'itself'. But in this way it can play a part in moving the drama back from the brink of an otherwise inescapable devastation of the sovereignty which it is the project's ideological desire to underwrite.

The depredation of the event in *Lear* is framed by the conservative metaphysics, and the dramatic shape, of the play's project seeking to legitimate what it can nonetheless barely represent, still less – in the event – successfully defend. To construct its ideological and aesthetic strategies of legitimation – and especially to delimit the crisis it cannot help but articulate – the text is constrained to establish the pseudo-historiography of the temporal structure of the project, inventing the simplified phenomena of its 'old' and 'new', residual and emergent forms. In the event these symbologies, behaviours, 'values' and characterisations are often quizzically and uncertainly located in the play's historical schema: it is certainly difficult to believe that 'feudalism' (and still less Tudor Absolutism) was ever in fact animated by some inner Cordelian principle of chaste and natural modesty – rather than, say, the ruthless exploitation of the rural populace. But the project seeks to make such an interpretation compelling, by the necessity of its imaginary temporality. The ideal of restoration – by definition the restoration of the old – precisely in as much as it is both the ideal and also temporalised in this way, simultaneously discloses and betrays the desire of the project and the necessity therefore of the screen of the final compromise formation. The text cannot help but code ideal presence – the tranquil, the ordered, the hierarchised, in short the *sovereign* – as lying in the past. And indeed, a general structure – although not the entire dialectic – of Shakespearean tragedy consists in this figure, of the location of the present in the past.

*   *   *

Lear ends in textual and discursive compromise. Its closing formation achieves a partial reinvestment of the 'sacred' land under central rule, although the very diminution in affect and symbolic charge serves to point up the fragile character of the achievement of the project against all the odds of the 'deconsecration' otherwise admitted into the system of the play's representations. It would be equally worth remarking in *Hamlet* the same symbolism of the land imbricated with a similar politics of representation, although also figured, in the event, in the form of decay from an erstwhile sovereignty. Despite the tendency of the play to produce its action in the interiors and precincts of the court, foregrounding tableaux of state power, together with the somewhat furtive conspiratorial underside of its absolutism, only a slight recentering of the play, a minor shift in the depth of field, brings into view an understated but important set of representations of the realm as symbolically coded of course, but in decline or deviation from those master-codes. If, in *Lear*, the legitimacy of rule is representationally evoked in, among other things, an image of the land as whole and abundant, then the counterimage of *Hamlet* – in which the land is darkened and oppressed, militarily threatened at the start, uneasily traversed by armies in its course, and violated at the end – 'grounds', as it were, that thoroughgoing depredation which affects the state itself. One could pursue through the play thus – as it is possible to do with *Lear* – the mutations of the symbolic form of the realm, from, indeed, the 'ground' (I.i.16) guarded at the outset by the sentries of the watch, through, say, Marcellus's view of the state in which 'something is rotten' (I.iv.90) or Hamlet's view of Denmark as a prison (II.ii.243), to another 'compromised' reinvestment of the centre in Fortinbras's eventual assumption of power at the end. Each is a 'structural metaphor' of the 'place' of the drama. Or in the same vein, it would also be instructive to trace the wider 'geopolitical' map of sovereign territory the play constructs, to understand its investment both in the particular figurations it produces of 'Denmark', 'Norway', 'Poland', 'Germany',

'France' and, of course, 'England' itself, and in precisely this set of depicted 'relations' among them. And beyond that, in what would be a slightly narrower reading of the political application of the criticisms or admonitions the play functions to announce, it would be important to explore the extent to which the text's imagined Denmark should be taken either to be, or to stand in for, a real or imagined England.

If there are then, in *Hamlet* too, significant forms of the land, and the realm, not least does the figure of invasion here again play an important subterranean part. The question of the initial threat offered by Fortinbras to a tract of Danish territory plays a crucial part in the specious but efficient discourse of the legitimation of Claudius's rule. Perhaps it would be overstated to speak of the land dispute of Act I in terms of actual invasion, although *war* is threatened, and invasion is a critical, and not simply a descriptive concept. But at any rate the spectacle of Claudius successfully managing the challenge to Danish territorial sovereignty is one of the marks of effective rule (even if we would want to say that from another point of view it is clear that the opening of *Hamlet* has already had to forsake any representation of symbolic majesty, and that it is more a question, in Claudius, of the factitious appearance of legitimacy). And of course at the literal level of the event of the play's fiction, Denmark is actually invaded at the end; for we should not suppose that Fortinbras marches into Act V unarmed and alone. The violation and defence of the sovereign realm is again at stake in these representations.

This is not to say that other signs of crisis are not very much to the fore. Indeed, near the beginning, amid intense discussion of likeness and repetition – to which we shall return – the ghost of a father who was also a king says insistently 'remember me'. At the end the son, now also dying, begs his friend Horatio to survive in order to tell the story. It is the most important thing. If in *Lear* the structural and representational pastness of the present describes one essential contour of its tragic figuration of history, here, in *Hamlet*, a 'culture' is losing its memory. And between this beginning in an injunction to remember and an ending in injunction to narrate, there is a persistent thematic strand of discussion of memory as a set of cultural practices which are coded as essential, but which in the event are

either absent or crucially compromised. The damage to those practices, to their representation and their ability *to be represented* can be
read as crisis in politically effective, symbolically sanctioned discourse, and in the possibility of the representation of sovereignty.
This in turn is linked to the fact that the formations of personal and
communal memory signify, beyond that, an even wider attention –
or lack of it – both to the play's representation of the issue of history
and historicity, and to its own historical status as historical representation.

There is some strain in the voice that prompts the need of memory.
The voice that reminds speaks in pain from beyond the grave, from
that undiscover'd country from whose bourn at least this traveller
does in fact partially return (III.i.79–80). The tremulous quality of
the voice, at once demanding and despairing, authoritative and at the
same time hesitant of its own weight, is also a potent marker of the
difficulty of true narration – and even of narration at all – which, if it
is to become important in the play's repertoire of signs of cultural
crisis (and not least in that dying command of Hamlet's), is already
powerfully problematical here. The story of the unlawful killing of the
legitimate king struggles to be heard across the line between life and
death, curiously half-embodied, and finally poignant in its last
insistence when it must return to the other world at cockcrow: 'Adieu,
adieu, adieu. *Remember me.*' (I.v.91–112, emphasis added) Adieu and
memory cannot substitute for or allay each other, but must not be
separated either: adieu must not be a sign of absence, memory will
not be presence enough.
    If there is a certain audile difficulty in the father's voice, there is a
compensatory extravagance in the son's response: 'Remember thee?/
Ay, thou poor ghost, whiles memory holds a seat/In this distracted
globe.' (I.v.91–112) A metaphor which maps the globe of the skull that
contains the already-distracted brain onto the globe of the world itself
is a lonely but not a particularly modest one. It betrays itself in any
case in its extravagance. 'Remember thee?/Yea, from the table of my
memory/I'll wipe all trivial fond records,/All saws of books, all forms,
all pressures past/That youth and observation copied there' (I.v.91–
112). Without any benefit of hindsight we can be sure that memory
will not long hold a seat in the great world, and nor will the total

commitment to wiping the individual memory clean so that this one all-important document can remain preserved in it, will not be, in the event, a simple matter. In particular, despite Hamlet's insistence that the memory of 'thy commandments all alone shall live/Within the book and volume of my brain,/Unmix'd with baser matter ... ' (I.v.91–112), the language of his promise is all connected, of course, with the materiality of recording and script: 'the table of my memory' (which is capable of being wiped), 'records', 'books' and volumes are clear enough, and even a word like 'commandments' summons up tablets of stone. It might be suspected that nothing can in fact 'live alone', but when it comes to this emphasis on writing – and even graving – clearly we are not dealing with any living voice. His father is after all a ghost, and these signs pertain to the difficult matter of writing. Certainly it is significant that he says both that it is a question of 'forms', and that what is held in memory is 'copied there'; a representation, a copy, and not, of course, the thing itself. Certainly *with* the benefit of the hindsight of Hamlet's near interminable delay, the problem of memory prompting action is only confirmed. This entire insistence reveals just how contaminated the act and practice – even the technology – of memory has become in an already-prejudiced polity (and the cultural significance of the effort to remember and its difficulty *is* finally a matter of the representation of the polity, rather than a simply technical problem of memory). Anything but the living urgency of a full voice, narration of the past or the present is caught up in the problematics of simulation, where it becomes impossible to tell how much dissembling intervenes between representation and similitude.

Hamlet is obsessed by and incensed with unlikeness and in particular with the unlikeness (and, through dissimilitude, unfitness to be king) of Claudius to his father. The unlikeness is mediated through a kind of ground – unstable as it may turn out to be – of representation, signs of the literary-mythological tradition, and tokens of visual representation, providing in principle, like the horizon of the fantasy of the secure ground and the sovereign past in *Lear*, an uncontestably established 'third term' on the basis of which to articulate the likeness, or in this case the disidentity, of the king. Hamlet speaks of his father as, for example, 'So excellent a king, that was to this/Hyperion to a satyr ...' (I.ii.139–40), or he establishes the comparative lack of comparison in terms like these: 'My father's brother – but no more like my father/Than I to Hercules.' (I.ii.152–3). But it seems that it is necessary to invoke the representation which is already representation, or copy, to ascertain the comparison, or lack of it. Much later in the play (for this is not merely an initial theme) he compares the two portraits: 'Look here upon this picture, and on this,/The counterfeit presentment of two brothers' (III.iv.53–4). Again not only is a comparison at stake – and, moreover, a comparison of likeness – but the language is overtly that of – painterly – representation. And the representations are 'counterfeit', in a word which links – as it does in *Lear* – representation to the dissimulation of sovereign authority (and an authority moreover, to make, in coin, what are at that tokens, symbolic values, representations). Not only is there this insistent emphasis on likeness and unlikeness, but it is necessarily mediated through overt, almost self-conscious, signs of representation. Each of these examples draws a kind of four-point diagram: 'so excellent a king'; 'this'; 'Hyperion'; 'a satyr' (and it is worth noting that, within this multiplex comparison, the satyr is itself already a doubled, monstrous form). Or, 'my father's brother'; 'my father'; 'I'; 'Hercules'. Or, the picture of Hamlet senior; the picture of Claudius; Hamlet 'himself'; Claudius 'himself'. It isn't enough, it seems, simply to liken, but to liken likeness to likeness. Comparison has to be compared, and in the process, I suspect, more troubled than confirmed, as if an extra effort has to be made to pin down and represent identity that even as it is intensively represented slips away from representation at every point.

In any case, if Claudius is a bad or questionable copy of a copy of the king, so is the king, or at least his ghost. The *'prompt'* for this emphasis on memory, is itself somewhat prejudiced. Among the figures of past wholeness which the tragedies engender as the horizon against which the actual events of their own internal political history is set, this one is more weakly realised in its alleged plenitude even than the rich champains of Lear's abundant, if empty, map. If that image of the presence of the sovereign land is at once ideal and immediately torn to shreds, no more complete or viable is the representation of the sovereign in *Hamlet*, even if in both cases the idea of such integrity is nonetheless invoked. Here, the prompt of memory is not only already existentially a ghost – of uncertain reality, it might be thought; insubstantial in any case and of equivocal status as a presence – but it is also caught up in the difficulties of likeness and unlikeness which in the very insistence of their repetitiveness bespeak an anxiety, an anxiety about speaking which belies the authority of the narrative of traditional power. Even if there is the possibility of a somewhat traditional *epistemological* discussion concerning the veracity of ghosts in particular, unlikeness – disidentity – and the difficulty of narration trouble the problematic of representation throughout the play. The trouble is powerfully initiated here at the beginning, however, as, variously, Marcellus, Barnardo and Horatio countenance the likeness of the apparition: 'Look where it comes again'; 'In the same figure like the King that's dead'; 'Looks a not like the King? Mark it, Horatio'; 'Most like. It harrows me with fear and wonder' (I.i.43–7). Both Marcellus and Barnardo – the repetition is again important – notice that the ghost will be 'spoke to', and Marcellus urges Horatio to question it: 'Thou art a scholar, speak to it' (I.i.43–7). The terms in which Horatio addresses the apparition are significant: 'What art thou that usurp'st this time of night,/ Together with that fair and warlike form/In which the majesty of buried Denmark/Did sometimes march?' (I.i.49–52) It is the *same* 'figure' which is '*like*' the king. If the word 'figure' already comes from the language of representation – in the register of the diagram, or of the rhetorical figure or, as we say, 'figure of speech' – equally there is some dubiety of course in 'same' and 'like' which, in saying that the ghost resembles the king, indicates precisely that it dissembles the king, that it cannot *be* the king, especially not 'the King *that's dead*'. It is a figure which will need a scholar to address it because, in a further instance of the invocation of the representational grounds of comparison and disidentity in Hamlet's ejaculations against Claudius, if scholars may claim a traditional skill it is presumably in reading books and deciphering texts. The figure is like and unlike, both 'fair' and 'warlike', but in any case something which, in the language of the text here, usurps both time and form. Setting aside, for the moment, the role of time as a fundamentally contested signifier in the crisis of sovereign order, it is again the language of outline or shape, of *form* and not of substance, that insists here. And above all, that significant 'usurps' connects this hollowing of representation to its properly political register: the ghost is a form which threatens to supplant the 'majesty' of buried Denmark, although in another equivocation, only 'sometime'. It has become simply difficult to tell in buried Denmark. Representation has come for them to mean difficulty of telling in both the interleaved senses of colloquial speech: that it is difficult to know, and difficult to narrate.

The instances repeat themselves and proliferate as Marcellus, Barnardo and Horatio try to speak convincingly to each other, and later to Hamlet, of what they have seen. There are doubtful likenesses of doubtful likeness; the anxious repetition of repetition. Here is another example, one of Barnardo's attempts to convince Horatio: 'Sit down awhile,/And let us once again assail your ears,/That are so fortified against our story,/What we have two nights seen' (I.i.33–6). We should note here both the difficulty of conveying the message in the metaphor of having to 'assail' ears that are 'fortified', and that insistence in repetition of 'once again' and the 'two nights', which key into the repetitive emphases in this scene more widely on, precisely, *repeated* seeing and trying to tell.

The repetition doubles the need invested in the assertion that because the ghost is like the king, it *is* the king: or at least, faithfully represents him. But the anxiety of the insistence resides in the nagging potential of the gap between the likeness of representation on the one hand, and identity on the other, which the repetition and multiplication of comparisons fails convincingly and satisfyingly to close. Horatio's 'I knew your father;/These hands are not more like' (I.ii.211–2) seeks to close by a natural simile the distance of representation in his earlier 'a figure like your father' (I.ii.199) – where 'figure' came from the lexicon of representation and not from that of 'natural' identity. The most apparently natural of natural identifications has to be brought into play to try to ascertain the ghost as king, but in a form so interrogative, that the result is another of these four-term diagrams: 'Is it not like the King?', Marcellus asks Horatio, 'As thou art to thyself' (I.i.61–2) is the reply. Rather than the identity of the ghost and the king being fixed by virtue of a comparison with the likeness of a natural self to itself, the equivocal unlikeness of the ghost to the king tends rather to open a gap within 'natural' self-identity 'itself'. In any case, given what we know, here and elsewhere, of Shakespearean representations of identity, especially of the 'normality' of the displacement into identity so strangely evident in *Lear*, how like 'himself' *is* Hamlet exactly?

It is not necessary to credit the existence of centred identity as historically fundamental to have some palpable respect for the effectivity of the historical forms of the ideologies and practices of

C

this punctual selfhood. Indeed, it is significant here that – rather than a deconstructive fantasy of universal slippage from identity – the initiation, in the context of troubled likeness, of the theme of the need of memory is linked intrinsically to – the depredation of – the text's symbology of sovereignty and power. It is not merely any figure that is only equivocally like itself, and which must become, if only it were ascertainable, the object and content – as well as the represented prompt – of necessary memory. It is not *indifferent* that it is the figure of an – indubitably legitimate – king: 'Well may it sort that this portentous figure/Comes armed through our watch so like the King/That was and is the question of these wars.' (I.i.112–4)

If it were not so difficult to tell, that is. The image of the true king is already compromised by the problematic of representation adrift from itself, and in the event of the text we are presented with two kings: one dead, one alive; both unlike. The kings in question – like those of *Lear* – are, in practice rather than in form, unable to centre in representation any effective symbology of absolute power, however much that centrality remains extant *in principle* at the level of the ideology of the text's project. The text is thus set up, not universally but situatedly, against a horizon of the fullness of the sovereign past, but is then in the event unable to dramatise that sovereign plenitude except in its promissory, 'deep-structural' form as indeed the figure of the normal and the normative, this side of which we are constrained to deprecate the depredation of the present and to register the crisis, thus, as crisis. At the same time, we cannot help but read, in the event, the incapacity of the text to underwrite its sovereign figures. The desire – both authoritative and plaintive – for the sovereign to be re-membered, for its body to be reconstituted, fails to be satisfied in the history of a text and a drama which is nonetheless symbologically and ideologically predicated on that drive and that voice.

The discourse of the text must be oblique. If memory itself must perdure, but the representation of sovereignty cannot be sustained, then the text must resort to a strategic displacement. These drives – to sovereign recall and to the representation of depredation – are constituted as the reverse of each other. The result of which is that the discourse of sovereignty, in the nostalgic, 'negative' form we have so far come to expect in *Lear*, or in that of the insistence here in *Hamlet* on necessary memory, both struggle for existence. But they are forced into forms dislocated from the historical register in which they were generated and in which alone they could make historical sense. Thus, once initiated, the theme of necessary memory in *Hamlet* is carried through both the dominant, projective discourse of the play and also through the discrepant sub-texts of the event in the form not of sovereign history – and still less in that of some more radical historicity – but in that of mourning or, more frequently, the failed mourning which makes a subterranean way between both the injunction to remember and the difficulty of telling at the beginning, and the remaining problematic insistence on narration at the end. Hamlet's sardonic 'O heavens, die two months ago and not forgotten yet! Then there's hope a great man's memory may outlive his life half a year' (III.ii.128–30), is characteristic of the obliquity of the commentary on the disjointness of the times, combining as it does the issue itself – the unremembering of his father the king – and the throwaway form which is pregnant but itself disconnected, spoken only to the side in the face of the massive difficulty of telling that afflicts the play's representations. But it also exemplifies how, under the form of this dislocation of historical memory onto mourning, the play defines as what is crucial, as that which must be remembered and without which there will be no memory, as the remembering of the dead.

The structure of the displacement is, however, still further complex. It doesn't simply substitute one form of memory for another, but produces instead – at the level of what is substituted for historical memory – a dilemma. It is important to see how mourning in the play takes thus two forms, in the difference between the apparent personalism of a son remembering his dead father – grief, that aspect of mourning which is frequently thought of as belonging to the private – and another, public and ritualised form, 'commemoration', remembering together. The very design of this difference needs inspection, of course: there is, in the end, nothing 'private' in the sense of being simply personal and uncoded or undetermined by social practice, nor anything truly 'public' in the sense of a transparent objective sphere which is neither suborned by power nor traversed by influence. The form and the ideology of this disjunction, however, is powerfully inscribed in modern and early modern

Western society, and in the tendency of the culture – constituted, as in large measure it is, by this very structure – to accept the *caesura* between the public and the private in the first place and then to dehistoricise half or more of what is 'in fact' indifferently social life; and then to inhabit the consequences both of this structure and its 'illusion'. *Hamlet* comes to be organised by these separations, on the threshold of whose modernity it stands. By virtue of them, the displacement is able to set up a false option between grief and commemoration as it figures these two forms, offering a faulty solution to a spurious problem. From different perspectives, each appears a preferable alternative to the other. While what is privately remembered remains secret – as power obliterates public memory – it is made nonetheless to seem that only personal witness can be authentically counterposed to power. And yet grief, already hard to narrate, remains powerless, redoubled in both its poignancy and its impotence. By the same token, however, neither is collective memorialisation – in the morbid form the play deploys – an answer to the problem of the access to, and practice of, history. This 'solution', the choice of commemoration over grief, not only leaves intact the 'original substitution' which effaced the historical in the first place, but also offers a vitiated and empty form as its alternative. Thus, if Hamlet's grief cannot be historical memory and the prompt of action – certainly not for what might be called 'historical action', or 'practice' – commemorations in the form, at least, of funerals, are also flawed and truncated as in the case of Ophelia's, or are otherwise perceived as inadequate – secret rather than public – as is that of Polonius; and in any case, they are quickly forgotten, or 'superceded' like that of Hamlet's father. The representation of individual death has obscured historical continuity – or discontinuity – in the discourse of the text, and then both private grief and public commemoration of the individual death also break down as personal and 'collective' acts of mourning fail. The reaction to tragic death – as it is today – is doubly located, both within the private – familial and personal – space, and also in the public realm; with consequences of equal deleteriousness. The 'public' forms feel alien, ludicrous, perfunctory or even a betrayal of the dead, intrusively imposed on, and unfeelingly substituting themselves for authentically personal grief. Private grief radically denies the historical sociality of death, just as the society denies the sociality of life. Although it is as rooted in history as anything can be said to be 'rooted' in history, the radicalism both of grief, and of the public and historical being of the dead, is only obscured in the private condition.

The memory of the dead – and, it should be remembered, in the case of the two fathers, the *murdered* dead – is both the prompt of memory as such and the arena of its suspension and current impossibility. Constituted by an originary displacement, disempowered grief and inadequate commemoration provide the organising metaphors for the impossibility of memory as such.

But perhaps in turn this impossibility is itself a symptomatic sign of the invasion of the historical memory for which these forms were substituted, a registration doubtless of the crisis, if not eventually a marking – albeit more or less unwitting one – of the site and the limits of the original displacement? It is as if, in the very failure, it is somehow acknowledged that neither of these forms can do the historical work of that which they have been substituted for, and whose burden they cannot carry. Hamlet's antic discourse – even at its most intransitive – contains within it, and even enacts, a sense both that the assassination of the sovereign has been concealed, and that the life of his father is effaced. And in his case, as in that of Laertes, this is the prompt – with varying degrees in either case of supplementary delay – of violent response to these forgettings. The failure to sustain and save, even by way of displacement, what the text codes as the sovereign – in the restricted and extended senses – is betrayed by these signs of the depredation which is its consequence. In any case the king is obscured and the proper telling discontinued. The continuity of the traditional story looks like an illusion now, and violence must ensue.

As indeed, in the historicity of tragedy under discussion here, it does. In very profound senses, the Shakespearean tragic text is an information of violence in the wake of the discontinuity that becomes inscribed in the formation not just of the power of sovereignty's traditional story, but also in the story of its traditional power.

In *Hamlet*, memory has entered the curious supplementary condition Ophelia speaks of when she says ''Tis in my memory lock'd,/And you yourself shall keep the key of it.' (I.iii.85–6) What is remembered is something locked in, confined, preserved but suspended, present somewhere and yet denied effect in the world as discursive or other practice: hostage to another who is nonetheless incapable of it. Hamlet's frequent expostulations on his own inaction rehearse this form. But among the play's mnemonic figures that 'locking' of memory in the mouth of Ophelia is not without significance. Ophelia's role, and her engendered discourse in the play, up to the point of her so-called madness, has been either that of an object or an instrument in the conspiratorial action by power. Whether as a snare for Hamlet in some diagnostic or forensic trap, recipient of his impassioned denunciation, receptacle for pompous but admonitory advice from either her father, her brother or both at once, or for apparently kindly but actually coercive discourse from the king, she is the object of all that – masculine – discourse which seeks, along with the text itself, at once to use and to control her, allotting her a passivity and marginality which is both poignant and repulsive.

But when it comes, Ophelia's response is different from those of Hamlet or Laertes. Where in them inadequate commemoration prompts to violence, in her it prompts to breakdown (but also to a kind of empowerment), when at last she interrupts the action and finds a voice. Although when she does eventually speak in her own voice – powerfully, certainly disruptively, of this scene and its polity – the voice is not, of course, 'her own'. At least it is not the voice of a rational and centred, of a rationally centred, subject. Even setting aside here the question of whether there are in reality such entities, it is impossible not to see that Ophelia speaks in a voice which is both weirder and truer than rational discourse. After all, it is the alienated official rationality of Claudius's public statesmanship which sets the specious, factitious, plausible tone of what in public counts as truth and works as power, but which is built, of course, on both contingent and structural lies. If Ophelia's dispossessed speech is truer than what passes for rational discourse, arguably its 'folk' idiom, even although this is probably inevitably Shakespearean pastiche, is cognate with the register of the 'discourse of the heath'; a language is again heard which not only does not serve power, but which, even as it resists, takes its own way, apparently departing from the nameable identity of the register that makes these distinctions in the first place. Once again, out of somewhere in the textual unconscious comes an 'alternative' voice.

When the woman at last speaks in the play, she speaks in and from what the dominant can only conceive as another, strange, place, and in another tongue.

The form of her language is nonetheless framed and positioned by the dominant discourse, not least in such a way that it can be spoken of by the other characters at the scene of her madness in recuperative and sage ways, as if it were simply *'grief'* that was too much for her, without disclosing the conditions, which the dominant itself has made, of the possibility of her speech as such. Even ranting hyperbole in the male characters is not contained within the condescending pathos, the patronising compassion, that surrounds what in Ophelia is, arguably, extreme rage. The project of the Shakespearean text, as we know, is not reluctant – arguably this 'drive' is constitutive – to idealise, to demonise, or otherwise absentiate its representation of what it constructs as 'women': Goneril, Regan, Cordelia – and their mother – are the efficient instances. To be sure, Ophelia's speech is difficult to interpret. Or rather, the difficulty of interpretation, which has tended to be taken too much at face value by critics, is strongly signalled: the unfixity of her 'mad' speech is the form of its articulation. According to the gentleman who announces her deranged presence 'Her speech is nothing, /Yet the unshaped use of it doth move/The hearers to collection.' (IV.v.7–13) Her hearers 'aim' at her discourse and have to 'botch the words up fit to their own thoughts'. Ophelia's 'winks and nods and gestures .../Indeed would make one think there might be thought,/Though nothing sure, yet much unhappily'. (IV.v.7–13) The text puts it as though there were in her language nothing sure but much unhappily –, but which even empirically is only partially true of her discourse – this passage more *signifies* the 'madness' of her speech than it describes or instantiates its lack of meaning. Indeterminacy plays a part, but is by no means the entire texture of the 'nothing' of Ophelia's discourse, which can be resolved neither into simple expressivity, to be sure, but nor yet into inherent linguistic slippage of meaning from itself. In fact it is quite possible to determine in her songs and speech, even in the excess of their 'poetry' over 'ordinary' discourse, pertinent, cogent emphases on sexual betrayal, and on separation and loss. And, quite explicitly, on the burden of memory: 'There's rosemary, that's for remembrance – pray you, love, remember. And there is pansies, that's for thoughts.' (IV.v.173–7) As the gentleman also remarks, 'She speaks much of her father' (IV.v.4), and to be sure, her distracted speech and its plea for remembrance is obsessively and oppressively caught up in the patriarchal remembering of fathers and kings. But it is also in Laertes's estimation, 'A document in madness: thoughts and remembrance fitted.' (IV.v.173–7). It is a *document* of memory, where memory has already become, as we have seen, a copy or representation, a text, and one which is symptomatic of the crisis in that when in this world thoughts and rememberance *are* fitted, and become discourse – in the 'language of flowers' the world calls the result – sympathetically of course – 'madness'. On the heath in *Lear* we have already come across another context where disidentity and dispossession are called 'mad'; here the discourse of the need of the memory of dispossession, a similar disidentity, attracts the same label, even though it avowedly expresses 'thought'. And the upshot here, as I have suggested, is not the dramatised violence – verbal or otherwise – of elite figures like Hamlet and Laertes, but the off-stage, 'undecideable', death of the subject, 'Ophelia', herself, which not least in as much as it may have entailed violence against the self, however, becomes itself the object of inadequate commemoration.

In the dramatic sequence it is at the scene of Ophelia's death, or rather of its inadequate commemoration, that the last reaches of the action begin, at the juncture of Hamlet's return from England. And in that it articulates and refocuses the bad remembering of the play so far. It is by her semi-obscure grave, that we hear the discussion between the grave-digger and the clown which bears on the question of whether Ophelia's death was suicide and thus permissable or impermissable of Christian burial. This is picked up again in the speeches of the priest later which admit the 'doubtful' character of her death, with the obsequies, by fiat of power, enlarged as much as possible. Criticism has reproduced the inadequacy of commemoration and focused on Hamlet's further reflections on mortality, famously that of Yoric, and in effect repressed the memory of what is already a furtive, truncated, barely ceremonial burial, conducted under cover of darkness. Neither an 'authentic' expression of grief nor an effective public ritual – in the senses of that opposition which the play, or perhaps its romantic and post-romantic readings, has tried to establish – the practice of memory is shattered by the spectacle of Laertes and Hamlet at each other's throats in the grave itself, the funeral disrupted by their towering, competitive, violent anger. The 'woman's' narrative is not so much subject to closure as abandonment (a figure also doubtless symptomatic of the wider formation), occulted by Hamlet's and Laertes's ranting and hyperbolic claims of grieving love for her; behind the noise of which, of course, Ophelia is forgotten.

And yet a compulsion to remember remains insistent, and provides what is effectively the last word. If the play begins with a ghost enjoining memory, it also ends with a dead man reaching for *post mortem* narrative.

Hamlet expends much of his last dying breath enjoining Horatio to remember and tell: 'Had I but time – as this fell sergeant, Death,/ Is strict in his arrest – O, I could tell you —/But let it be. Horatio, I am dead,/Thou livest. Report me and my cause aright/To the unsatisfied.' (V.ii.341–5) Nothing here suggests that the narration will be easy. It is as difficult to tell now as it has been throughout: time and narration cannot be fitted to each other, and the speaker is about to become not the commemorator but the commemorated. Hamlet dies, like his father, 'Things standing thus unknown' (V.ii.349–54); the only difference from pure repetition being, on the evidence available, that Hamlet, although he actually speaks of himself in the present tense as dead, as if already a ghost, utters the injunction to remember with his dying voice rather than from beyond the grave. A sequel text could be imagined, which would begin with the return of the ghost of Hamlet: except of course, he has no son, and even generation, that peculiar Shakespearean metaphor of – mystified – historical sequence, is unavailable here. The telling of the significant story is obliquely displaced into the narration of another to the *unsatisfied*. And the harshness of the environment in which the telling will have to be done signifies instead not some facile continuity of tradition, as the master-discourse of the project might have desired, but a strain like that in the voice of the original ghostly prompt: 'If thou didst ever hold me in thy heart,/Absent thee from felicity awhile,/And in this harsh world draw thy breath in pain/To tell my story.' (V.ii.349–54) It signals the difficulty, the interruption and hollowing, of the present, even as it articulates the ineluctability of the need to remember.

But if, at the end, memory is imbricated with the difficulty of telling that has problematised its deployment throughout, its persistence there is also marked, even as it is articulated, above all, by way of sovereign notions – however promissory – of sequence, and succession in the royal sense. 'Thus unknown' summons up more than the fear that some individual's memory will be lost, just as the original death of the elder Hamlet, as the political assassination of the legitimate king, signals more than 'mere' death. Memory is back on the tragic scene of the state. What has persisted in the play as mourning is translated back into what we might call the 'historical' form of narration, a historicity signalled in the play not least by the proximity of the injunction to remember and narrate to the death of the reigning monarch and to the question – both practical and meta-physical – of the succession. Although there is no evidence so far that Hamlet favoured him or his cause, Fortinbras nonetheless has Hamlet's dying voice: 'So tell him, with th'occurrents more and less/ Which have solicited – the rest is silence.' (V.ii.362–3) Compared with the all-important succession, there is nothing but silence, or untelling. The text has Horatio accept the task of memory and narrative, absenting himself from the felicity of death – an absence from absence – in order to tell: 'let me speak', he says, 'to th'yet unknowing world' (V.ii.384). In order that the 'world' not remain in ignorance, not only of the past but of the future which is about to be imposed on it, the continuation of rule becomes the main theme of narration's speech, and the apparently metaphysical void of 'unknownness', unnarration, unmemory takes on its historical significance – a significance located, of course, in the very register of the depredation of sovereign order itself. If the *text* strives for historicity, the *play* invokes the only form of historical legitimacy its project can imagine, in a compulsion which equates the fear of the void of unknowing with its real content, a fear of a vacuum in royal power.

And it seeks then to supply once more that absence. Fortinbras himself calls up the resources of the legitimation of continuity which historical memory, on this – conservative – construction, apparently can provide, to gloss his own practical assumption of the throne: 'I have some rights of memory in this kingdom,/Which now to claim my vantage doth invite me.' (V.ii.394–7) From the point of view of the dominant project of the text, the 'deep structure' which grounds and organises the representation of depredation – 'invasion' – *as* depre-

dation, the ending has to be achieved, against all the odds of inefficient narration, by a discourse of succession, couched in the terms of
a language of sovereign memory.

The formations of memory in *Hamlet*, whether they take the form of
mourning or are in a wider sense putatively, if barely, 'historical' –
and we have seen the way in which in the depth of the field of this text
one displaces and stands in for the other – are conservative and even
nostalgic. But the insistence of both kinds of memory marks the site
of the irreducibility, however deracinated, of historicity, if the text is
to make meaning at all. Indeed, the very trajectory of the representation of Hamlet's identity – and with it, it seems, all that is otherwise
crucial in the play – from claimed interior essence to *post mortem*
narration by another – and, indeed, to the narration of the story and
not the self – suggests that straining through the personalist cast of
the play's coding of memory as mourning for the individual dead is
the demand for cultural memory rather than signs of individuation.
Indeed it might be argued that the form of this potential is offered in
particular by the function of memory as it is represented by the
travelling players, and by the text's inscription of their existence and
activity. Their work, after all, is collective, and public; their sphere of
activity cultural, and their political valency arguably critical. And in
the event of the play, they have, as well as a function of telling and
recording in general, a particular and local role in the quasi-forensic
exercise of *The Mousetrap*; or because of one, the other. Both are
important, and both are involved in power and its counter-valuation,
in its representation and its unlikeness.

At first sight however, the players look like another formation of
personal memory. Hamlet warns Polonius to treat them well in these
terms: 'Do you hear, let them be well used, for they are the abstract
and brief chronicles of the time. After your death you were better
have a bad epitaph than their ill report while you live.' (II.ii.519–22) If
there is an equivocation between chronicles and epitaphs, between
history and death, it is the equivocation of the wider play. The idea of
the bad epitaph seems to link the function of the players simply to the
commemoration of the dead. But if so, it is as much by difference as
by similarity. If the report of the players can be like an epitaph, it is
one which belongs to the living. For it is *now*, in present time, that

they are brief chroniclers. And if they are recorders of the time, it is not simply in the form of some complacent celebration of life or commemoration of the great after death, but in a *critical* mode: it is their *ill* report that is to be avoided. Commentators have remarked that it is the description of the general role of the actor in Hamlet's 'O what a rogue and peasant slave' soliloquy (II.ii.544–601), where the function of the player includes that of making mad the guilty and appalling the free, which prompts their particular use in *Hamlet*. And it is in such an oppositional role that the players in the play *Hamlet* are cast – in the forensic device of exposing the guilt of the murderous usurper Claudius. There has been considerable debate as to whether the theatre underwrites, opposes or even 'negotiates' state power, but here, at any rate, it appears to be enlisted against con- temporary power (even if a compensatory romanticism – at bottom legitimatory – of Shakespeare's theatre, rather than the vagabond players', is at work here). For the players, as Hamlet himself remarks during their performance, 'cannot keep counsel: they'll tell all'. Given the difficulty of narration which has otherwise organised the text, this in itself is indeed remarkable. And if Hamlet's declaration about the conscience of the king is famous, the preceding line is at least as instructive: 'I'll have grounds/More relative than this. The play's the thing/Wherein I'll catch the conscience of the king.' (II.ii.599–601) As he says this, Hamlet is, of course, planning the play within the play which will stage the murder of his father in the public gaze, or rather in the gaze of the king, which amounts to the same thing here, where the absolutely sovereign is in principle both subject and object, ideologically both foundation and spectacle. His purpose is to have Claudius perform signs of his guilt: hence his fierce instructions to Horatio to observe the King during the performance of the play within the play, and hence all the critical and scholarly writing that has been engendered by Claudius's failure to respond to the dumbshow which precedes the dialogue of *The Murder of Gonzago*. And above all it is important here that Hamlet wants both 'grounds', a word rich with meanings in respect both of representation and land; and also grounds more 'relative', a word which is usually glossed as 'cogent' or even 'relevant', but has importantly also the meaning 'relatable' or able to be told to the public. Uncontestable foundation and the possibility of true narration are what the players will help him 'have'. The point of *The Mousetrap* is not so much to ascertain the guilt of Claudius as to prove it, or at least to force it into the open, to retrieve it from secrecy. If the players 'tell all', this is positioned both dramatically and discursively – 'telling' seems otherwise impossible in Denmark – in opposition to the official forgetting of Claudius's account of the death of the elder Hamlet, and to the wider, chronic weight of mnemonic occlusion which distresses in various ways both the text and the society of the play as a whole.

But on the other hand, if the players represent the possibility of a disclosure, of a narration in present time against secret oppression or hidden and forgotten right in *'buried'* Denmark, the fact that the power the players are used to undermine is a *usurped* one, may give to their function a conservative cast. Although operative in respect of present time rather than for memory coded as mourning, they are nonetheless engaged on the side of Hamlet and *Hamlet*'s project which originates in, and on the surface of the play is motivated by, the command of the father in a framework of the desire for the restitution – or at least the vindication – of past legitimacy.

In fact there is a double – dialectical – formation of contradictory drives at work here. From one point of view, clearly, it would take massive re-writing to make this kind of tragedy radical. In as much as it is linked to restitution and the past, even in its present-time forms the narrational ability of the players would argue a conservatism, if not a nostalgia at the level of what I have been calling the 'deep-structural' or the subterranean, which informs the tragic formation as such. The mode of the critique of memory loss in the players, in the represented intentions of the character Hamlet, and in the play's wider thematics of commemoration, is not (as with everything else in the play) uncontaminated by the *project*, which *is* conservative and seeks to underwrite the patriarchal, monarchic authority it takes to be extant, even as it idealises it. Its past, like *Lear*'s, is a tragic fiction. At the same time, the function of the players must be seen within what might have to be called a political epistemology which – *even if it uses the signifier of the past* – is engaged in a retrieval of the forgotten from the occluded secrecy of present time. This is their narrational-critical purpose, where the narrational *is* critical, in as much as in itself narration runs against the grain of the representational – and indeed ontological – situation of the text's empowered representation of 'reality', which power itself constitutes as constitutively involving what is critical being officially and powerfully forgotten. As narrators under the auspices of the project of restoration they must perforce tell a retrogressive tale; as historians where the preservation of contemporary power depends upon the occlusion of the past, they are, by that very gesture, critically dislocated from the sovereign amnesia which they can only badly serve.

If the problematicity of remembering and telling remains in, and is renewed by, Hamlet's injunction that Horatio survive and narrate the full story, it should also be said that under the pressure of the dialectic between the sovereign desire for continuity on its own terms and the representation of its impossibility – the impossibility under determinate historical circumstances of its representation – in the tragic text, the question is always finally truncated by the compromise-formation which, in hope and default of full closure in the re-institution of sovereign plenitude, at least ends each of these 'high' tragedies of state. The project, the master-narrative of *Hamlet*, moves from the opening issue of legitimacy and usurpation to a closure in reinvested central rule. But although traces of the Elizabethan theory and symbology of majesty persist near the end – 'such divinity doth hedge a king' (IV.v.123) – what the play dramatises in the event is the diminished sequence which traces a difficult line from the equivocal identity of the hardly remembered king-in-representation at the beginning, to the opportunist and doubtful legitimacy – and still more doubtful symbolic efficacy – of the eventual rule of Fortinbras. If Hamlet's naming Fortinbras as in effect his heir and in practice *his* successor seems arbitrary, still less does it appear that Fortinbras has any legitimate objective claim on the crown based on either blood or law. In practice his assumption is based on the power that he alone now has, while structurally it mediates the central dialectic of the project and the event. On the one hand, memory manifestly doesn't work; but on the other, the king must not die. The depredation of the event offers the destruction of the sovereignty which the master-discourse still takes to be extant. But the subject is still capable of introjecting an 'unless': destruction unless the 'structure' of the society – that is, its power-structure as coded by the still dominant but residualising ideology – can be kept alive. But in the event, in turn, it can only be revived by force, or as we might say, by Fortinbras. The centre, or at least central rule, is, in Fortinbras, reinvested and reinvented. But the force kills the project: the diminution of affect at the end gives the game of symbology away, the sacred is embarrassingly made secular, and power nakedly materialised. Like *Lear*, the play ends not in succession but invasion, not in the restitution of either represented or symbolic sovereignty, but in the compromise of the pragmatic legitimacy of the figure of Fortinbras, as, in order to solve its ideological and aesthetic problems, the text imposes military rule on itself. Memory, once again in the form of forgetting.

But if the conservatively-constituted memorialisations and the radically inflected narrational-critical practices tend in the event to merge, are we then to hand over the text and the sub-texts to the reaction of their dominant project? Perhaps not entirely, because of the very signs, however transmuted into forms of nostalgia and morbidity, of history – or 'historicity' – which are at stake. The need of memory, or, now, *history*, need have nothing nostalgic about it: this, quite apart from anything which might be brought to bear on the question later, is signalled by the 'radical' side of the players. At stake is not just the loss of what the play conservatively imagines as the whole substance of the past, but the loss of the dimension of *historicity* defined as the social capacity to remember and to narrate, not in order to preserve the official content of the past, but on the contrary – as in the players' present-time, narrational-critical function, and the other signs of the perdurance of memory – to be able to inscribe the historical character of the present, both as structure and event. Despite the forgetting with which the master-narrative has defined sovereign history, the loss of this capacity is to lose the ability to establish, and make meaningful in the future, those significant parallax senses of the the difference of the past; it would be to lose the power to unfix and overcome the tyranny of the facticity of the present.

If in *Hamlet* the terms of the dialectic appear to converge, it is because a society that loses its memory dies.

*   *   *

The death of history is also engaged in *Macbeth*. The assault on what counts in the depicted society of that text as history, is bloody, violent and eventually resolute.

In any case, the play begins in a moment of decision from its own pre-history, with the 'hurly burly' of both insurrection and invasion.

If, in the Shakespearean text, sovereignty is marked in the projective inviolability of the land, and by absolute definition in the authority of the monarch, both are breached in the opening gesture of *Macbeth*. And, like *Lear* and *Hamlet*, it also ends with invasion. Together these figures set the play in a *dispositif* of violation and defence of the sovereign land, which constitute its politico-symbolic frame.

But surely then we should think of *Macbeth* as a comedy? For if it opens with rebellion against the legitimate king and incursion by the rebels' foreign allies, this threat to territorial integrity and sovereign authority is successfully crushed. Do we not see in the opening of the history of the drama not the depredation of the realm, but its successful defence; and in the wider sense thus – given the way the master-signifiers work – the underwriting of the sovereign rather than its undermining? The invasion of the end – like, but less ambiguous than, Cordelia's return to Britain to vindicate Lear's right – is one carried out in the name of restitution. And it is one which successfully restores the royal line to the throne, ensures the succession in physical and metaphysical senses, and re-legitimates, after the interim of usurpation, not only the ruling house but the signification of sovereign order itself. There is no *founding* question of succession in *Macbeth* as there is in *Hamlet* and *Lear*, nor is there in the proper succession of Malcolm at the end – whatever the depredations of the interim – any remaining void in the sequencing of sovereign rule on into a restored future. And in an important sense *Macbeth* comes closest among the tragedies (in a dramatic manner much like that of the English Histories) actually to dramatising, in the figuration of Duncan, and the sacred language that surrounds his person, the full presence of the king. As an ideological text it is altogether closest to achieving the representation of the sovereign project in its positivity. Rather than the ever-just-having-become-absent character of kingship that hollows sovereign representation in *Lear* and *Hamlet*, in *Macbeth*, surely, the sovereign appears in person, fully embodied, socially and symbologically?

But *Macbeth* is not a comedy. It is not a play of plenitude but of crisis, and of a very violent interim indeed, in which it is not so much the representation of presence that is most fully articulated, as its violent absentiation that organises the tensions which shape the text. Indeed to address *Macbeth* is inevitably to address violence. Or rather, two violences, as the Shakespearean tragic text swerves between, on one hand, the demonisation of violence, and on the other the contemplation of violent solutions to the historical blockages and depredations which form the nexus of its event.

If there is crisis, certainly little in *Macbeth* is identical with itself. And once the King is dead, nothing.

If the frame, and much of the substance of the drama, discloses political disruption in the large structures of sovereignty, to no less a degree is the representation of the individual also in crisis. And it is so in a fashion that finds its proper language not in the ineffability of personal essences (which the text presupposes, invokes and valorises), but in the forms of disidentity that texture its actual practice. It is a process of naming and renaming that first discloses the identity question in *Macbeth*, as 'Macbeth' or 'Glamis' becomes successively 'Cawdor' and eventually 'King'. There is, in any case, difficulty – analogous to that which inflects the ghostly status of the discourse of the elder Hamlet – in ascertaining either the ontological or the epistemological reliability of the witches' prognostications. Moreover, the opening sequences of the play, subtend a relative alienation of the signifier, where the name, and the process of naming is not so much essentially naturalised as discursively deployed, where there is an uncertain fissuring between the name and what is named. From the first the text establishes Macbeth not by character and essence but by function, as militarily efficient, and both politically and – in the sense in which the play defines the social – 'socially', loyal; loyal that is to the form and substance of its sovereignty. But even then, its problematic handling of 'identity' is disclosed in something like the sliding ambiguity of an appellation such as the Captain's 'brave Macbeth (well he deserves that name)' (I.ii.16) where 'name' slips from noun to adjective and back. Is it the name 'brave' he deserves – this is the evident meaning – or the nomination 'Macbeth', which is the only name proper? And if it is the latter, who – or what – is the 'he' that deserves: an unnamed – perhaps unnameable – indifferent, neutral substance, a mere '*träger*' of the name which 'Macbeth' in any case already bears? Even within the reported, 'objective' character of the introduction of Macbeth to the tragedy which bears his name, we find, before Macbeth can appear 'in person', puzzling formulations like those of Rosse's account of

Macbeth's encounter with the rebel Thane of Cawdor, whose name he soon acquires. Macbeth is described as having 'Confronted him with self-comparisons' (I.ii.56). ... We may wonder why such an emphasis on likeness with the rebel enemy, rather than difference, should inform the pre-dramatic construction of the identity of the epitome of loyalty. The error of names and titles in the first act sets in train in *Macbeth* the problematisation of identity which is such a powerful component of the Shakespearean tragic formation more widely. In *Lear* and *Hamlet*, and again here in *Macbeth*, is enacted more a dispersal of self among patterns of likeness – comparison – and representation, than a fixing of self in whatever models of old or new identity might be available.

This problematising of identity insists, and persists, through such crucial moments of textual negotiation as Macbeth's animadversions, in the face of the contemplation of the royal murder, on what it is to be a man – against the minatory limits provided by an apprehension of transcendent aspiration as unnatural hubris, or declination from nature into bestiality – and Lady Macbeth's famous rejection, in the same circumstances, of traditional gender-identifications, with all the misogynistic charge invoked by her unsexed willingness to dash out the brains of her child. It leads ultimately to a distance from self-possession analogous to Lear's, when 'To know my deed, 'twere best not know myself' (II.ii.72). This is a troubling of the normative ensemble of the knowing self and that which is known. If the identity of the objective, reported Macbeth of Act I Scene II was in a sense defined by the deed, here to know the deed is figured as a deracination of the self, splitting it from, rather than identifying it with, either the objective deed or the self that is uttered. It offers up again that structure of disidentity which tends in the event to be the rule rather than the exception.

It is a complex structure as we have seen in *Lear* and *Hamlet*, because the desire of identity fixation which is the – unperformable – background norm against which disidentity is implicitly defined as aberration, is not itself undifferentiated. In fact, two different general forms of 'identity' are in transitional contestation with each other. A residual definition by relation to the king – whether 'social' in the sense of being inscribed in the representation of feudal rank, or 'moral' in the sense of loyalty (that is, in fact, diligent service to the sovereign) – is in the course of historical supplementation and supersession by an identity defined as subjectivity (configured within an equally emergent sense of the individual deed, a new secular activism replacing the residual ethic of service and obligation). And we should note that in addition there is no simple characterological unity here either: the line dividing the old and the new does not actually run between 'characters', but is constituted among dimensions of the figuration of 'single' characters. The vacillations of 'Macbeth', for example, mix old-style duty and new-style individualistic aspiration, plagued by the guilty conscience which is apparently a major component of subjectivity itself.

In any case, neither kind of definition of identity is ever quite stabilised in *Macbeth*. This is not least because in *Macbeth*, like *Hamlet*, individuals are not normally attributed essences but writings. Lady Macbeth: 'Your face, my Thane, is as a book, where men/May read strange matters' (I.v.62–3). In this resonant phrase there seems to be an imputation of writing which is, in principle, interpretable – men may read there. But in practice what they will find is at best 'strange matters'. And in any case, the statement is made in the name of one of Lady Macbeth's characteristic injunctions to Macbeth to perform a false signification: 'To beguile the time,/Look like the time; bear welcome in your eye ...' (I.v.63–4). Beguilement is about the least of the violences eventually perpetrated on time, as we shall see below; but if here there is merely guile, elsewhere there are books of the self where the reading is altogether more difficult. If the gaze of the king himself – or, as we might say, the sovereign *itself* – encounters the problem that 'There's no art/To find the mind's construction in the face' (I.iv.11–12), clearly something is profoundly wounded in the representation of the transparency to sovereign power of the erstwhile loyal subject. But nor should this be taken to mean that the problem is one of a merely local and aberrational difficulty of interpreting from the outside what is within, because the difficulty is 'interior' too: the emphasis is not just on the failure of interpretative 'art', but on the very 'construction' of the mind in the face. The difference caught in the metaphorics of writing, is, so to speak, essential; constitutive of what in practice counts as the individual, which turns out to be unrepresentable in any form of undifferentiated identity, much as such representation informs the desire and assumption of the project. This, by the way, is one of the reasons why the traditional model of 'seeming' is so inadequate: it

presupposes plain truth behind the mask, but the difficulty of identity
is inherent to the self, not simply hidden by a false covering or
'appearance'.

But on the other hand, the uncertainty, the disidentity – an
'undecideability' repugnant equally to the Shakespearean project and
the humanist tradition on whose threshold it stands – should not
provide a mirror image of that tradition in the sense of legitimating
some deconstructive notion of universal error from self as in fact the
norm. Rather than a given condition, there is context here for the
limit of the king's gaze. It is insurrectionary violence against him; an
interruption of the sovereign power which is, as it were, historical
rather than universal, and in which the equally historical crisis of
representation is imbricated.

We have seen in *Hamlet* that memory, whether 'personal' or
'social', is an important site of crisis. No less does *Macbeth*, by
turning it into text, trouble any easily settled sense of memory: 'my
dull brain was wrought/With things forgotten. Kind gentlemen, your
pains/Are register'd where every day I turn/The leaf to read them.'
(I.iv.150–3) But as with Hamlet's 'distracted globe', turning the mind
into book doesn't produce the centred certainty of an essential subject
located both spatially ('socially') and temporally (in an historical continuum), but an image of identity decentred, at a remove from itself
both in space and time, incapable of the likeness of representation,
and without access to appropriate forms of continuity. In the very
moment of saying that he doesn't hear because he is preoccupied
with 'things forgotten', Macbeth also vouchsafes that the said of the
utterance is nonetheless registered in the book of the memory which
he may consult daily. Implicit in his formulation is an ontological
assumption about a certain lived continuity of experience being only
apprehendable as continuity – and therefore, as experience – by the
use of memory. But even if we knew nothing of the problematic of
writing and merely took for granted normal and normative accounts
of memory as intimate to, if not actually definitive of, self, who here is
'he', or 'I', figured at that distance from self across which self does not
inhabit either the place or discourse of the self, but speaks of self as
an objective other? The problem becomes diagnostic, and indeed
'objective' – or at least external – again when, during Lady
Macbeth's final displacement from self, Macbeth both plaintively and
angrily demands of the doctor whether he cannot, in order to

'minister to a mind diseas'd', 'Pluck from the r
sorrow' and 'Raze out the written troubles of the b
surgery or erasure of inscription is possible: †
oblivious antidote' to 'Cleanse the stuff'd bosom'
doctor washes his hands of any such attempt to re-centre ᴜ.
The 'troubles' are figured not simply in some abstract discussion oɪ,
say, 'evil', or, in a more modern register, pathology, but rather as ones
which, because of their writtenness – which is in turn caught up in
the thematics of the necessity and difficulty of memory – throw into
relief the problematicity of identity-in-representation. Only memory
will hold the centre, only oblivion will cure the ill of the self. Taking
the theme as a whole in *Macbeth*, we glimpse a simultaneous
identification of memory, as both impossible and essential. Because
the radical sorrow, which is now *both* her self *and* her aberration,
cannot be plucked out, 'I', at a distance from itself, will always be
eccentric to what 'I' is defined by. In sum, the problematicity of the
self constitutes an ideological impasse that cannot be resolved but
only evaded, in another rehearsal of the form of compromise we have
noted in the tragic formation already. It is simply cancelled, by stoic
narrowing and death.

But as in *Lear* and *Hamlet*, so in *Macbeth*, the link should be stressed
between the disidentity inscribed in the individual, and discontinuity
in the historical sense. The text imbricates its powerful evocations of
disidentity, or absence of identity, with the uncontainable act of
absolute violence that lies at its centre: the assassination of the king.
The failure of personal and cultural memory is articulated with the
demise of the sovereign, with the absentiation of what alone the
master-discourse of the text is capable of conceiving as historical
sense. And by the same token, whether identity is inscribed in old-
style feudal-hierarchic terms (as the text imagines the past), or in the
new-style emergent, essential and interiorate form, the elimination of
the king entails inherent disfunction of memory and identity.

As we have seen, the instability of represented identity is inscribed
in the process of naming and renaming of Act I. If memory and
violence are not strangers to each other, neither do acts of naming
entirely lack a violent dimension. Indeed the process of renaming,
and the insistent destabilisation of identity-in-representation disclosed

hereby, comes first out of the violence of the war: Macbeth wins new names by force of arms. Renaming is fundamentally part of the process by which Macbeth approaches the central violation of the sovereign. And when the assassination is done, there is a powerful consequential effect on identity in all of the play's metaphoric and metonymic registers. When the king is dead Macbeth's clothes – to cite but one of these metaphoric 'chains' in which identity and its breakdown is inscribed – don't fit. If an uneasy sense of 'borrowed robes' precedes the murder of Duncan, the effect is intensified to the limit afterwards. Given the imbrication of the symbolisation of the sovereign in the body of the king, Macbeth's feeling ill at ease in his costume is probably at root a distance from his own body. Lady Macbeth, in the desire to be 'unsexed', seems to name this for what it is. The unfitness of clothing before and after the murder replicates the initial, unfamiliar naming, as preparation for, and consequence of, the truly central act of false naming and wrong dressing: Macbeth's assumption, after the regicide, of the name and costume of the king. True names, proper dress, identical and natural bodies, disappear into the past, along with the king. That this is thus a *nostalgia* for fitness may betray, in the event of the play, the suspicion that the 'identity' which is not itself, which is displaced and doubled, is not aberrant but – in the 'actual' – the absolutely normal. In any case, it is intimately part of the assault on the sovereign that lies at the heart of the text.

Macbeth is, throughout, a play of hurt and violence. It begins and ends in violent insurrection and invasion; coupled at the beginning, merged at the end. And of the high tragedies, *Macbeth* is without doubt the most bloody, both in terms of the violence of events and of the symbolisation of the blood that has fascinated so many commentators. The initial designation of Macbeth as warrior and fighting machine, and the graphic and particularly bodily account of his deeds against the rebels and invaders, in particular the manner in which, in the Captain's account, he destroys Macdonwald, 'unseam'd him from the nave to th'chops,/And fix'd his head upon our battlements' (I.ii.21–2), paves the way not only for the central assassination, and perhaps ultimately for the eventual display of Macbeth's own severed head – 'self-comparison' indeed – but also for the reign of both physical and metaphysical terror which Macbeth's rule is to become. The serial is soon remorseless, in both ethical and deterministic senses, of murder after murder, forming, after the killing of Duncan, the main narrative action of the play. It is a sequence which is a ghastly parody of historical process as the sovereign project would have a benign monarchical history represented; perhaps it is a revealing one.

But, of course, the way in which *Macbeth* installs violence in itself as a text is as significant as the empirical violence of the action. It is not just that violence is depicted, but that the text is instinct with violence in its very constitution as tragedy. Violence is a critical and not only a descriptive term.

At the heart of it is indeed the death of Duncan. For if *Macbeth* is the tragedy that comes closest to dramatising the monarch in presence (and I remarked earlier on the relative positivity of invasion and rebellion defeated and eventual succession achieved), equally it comes closest to dramatising, only just in the wings, the violent overthrow of that same sovereignty. Although for ideologico-aesthetic reasons the assassination of Duncan does not actually take place on stage, and in this sense is not represented, it nonetheless occupies a place in *Macbeth* whose importance can hardly be overstated; not least its importance for the discourse of sovereignty which is both underwritten and violently assaulted in it. Before the event, the text has already endowed the person of Duncan with the qualities and properties of specifically sacred monarchy. In the event of the assassination, the violation of the body of the king is then put into these terms: 'Most sacrilegious Murther hath broke ope/The Lord's annointed Temple' (II.iii.66–7); and his wounds are said to be no less than 'a breach in nature' (II.iii.111). Much has been written, and it is not necessary to rehearse it all here, about the sacred symbolism of the discourse that surrounds Duncan, and about the language in which the horror of the act, and of the implications of the act, of killing him is couched. This is language which looks extraordinary today because it is, as it were, global: what is at stake is not 'merely' the death of an individual, but of something more, of an entire ideological and social system, a whole symbolic order.

But if in *Macbeth* there are signs of the underwriting of important sovereign forms, signs, as it were, of counter-invasion, and the king is, for what turns out to be nonetheless a rather fleeting period, dramatically 'present', so much the more graphic is the violence of the sovereign's elimination from history. The foregrounding – in comparison with the other plays – of that great act of violence, the killing of the king, throws into relief the unrepresentability of that allegedly full sovereignty to an even greater degree than the decay from power of *Lear* and the dramatic argument about legitimacy in *Hamlet*. If *Macbeth* displays the 'most body' of the king, then the murder of Duncan is, as it were, the 'most' violence. Sacred terms define the inviolability of the sovereign, and thus measure and demonise the enormity of the transgression entailed in the murder. (The 'secular,' but no less 'anthropological', prohibitions – on the killing of a guest, for example – are also not unimportant markers of the boundary of what is sanctioned.) But it is also important to remark the violation itself and the way in which these sanctions –and the wider underwriting of the sovereign formation – thus serve, in the event, both to confirm the ideology of kingship in an unassailable positivity, and also to heighten and intensify the assault on that ideology which inheres in the act of political murder and 'social' violation at the centre of the play. If there is presence here, it is only in as much as the act concentrates the perpetrated absentiation of the king and the sovereign. This is the doubly tensioned formation of the tragic. The 'ruse', as it were, of the project consists in the wager that 'most presence' intensifies the demonisation of the absence of the sovereign. But the event 'responds' with that absentiation, with the failure of the project to be able to sustain the presence as an effective and practical, as well as a symbolically inviolate, deployment.

One of Hamlet's symbolisations of the general crisis, and of his own critical predicament, mobilises the language of the time which is 'out of joint' (I.v.196). In *Macbeth* too, the apparently definitive assault on sovereignty is also an absolutely sense-destroying violence, the assassination of the king both producing and symbolising the ultimate disruption of the absolute metaphysical frame – ideology at its most pervasively effective. As in *Hamlet*, this assault on sovereignty co-involves the dismantling even of time itself. Certainly *Macbeth* is a text extraordinarily marked by signs of time. It is full, replete to the point of fracture in fact, with references to the time and times in which – and out of which – the action takes place. But the time of the play is neither, coherently, the artificially 'real' time of the classical and neo-classical unities, nor the quotidian time of realism or naturalism, the time of the positivist novel and certain more recent forms of drama. For if in *Lear* formations of the representation and disrepresentation of the land mutate and distort, so in *Macbeth*, in addition, there is a similar self-discrepant complex of forms of time, similarly underlining the deformation of what might otherwise be taken to be both a fundamental and an immutable regularity in the order of reality itself. The marks of time vary, in *Macbeth*, in their symbolic density as on a spectrum (although there are also some sharp breaks between the kinds of time at work, as well as some shading of one into another). At one end of the range there are indeed mundane markers of the time of day or night, by which barely a scene passes without some reference to the time of its event. Although in each particular case they are frequently 'realistic', taken together these markers amount not so much to a coherent realistic time of the kind which would allow a chronological chart of the action of the play to be drawn up – this could probably be done, at least for stretches of the action, but it is not the point – as to an effect of urgency, even anxiety, in the general 'atmosphere' of the play's representations. This in turn is linked to such intransitive but insistent examples as the witches' numinous 'Tis time, 'tis time' (IV.i.3), which conveys a sense of imminent eventuality. But even at their most chronographically ordinary, these markers of time are extraordinary for their number and insistence: as many such temporal deictics can surely hardly be equalled in a work of this type and length.

But then these kinds of reference to time impinge in turn on others which have a certain symbolic profile, hinging 'ordinary', chronometric time onto the various characterisations – in which the text inscribes much of its account of the crisis it 'represents' – of 'the times', or even Time as such. In, for example, the exchange between Macbeth and Banquo at the beginning of Act III, apparently ordinary references to the timing of the coming banquet take on an urgency and a symbolic colouration, as time becomes the charged space of danger, and the medium to master, or in which to be mastered: Macbeth's 'Let every man be master of his time' (III.i.40) takes on a sinister register when followed immediately by his interview with the murderers which sets the trap for Banquo's assassination. And in turn, these semi-symbolic references to time reach towards the more conceptually elaborate passages where the character of the time and its lack of joint is evoked. For if to call the times 'cruel' in an example like Rosse's 'But cruel are the times, when we are traitors,/And do not know ourselves' (IV.ii.18–19), is, as an epithet, more or less a cliché, the association with not knowing ourselves – with that ontological and epistemological dissimulation of identity which is so significant in the Shakespearean tragic formation – nonetheless imbricates Rosse's remark in a discourse of the profound denaturing of time, of the kind where, elsewhere in the text, even a sign as extreme as the monstrosity of the walking dead, unholy resurrection, is not at all unusual. Macbeth's expostulation that 'the time has been,/That, when the brains were out, the man would die,/And there an end; but now, they rise again' (III.iv.77–9), marks this sense of the denaturing of time, and also evokes, by the way, the failure of what is elsewhere called 'the deed' – defined as the infliction of violent death – to achieve the punctuality it seemed to offer.

But whatever their degree of mundanity, symbolic richness or conceptual abstraction, overarchingly the time-markers are located in – and locate – the discrepancy between a nostalgic project or projection of time, and the actual dramatisation of a quite different, 'existential' disorganisation of reality. A present disjointedness in the body of time is compared unfavourably with a former period of implied temporal coherence; a time, of course, of the fullness of the king's body. Such a nostalgia is even registered in Macbeth's wish that the present horror be taken from 'the time,/Which now suits with it' (II.i.59–60). Whatever it was that might once have been fit in time, and may have guaranteed the fitness of this most fundamental sign of coherence, or whatever might in the project of the play eventually be restored to time, now, in the violent present, as Macbeth understands, it is only 'horror' that 'suits' with the temporality of the present.

This discrepancy between an older, full time and a hollowed present time of horror is, however, a somewhat facile ideological structure: although in the form of its antithetical opposite, the latter even belongs to the same problematic as the former, 'original' time of the king. But if the disjunction between these two forms of time is symptomatic of the crisis, that crisis insists even more profoundly beneath this opposition: the real horror, in the estimation of the play's dominant discourse, is of an activism which will offer to make time fit into a new form, within a problematic, and with ideological implications that the text will not, dominantly, tolerate. Thus even horror turns out to be a relatively full temporality when compared with another of the forms which the text will soon inflict. As with so much else that is actually dynamic in the text, it is initially more Lady Macbeth than Macbeth who is associated with this activism that the play will demonise. She grasps what is essential: that the potential exists for remaking time, 'Thy letter hath transported me beyond/ This ignorant present, and I feel now/The future in the instant.' (I.v.56–8) If, for her, the present is a time of ignorance – and many have characterised 'feudal stagnation' in this way – the letter, significantly enough, prompts an aspiration which is prepared dynamically to reshape time in a quasi-modernist, if not almost revolutionary, apprehension of the present 'instant' as a constellation pregnant, shot through, with a desired future. Against Macbeth's hesitations in the face of proper limits – 'I dare do all that may become a man;/Who dares do more, is none' (I.vii.46–7) – Lady Macbeth will incite this very activism, which she counterposes to Macbeth's current hesitations, urging upon him a willingness to seize time and make it fit: 'Nor time, nor place,/Did then adhere, and yet you would make them both' (I.vii. 51–2).

To *make* time and place adhere, however, contains ideological implications which are not acceptable to the master-discourse of the text: appearing too secular, too reliant on individualised and individuated human action, and too clearly located on that historical interface where Renaissance aspiration begins to look like a form of new, and newly historical, praxis which will contemplate the use of any means that serves its ends. In respect of the totalisation of the discourse of kingship at stake, it would begin to be right to talk about the insurrectionary, if not revolutionary, character of Macbeth's deed, *in so far as* (and the qualification needs to be stressed) it offers not 'simply' to kill Duncan, the king, but to change – in the order of discourses of sovereignty – the entire order of things as such, to effect an *historical* discontinuity in its transgression of all that is symbolically 'holy' and politically hegemonic. And, of course, like all revolutionary action, this entails not only the physical act of seizure of effective power, but the ideological reshaping, to the most 'fundamental' level, of the practices and discourses of socio-political and 'personal' life. Or, to put it more precisely, no revolutionary act is revolutionary – let alone historically successful – unless it also grows out of such a reshaping.

There are a number of ways in which it is possible to see such a transformation offered – or rather, threatened – in *Macbeth*. The discourse of Lady Macbeth in particular – even demonised as it is by the text – implies, seeks, and desires the quite profound transmutation of central assumptions about ethical action, and offers, in doing so, quite new perspectives for action; for seizing the time, rather than subordinately inhabiting its ever-pre-established order. But the text is not content to represent things in this way. On the contrary, even if the dominant discourse of the play – what I have been calling the project of the tragedies – cannot sustain itself, and must admit what it seeks to forestall, at its strongest ending only in a compromise formation with what it fears, it nonetheless exists precisely to warn against such an alteration in the sovereign order. It is thus probably neither accidental nor gratuitous that it is into the mouth of the character or figure of a woman that these and similar remarks about the potential for the active transformation of time and with it the implicit sovereign order are put. The resources of misogyny make the demonisation of this unacceptable ideologeme easy. If such a sacrilegious account – ultimately it is an account of an orientation toward history – is given to a 'woman' who has not only a heterodox account of manhood, but is willing to unsex herself and become such a man, to murder her children in the cause, it is, of course, disqualified from the start, as Edmund's discourse, in a different way, is also precisely, originally 'illegitimate'. The dialectic of reversals of gender roles, between Macbeth – too full of the milk of human kindness – and the 'strong' Lady Macbeth, has been much remarked: but even if her unsexing is thought as not one of becoming man in order to act, to do what Macbeth himself shrinks from, but a subversive slipping from definition by gender at all, this is no less unacceptable to the play itself. Indeed, the double-bind masquerading as dialectic is thus able to revolve powerfully and on itself: monstrous activism is female, and therefore monstrous when femalely active, and so on. It is the same set of ideological resources as those which frame Goneril and Regan, or lead, alternatively, an Ophelia from silence and passivity to a speech which is called mad, and an 'action' that is her own dying.

But even if there is, in the violence offered to sacred majesty by

Macbeth and Lady Macbeth, the potential for decisive, quasi-historical intervention, their regime nonetheless fails in this reshaping of life; or rather, it is not allowed to be represented as succeeding. The text ensures, as best it can, that its characterisation of Macbeth's deed, and the terms of Lady Macbeth's prompting to assassination, are ones of symbological vandalism and profanation, of monstrous, unnatural, sense-destroying horror. Through their demonisation the text builds into its representations in a very fundamental way not only the sense that the act is a violation which is absolute, but that any activism is equally and inevitably a hideous violence, and hence proscribed. A deep submissiveness in respect of authority is characteristically Shakespearean, as many have noticed, although I come to rather different conclusions than some about the political significance of this. But even if Macbeth's tyranny is read as the *critical* reflex of an unmitigated Absolutism, as minatory not merely against historical change from below, but also against monarchical rule gone beyond some proper, if imagined, limits (and such a reading is not without its credit), the fundamental ideological point is in any case the same: only proper authority and proper submission to that authority will do.

Of course, in the process of the demonised representation of the life and the death that activists commit themselves to, *Macbeth* becomes almost lyrical – if by virtue of a negative lyricism – in the way it puts into language the solitude of violence. But a certain 'textual bad faith' operates in the difference between the project and the drama, a difference which marks one of the determinate hierarchisations of the discourses of a text which is not at one with itself, and through which it is possible to read against the grain. *Macbeth* has, after all, no compunction about the violence of its own resolution, even going as far – a little unusually in tragedy – as depicting actual battle. At the level of the project, the violence of Malcolm's campaign against Macbeth can, no doubt, be said to be 'necessitated' by the original violence of Macbeth's murder of the king. But if even that much is conceded, it is important that this is not some early modern liberalism clinging to the Shakespearean project: it unleashes without compunction the violence of what it counts as justice. The appearance is no doubt saved – in a sense of the term I have used already – by this violence being conducted in a good cause. That is to say, as long as it is a violence in the name of the restitution of legitimacy, marked in this case by both elective and dynastic descent from Duncan (and overdetermined by the Englishness of the origins and resources of the purge), it is wholly to be sanctioned. As is so often the case with ruling ideologies, the spiritual charge – of Edward's saintly kingship – is neatly separated from, although simultaneously supported by, the physical violence needed to put its purging efficacy into practice.

If the activism that will offer to make time and place fit not in the fantasy of old symbolic harmony but in a present-time activism is demonised from the start, equally it is punished savagely by the play. The fear of transgression – in the face of which Macbeth vacillates, and against which Lady Macbeth speaks so powerfully – can only be represented within an insistence on the transgressive deed which would have it run uncontrollably through unimagined – that is, horrifyingly imaginable – consequences. It is an anxiety in respect of action which is thoroughly Shakespearean (as Hamlet's hesitation – merely the most well-known example – amply illustrates): 'If it were done, when 'tis done, then 'twere well/It were done quickly: if th'assassination/Could trammel up the consequence, and catch/ With his surcease success' (I.vii.1–7). Macbeth's desire is represented here as one organised for pure deed, pure action, punctual and definitive, and in quick time. Activism is demonised as that which seeks to kill. But even then it takes the form of an 'if only', leaving intact the old fantasy and its politically grounded symbolic taboos, even as their 'inexistence' is dramatised. '[T]hat but this blow/Might be the be-all and the end-all – here,/But here, upon this bank and shoal of time,/We'd jump the life to come. (I.vii.1–7) We have already noted Macbeth's deed as the deracination of identity. Here the play induces an interpretation of activism as the problematic inlaying of present time as a dimension which is instinct not with Lady Macbeth's transformed future, but with the inhibitions of *post-mortem* existence which the deed cannot stop *dead*. It is only this – to modern ears – quasi-fascist account of historical activity as pure deed, that the play can imagine.

The price of activism, in contrast to the comparatively full time even of horror – let alone to that of the old temporal plenitude of the king – is to live, and eventually die, in, and into, empty time: 'I have liv'd long enough' Macbeth says, 'my way of life/Is fall'n into the sere, the yellow leaf;/And that which should accompany old age,/As

honour, love, obedience, troops of friends,/I must not look to have ...'
(V.iii.22–8) In tune with an increasing isolation, the last flickers of
action both in, and against, time are caught in the bound constraint
and fierce defiance of the image of the fighting bear: 'They have tied
me to a stake: I cannot fly,/But, bear-like, I must fight the course'
(V.vii.1–2); or the determination, which contains both stoic resigna-
tion and militant resistance, to die in arms but also under restraint:
'There is nor flying hence, nor tarrying here./I'gin to be aweary of the
sun,/... Blow, wind! come, wrack!/At least we'll die with harness on
our back.' (V.v.47–52) Macbeth the initial warrior, and the activist he
becomes, is fastened into this reductive condition, and soon violently
eliminated. Time is now something that has run out (no longer a
quality but a quantity). Secularised, it becomes the medium of action
or history, but also, in this demonising representation, it expires,
runs away, runs out: 'Had I but died an hour before this chance,/I
had liv'd a blessed time; for, from this instant,/There's nothing serious in mortality;/All is but toys: renown, and grace, is dead;/The wine
of life is drawn, and the mere lees/Is left this vault to brag of.'
(II.iii.89–94) Now, the fit moment is in the past, and the 'instant', if
it encodes a future, evokes one of bitter emptiness. And the same is
true of Lady Macbeth's death as of the last part of Macbeth's life.
Macbeth's protest that 'She should have died hereafter:/There would
have been a time for such a word' (V.v.17–28), prompts his famous
reflections on the emptiness of time as vacant repetition – 'To-morrow, and to-morrow, and to-morrow' – and as the *mise-en-scène* of a
morbid and sterile mortality: 'And all our yesterdays have lighted
fools/The way to dusty death.' (V.v.17–28) 'Signifying', as he says,
'nothing' (V.v.17–28), time becomes not succession, hardly even sequence, but mere successiveness. And, doubtless, to die is now to die
out of empty time into empty time, where eternity, if it can be
conceived at all, lies not transcendently outside of time, but is constituted at best as infinite, meaningless duration. There will be no
commemoration. And history, even in the degraded form which the
representation of demonised activism allows it, is closed down again
to secure for the master discourse of the project a kind of restitution.

The formation produces what is a form of the characteristic Shakespearean seduction. It offers impossible choices between, on the one

hand, sacred time – the non-time, the non-narrative fullness of the old imagined king; or its complementary opposite, the time of tyranny, mere continuance – and the instrumental time of emergent, means-ends structures on the other. In order to provide something approximating to the necessary closure, it is obliged to compromise among these mutually impossible perspectives (although it should be said that in so far as the empirical ending of the play alone is concerned, *Macbeth* is unique among the tragedies in the extent to which it is able to dramatise the appearance of restoration).

In Act V as the invading forces close in on Macbeth, Siward is able to speak of the approach or re-approach of a time of normality which will apparently restore, if not the timelessness of former time, at least a certain clarity: 'The time approaches,/That will with due decision make us know/What we shall say we have, and what we owe.' (V.iv.16–18) Compared with the distortion of time associated with the assassination of Duncan – a distortion measured, as I have suggested, not against the 'real' but against the play's project(ion) of a nostalgic erstwhile normality – now, rather, it is possible to glimpse again a time when due order, limit, obligation and possession, if not self-possession, will once more make sense. The significant metaphor insists; in Macduff's triumphant (and submissive) 'Hail, King! for so thou art. Behold, where stands/Th'usurper's cursed head: the time is free' (V.ix.20–1): the restoration of the king, the overthrow of the usurper, and the freedom of time are sedimented into two lines. But, taken by itself, this is too triumphalist, for compacted into Malcolm's speech of accession are both significant poles of the compromise by which the text is in fact closed off. On the one hand, at the level of the project, with the death of the usurper and the institution of a legitimate king, time will now be free, and, in Malcolm's words, measure, time and place restored: 'What's more to do,/Which would be planted newly with the time/... this, and what needful else/That calls upon us, by the grace of Grace,/We will perform in measure, time and place.' (V.ix.26–41) Yet, on the other hand, in close proximity to this conservative idealism is that jarring note of mercenary reckoning – distinctly at odds with the ideal symbology – which marks the end of each of these plays. Rather than the gratuitous gratitude of Grace, we have instead a figure of the ethical register of the new – the nexus of cash payment for secular services rendered. Like the terms of Albany's equivalent speech in

Lear where 'wages' of virtue are promised (V.iii.302); or like those in *Hamlet* of the returning Ambassadors' querulous search for recompense, whose response to the spectacle of tragic slaughter is 'The ears are senseless that should give us hearing/.... Where should we have our thanks?' (V.ii.374–7); so in *Macbeth*, as well as Siward's 'have' and 'owe', there is Malcolm's own deployment of the identical lexicon of money payment in a settlement which is also one of debt and reckoning, even inflected – significantly enough – through the metaphor of time: 'We shall not spend a large expense of time,/Before we reckon with your several loves,/And make us even with you.' (V.ix.26–41) It is even appropriate to notice the distribution of honours which usually glosses the more material division of the spoils. Here, importantly, they are 'English' ones: 'My Thanes and kinsmen,/Henceforth be Earls; the first that ever Scotland/In such an honour nam'd.' (V.ix.26–41) The dialectic closed out by compromise, in a similar fashion to the endings of *Lear* and *Hamlet*, has produced what looks like a restoration, but which is yet also the occurrence of a still new form of time, in which metaphors of monetary settlement in what was once a sacred medium have been allowed their currency. If the vindication of the sovereign has been to some degree achieved, it has nevertheless paid a heavy symbolic price.

This secular, even demystified, materialist moment, which coexists at the end in compromise with the restorative drive of the project, takes in *Macbeth* the form of a trace. For reasons of the overdetermination of the ending of this play, the compromise in *Macbeth* is an uneven one, giving more weight finally to the signs of restitution than to those of depredation. Certainly the compromise is not as reductively personified as it is in Albany or Fortinbras. But if the ending of *Macbeth* approximates most closely to some actualised restoration, it is important to note again that from first to last the discrepant formations of organised and disorganised time are founded upon the extent to which the king is or is not in place. It is around the figure of the sovereign that the nostalgic structure of the signs of the times being diminished and disjointed – compared with a past fixity where the joints of the anatomy made a sense – is arranged; and equally, it is in the attempt to relegitimate such sovereignty, that the ending aims so emphatically at their restitution. If at first, time, role, identity and the king are conceived – but barely able to be represented – as having been of a piece, in the depicted times of violence of the play, each is denatured, and the activist attempt to make time fit for another future, is coded and 'represented' as inevitably blasphemous violence. At the end a legitimate violence is unleashed and a crushing victory for reparation gained. But not without that trace of the decathexis of the sovereign symbology continuing to mark the text. And not without the lingering suspicion – however subject to overdetermination and closure – that the crisis disclosed in the depredation of the severe interim of the drama, must have been deep indeed to have necessitated a force sufficient to provide, against all the odds of *Macbeth*'s assault on sovereignty, the degree of sovereign redress it is able to achieve.

*   *   *

In seeing Shakespeare's art as very profoundly conservative, it is no part of my case to argue that the Shakespearean text constitutes an unproblematic underwriting of sovereign power in general or the historically actual regime of the Elizabethan and Jacobean monarchy in particular. On the contrary, mine is a dialectical reading. Certainly at one level it diagnoses a master-discourse, what I am calling the 'project' of the text, whose purpose is precisely to underwrite what it takes to be the order of extant sovereignty. But at another level, what we see actually dramatised, in what I am calling 'the event', is not the artistic realisation of that sovereign plenitude but its demise, its disruption, or, in the extended sense in which I am using the word, its invasion. This is the drama of the failure of the project to make the codes and signifiers of its imagined power adhere; the drama which often only finds that sovereignty in the form not of a substance but of the trace, and usually in that of nostalgic traces to boot.

And among the fragments, other voices sometimes sound; other readings than those the project could either imagine or tolerate might be possible.

At the level of the project itself there is no doubt that the master-discourse of the tragic text fundamentally subscribes to sovereignty in general and in particular. That chaos is anathema, hardly needs saying. In general, the project cannot conceive of life without a fixed, reduced, order in every department of the totality: 'social' order as much as governmental, familial as well as metaphysical; both cosmic

and mundane, individual and collective, and so on, in all the structures of life. Sovereignty is, of course, a matter of political authority
and governmental power, certainly; but it is also the name of the
organisation of reality in all its details, for these different reaches of
power and fixity are fundamentally instances of one and the same
coercive regime. There are a number of practical and metaphorical
forms in which this sovereignty is embodied and symbolised, the
king's inviolable body and the charged integrity of the realm being
the most relevant ones here. In its particularity the project recognises
and inscribes monarchy not only as the extant but as the sanctioned,
even sacred, form of sovereignty in general. Totalisation, singularity
and historicism here happily sustain each other.

But it probably also goes without saying that historically speaking,
even within the politics of the ruling class, this was also a
conservative project, although the point is debatable and it would
probably be possible to contextualise this formation among the quite
complex debates of the times concerning neo-feudal, Absolutist, and
modified or 'constitutional' absolutist forms of monarchical
government and administration. Shakespeare never seems quite to
know which he in fact supports, and the plays vary in detail among
these forms: _Macbeth_ can be read as an argument against Absolutism
in its most absolute forms, in favour of the imagined moderation of a
feudal or neo-feudal establishment; _Lear_ on the other hand might be
seen as articulating a need for absolutely strong and unnegotiable
leadership, by illustrating the consequences of its demise. But in any
case it is clear that whatever the topical and local forms, the
Shakespearean project imbricates itself in a fundamentalism of
commitment to domination – sovereignty is a polite form – as an
unnegotiable 'inner' structure of life itself.

However, it is not the case that by and large the project is either
positively represented or dramatically deployed, but rather, that it
functions to secure, in 'deep-structural' ways, what I am calling,
rather inadequately perhaps, the 'criteria of value': the foundational
ideological and symbological structures that have the power to define
the right, the sanctioned, the natural, the sacred, the real. Implicit is
the assumption that these are indeed powerful, sedimented, but not
unproblematical terms. There are examples elsewhere in the drama
where the underwriting of sovereign authority either takes the form
of a positivity by which powerful representations of sovereign majesty

are produced as spectacle, or that of triumphalist narrative strategies by which the monarch enacts his power. In Shakespearean tragedy, the representation of Duncan in *Macbeth* approximates the first; and arguably the English Histories, taken as a sequence overall, strive to produce the second – certainly in some of their particular deployments this is so. But the major strategy of the projective master-discourse of the tragic formation is to define what can or cannot be thought and imagined, to set the terms of such, and to demonise or exclude whatever transgresses those terms.

One of the ways in which the project functions, then, is to define 'value', the standard against which depredation can be seen as depredation. After all, it is not too difficult to imagine perspectives from which the assassination of the ruling monarch could be represented in wholly positive terms: this is not the perspective of Shakespearean tragedy. Even when historical actuality is depicted as aberrant from the master-codes, those codes are immanent in the very intelligibility of aberration as aberration, of crisis as crisis.

That the project works in this substructural way is the reason that the figure of invasion, and the ultimate 'saving' of central rule (of a kind), is so important. It is doubtful if there is any play of Shakespeare's that can be called a tragedy which does not inlay within itself, in however muted a form, the figure of invasion. In any case, we have noted the way in which each of the tragedies under discussion here is framed by this figure. The threat of war is part of the primal scene of *Hamlet*, where the contrast between the old king's individual martial virtue and Claudius's able policy, are set within the question of the integrity of the land, foreign threat, and where these can be connected in turn back to the more or less out-of-focus political narrative of that play and its invasive rupture of sovereignty. In a sense *Hamlet begins* with reduced rule, and that is its problem. It ends with invasion, by Fortinbras. A similar strategy keeps Albany in the wings to pronounce a settlement, however affectively and symbolically reduced, in order, contrastingly, to conduct away the disruptive charge of the invasion of Britain by France. But also in a strange way to fulfil it: in *Lear* the invasion is doubly inscribed, for it is conducted in the name of the restitution of original right, as Cordelia invades to restore Lear to the throne (if France may have had other motives). And *Macbeth* both begins, of course, and ends, in the couple of internal crisis and invasion from without. Although in

Macbeth too the final invasion is complex. In a sense it resembles Cordelia's, coming from within a 'true' tradition; but *Macbeth*'s coming closest of the high tragedies – and this is not wholly close – to an effective and affective restoration of legitimacy is complexly overdetermined. Even if we set aside the famous discussions of the extent to which this play was written either to flatter or admonish James, there are senses in which the invasion is legitimated by the fact that it comes from England, the place of saintly health contrasted to the sick barbarity of Scotland as the play has it, but it is also in a sense covertly weakened by the fact that in Malcolm true tradition has only been able to be preserved in its integrity, like Cordelia and all she 'represents', abroad. In the political geography of the play, in another country; in its metaphysics 'saved', but *elsewhere*.

The figure of invasion is significant here because it represents the most graphic form of the violation of the realm. It should not be taken solely empirically, descriptively and representationally, but as an evocation – and as analytic term – of the degree of the crisis in sovereignty. In each of the Shakespearean plays which deals centrally with these matters, there is some combination or *combinatoire* of internal and external threats. There is not much to choose between the form of tragedies and that of the Histories in this respect. In one sense it doesn't matter so much who the invaders or potential invaders are or what they might be said to represent; what matters is that in the ideological and affective structures of the texts they offer a threat, and a threat to something valuable and even sacred, or sovereign. This is how the texts do most of their ideological work, making something precious by showing it to be vulnerable and threatened. Enough, when the invader violates the land, is, for the English ruling mind, enough, especially when what are perceived as internal and external threats in Shakespeare are often displaced forms of each other: the *combinatoire* is a structure of mutual feints. This is a sign here of the metaphysical character of the figure of invasion which is not just about representations of the invasion of the land as more or less arbitrary narrative material, but about the reason why – historically – such empirical representations should be constructed at all, about the significance of such figures as affective and effective forms in the structure of the representations which we call Shakespeare, the tragedies, History, and so on. The figure of invasion is part of a subtle and coercive, powerful but naturalised, substructure of historicist 'obviousness' which functions representationally to draw a protective circle around what it presents as the encratically undifferentiated realm, rather than anything which might be thought of as the real-historical land and still less the rule of a particular – if historical – class and institutional regime. On the contrary, its purpose is to prevent that thought.

The figure from the Histories of the 'scepter'd isle', and all that it encodes in terms of an idealised, non-conflictual representation of the social formation as a moated house protected from the foreign threat of pestilence and war, is thus latent in the figure of invasion itself. Shores of English integrity are drawn around the rim of the fantasy kingdom. This last – the strategy of patriotic nationalism – is more insistent in the histories (although it is questionable to what extent it is sustained even there, much as their wider project may be to historicise and in this sense underwrite the Tudor dynasty). If the tragedies, in the event, hold the line around that precious sovereignty, and arguably the figure of the emergence of the dynasty is reversed, power mutating from sovereignty to violence, and to violation of the land, they are nonetheless predicated on the imagination of that wholeness.

The signs of invasion are thus complex indices at the site of the project's discourse of sovereignty. But it is above all important to notice that the outcome is the same in each case. With varying degrees of real or imagined legitimacy and continuity with the *status quo ante* (and also, to be sure, with varying degrees of loss both of affect and symbolic effectivity as well), central – monarchical – rule is re-established, and the text 'saved' for sovereignty. Or sovereignty is saved for it.

By working through the depiction of the interim, the Shakespearean project is also in that sense minatory. It depicts what happens if the king, or rather the sovereign – in the extended reaches of that word – is challenged, reduced or eliminated. It constitutes, by way of that profoundly conservative argument – totalised in the metaphysical person of the king – that all is one, and any part of the sovereign whole surrendered risks the loss of the whole as a whole, a warning against such insurrections. Sovereignty is one of the names of this megalomaniac paranoia. The project asks its audience to imagine, engage with and reject – rather, naturally, than to celebrate – the demise of the sovereign which it shows in its violation and invasion, and simultaneously in a strange way thereby codes as inviolable. It dramatises before them, and who knows if not even *in* them, the suffering, the tearing, the dislocation, the incoherence, the dissembling which attends on the disruption of that material and metaphysical order. It admonishes all who might rise against that order, that in doing so they offer not merely to change the government but to invade, pollute, distort and even destroy reality itself. And it shows them the price, in torment and alienation, that will be exacted. Nor is this just a fantasy: representation was not the only violent means by which sovereignty defended itself.

But if the sovereign project operates in these ways, establishing criteria of value and depicting threateningly the effects of their invasion, this has at least one inevitable consequence for its representational strategies: the representation of the sovereign in its positivity must be either temporally or spatially displaced. Cordelia's absence, for example, or the English character of Scottish restitution, are obvious forms of spatial displacement; more complex are the displacements 'into place' of the disguised Kent or Edgar. But more important, probably, even than these dislocations, is the temporal organisation of the drama, by which the sovereign, in the concise and the extended senses, is already, or is about to become, part of the past.

Although Shakespeare's writing does not predominantly enjoy the sentimental affects usually associated with nostalgia, its formation is – in its very structure – nonetheless nostalgic. If the representation of sovereignty is a matter of the viable depiction of legitimate monarchs (or depiction of legitimate monarchs in their viability), Duncan is soon destroyed, *Lear* begins with the absentiation of the king from himself, and the elder Hamlet is already a ghost; or if it is that that representation is a matter of the wider, 'deep-structural' figuration of sovereignty as the uncontested physics and metaphysics of order and possession, the authority and plenitude of the text's full desire, in each case sovereignty in its positivity forms a horizon of departure for the tragic text. It is a figure still powerful enough nonetheless to signature violation and a need for wholeness; but in that it can only register these as belonging to the past, the text, whether it likes it or not, is committed by its representational – and historical – formation to this perhaps unconscious but certainly nostalgic structure. It is the same figure which allows the language of the Shakespearean project to define the whole land as the erstwhile ground of an integrity whose passing the 'existential' actuality of the drama laments, even as it recruits that passing to a powerful denunciation of the present. Equally, the nostalgia articulates an anxiety to re-member in the sovereign, projective sequence – and at that level – the voice and the body of the king.

The nostalgic figure of the wholeness of the past operates at both social and individual levels. The minatory undoing, actual or fore-warned, threatened in transitive and intransitive senses, of political authority and power in its wider forms – transcoded, of course, as stability, reality, life as such – is symbolised forcefully and practically in the invasion of the king-body-land. But also at the individual level 'identity' comes undone. The cutting off of kings is made, in the formation, to equal the decision of the self: identity goes, memory becomes grief, and in either case the death of sovereignty is coercively figured. And thus is disidentity demonised as if the refusal to be a fixed self were first treasonous, and then even threatened the dissipa-tion of the very order of reality itself.

In Shakespeare the discontinuity of experience is linked to the discontinuity in 'cultural' tradition. But what is the cultural tradition, if not the symbolic hegemony which underpins, and in great measure *is* – as legitimation of the extant order of things – the ground of political authority? Alongside the discontinuities then, there are in this sense also false continuities established, within the Shakes-pearean text, and subsequently, with it. The substitution of tradition for history is an important representational figure here, producing what appears to stretch into the past and thus to legitimate the present by derivation or descent, but which is actually a contemporary discursive organisation of apparently old material produced out of the past for exactly those legitimatory purposes. With the benefit of hindsight we know that the symbology of the project, indeed *this* sovereignty, was on the threshold of its historical demise. But *within* the text it is residual in a very special sense. It is not that this discourse belongs properly to an earlier or passing historical formation which is somehow just still there, as an historical but archaic remnant, a 'survival'. It is rather a fictional construction in present time of a past which never existed. Thus the importance of the representation of long-dead kings, and even of elite fantasies like that initial ideological identification of the land as cleaned of the historical marks of its actual division and expropriation. A land which has become itself a sacred body like that of the king – or in other words, a realm – is inherent in the temporal structure: or, perhaps better, in the structure of the temporality of tragic formation. It is not necessary to believe that any such place ever existed, as if feudalism had once in reality been the contradiction-free plenitude the Shake-spearean project imagines, the hierarchy stabilised by loyal assent; nor to think that uncomplex, identical identity ever really fixed all subjects to their roles and stations. On the contrary, we know that identities and hierarchies are imposed and held in place by violence of direct as well as institutional and structural kinds. It is only necessary for the present argument to believe that the Shakespearean project, within a contemporary structure of conjunctural drives and powers, so believed: or rather, to see the deployment of that plenitude as the horizon of departure in the ways I have described here.

But of course, in as much as the representational strategy of which the project is in these ways criterial, minatory and nostalgic, it is also one – coercive as the power to define value can be – that is under threat. Certainly it is full of risk, and in the event it can barely hold the line against the depredation introduced into the representation of sovereign order. In particular it runs the risk that it is the *crisis* of political authority and power in its wider forms that is symbolised in the invasion of the king-body-land, and not the defensive warning against that interruption. The foundationally pre-protective risks becoming merely defensive. What in any case we are presented with, in the dramatic representation of the event is, after all, that depredation, in sometimes horrendous, poignant ways. And in dramatising the threat to the sovereignty which the project seeks to underwrite, even the project admits the possibility (even if it doesn't admit that it admits it), that this symbology of majesty is done for. At the very least we have to grasp as clearly as we can the paradoxical temporality of the tragic formation which I have noted above: that in as much as in the event it is incapable of dramatising the full, sovereign presence, the text cannot dramatise what is present at all. The present becomes part of the past.

It is probably because of this structural residuality in the project – that it is traditional in this sense – and because of the history that lies in and behind the fact that the tragic formation is as it is, that it is

possible to understand in the event of the drama its critical underside, to trace the negative – in almost the photographic sense – of the
project. We can read, in other words, the depredation of the event as
against – that is, 'against the grain' of – the way in which the project
seeks to define it as declination from sovereignty.

I suggest, in fact, that we can read against the grain in two ways: on
the one hand by taking from the project what, in a useful metaphor
from the lexicon of counter-espionage, I will call 'backbearings', reading indeed traces rather than positivities; and on the other hand, by
trying to listen for the other 'voices' – the ciphers of other 'position-
alities', the non-sovereign, displaced, dispossessed, disidentities –
which are just audible in despite of not only the project's desire for
mastery, but even its constitution of the representational formation
of tragedy in the first place. It is because it is an embattled formation
that the other registers of its anxiety are there.

On the first count, that of the negative contour of the project, it is
important to apprehend in particular the way in which that anxiety is
betrayed in what it deprecates, rejects or exscribes altogether. The
sign of the forgotten is like an amputation or a wound where what is
missing hurts most. If we look, for example, at the structure of tragic
forgetting, and then try to address the possible 'contents' of
nonetheless necessary memory, it is as if there were two 'substances'
becoming, or having become, actively forgotten in the tragic text.
There is that of the project, the master-discourse, which thematises
memory-loss as the loss of the king, or more widely the sovereign.
But there is also, if we stand back from the text, another set of
forgettings done by its very process of representation. At this other
level – that of which it doesn't speak rather than that of what is
positively thematised – is the land, as distinct, of course, from the
realm, the people in their autonomy and resistance, and even women,
independent of misogynistically constituted demonisations of
'women'. There is a violence, to which I shall return shortly, in the
depopulation and forgetting which is effected in the representational
strategies of these texts. But there is also a sense, albeit negative, in
which we can read the trace of that violence, and listen, with slightly
different inflection in each of the texts, to the silence which is its
effect. We have noted in *Lear* the emptiness of even the ideal terrain,
and the displaced 'return' of the people in the substitutional form of
the discourse of the heath; while loss of memory is instinct in *Hamlet*,

a play which has forgotten the people even before it has begun to problematise the forgetting of the king. In a strangely self-complicit way, the tragic text, at once peculiarly full and peculiarly empty, dramatises what it also deprecates; it is part of the process of diminution of the social – which in any case it can only imagine in forms which are nonetheless politically and historically conservative – even as it brings to light that very distortion. And let us not be afraid, by virtue of a fashionable critique of metaphysical essences, to say that it *is* a distortion: no society on earth so far has done without the earth, or without labouring masses, or ... women.

A further 'negative' impress of the force of the project may be traced in its representation of identity. Indeed, it is impossible to avoid interrogating the shifts and feints of the tragic text as it tries to sustain its main senses of *self-possession* in the face of the difficulty it simultaneously experiences in validating such a form. On the one hand, although it is hard to know how anything can be a property of itself, the language of selfhood is in principle at its most cogent when, paradoxically and incoherently, it defines the self thus as in its own possession. But on the other hand, the sharpest depiction of autonomous self-hood in practice resides in either the aggressive acquisitors, or the displaced dispossessed. In short, the text cannot fully think or figure the humanism of the self it otherwise vaunts: for either the self is defined by property and place, in which case it is a material dependency; or it is unpossessing or dispossessed, and, lacking self-possession, thus hardly a self at all in the definitions, conceptions and figures available. And yet its figuration of 'identity' is dynamic in ways that possession and self-possession cannot be. And this is also why, in *Lear*, it is in the condition of dispossession that normal identity – fixed subjection – is abnormally visible as the fragile, contingent, historical construct it is.

The Shakespearean tendency to substitute forms of dependency – identity predicated as property – and autochthony for each other, at least in the foreground, risks giving the game away. The text finds it near impossible in this sense to ground 'self-possession' as a fixity of the boundaries of self, as control or self-control of self, or as subjection in the sense of the 'voluntary' fixing of the 'person' into an order which is external to the self.

There is a danger of construing – as many have done recently – Shakespeare as progenitor of the problematic of disidentity, even of 'deconstruction' as this term has come to be loosely used, as signify-ing a nothing at which much 'theoretical' criticism aims. What is at stake is an historical crisis of representation, of, at this level, the representation of the self, and this is why I have taken so much trouble to emphasise the way the texts themselves deploy metaphors of writing and of other modes of representation when they discuss, in very troubled ways, formations of identity and disidentity. By the same token, the phrase 'crisis of identity' would be convenient only so long as it is clear from the overall context that it is not the psychologistic usage of traditional criticism that is implied. The representations at issue are not 'psychologies' to begin with, but, precisely, writings.

The discontinuity of experience in Shakespeare ought to be poignant for us, in as much as this century has not been without its erasures and fragmentations of the self – at theoretical and all too practical levels. Certainly the experience of identity, and the concept of the self, are the site of very intense conflicts, struggles and contradictions. And perhaps it is this that makes the underside of the Shakespearean project visible for us. At any rate, it is the contingency of the fixity of identity, especially as a mode of control – one of the instances of the intervention and exercise of power – which is actually foregrounded in the event of the text. There is a distance, in other words, between the Shakespearean discontinuities, real or imagined, in 'personal' experience and in cultural tradition, on the one hand, and what might be diagnosed in respect of that diagnosis on the other. On the surface of the text is the loss of the king and all that the sovereign embodies in the political symbology at work in and as the project. But there are other forces deep in the text's unconscious, in fact in the deep-structure of *its* amnesia. If we can, against the grain of the project, read the traces, we can see that the desired wholeness which is foundational of the project and the overall text would not have been even as imaginable as it is had those other forces received their due.

Perhaps some of that due is paid, however, in the way in which other, non-sovereign, displaced voices almost sound, very faintly, in what can only very inadequately be called the 'liberation' of the event. This is the other main way in which it is possible to try to read what under certain conditions evades the complex forgetting of the text. In what I have called the discourse of the heath, in Ophelia's mad speech, or in various other affects of what the text deploys as a reactionary pathos – when the figure of dispossession is used as the metaphor or metonym of the depredation of sovereignty – the voice of the permanently dispossessed, and *their* rage for justice and restitution can almost be heard. Even, in a very distorted fashion, in Lady Macbeth's aspiration beyond the fixity of location and time, it is possible to sense a dynamic which finds in the undoing of sense, order, reality, and so on, not a minatory blasphemy but a sense of possibility, if not a perspective of liberation; at least a will, a drive, which is before and beyond rage, to transgress the 'civilised norms' because it deeply knows – even if it cannot articulate how or why – that these normalities are on the side of a profound oppression. In as much as it is possible to interpret historically some of the forces that it demonises timelessly, we can see how the text admits into itself what it otherwise strives to prevent, glimpsing something, often in very critical form, beyond the dead order of the old. These other position-alities – which are actually non-positions, of their essence dis-locations – are not, and cannot be, represented as counter-positivities; the 'other' forces are demonised, always-already constituted as such by the project. But nonetheless, exceeding the ability of the project to contain its own anxiety, something is rendered of another historicity than that either of the project's nostalgic or of its minatory command.

Taking together the negative contour of the project, traceable in the event, and the discrepant voices and forces released, it is clear that the tragic formation risks representing the power of the sovereign as dissipated rather than affirmed; erased, if not overthrown. The voice of the king is barely audible through the event horizon, and some 'ultimate' prohibitions are shown to be breakable: the sovereign body in punctual, extended and universal senses is dismembered; the realm as the place of rule is invaded; fixed identity looks more like a prison than a viable way of life; the problematicity of gender definitions, rather than their functionality in a systemic way of allotting subjects to roles, comes to the fore; memory, which all agree is crucial, becomes more and more difficult, as voices of authority fade and become ghostly; the constraints of 'nature' are loosened and even the foundational media of being, like time itself, are cast into the secular arena where individual or collective action can offer apparently to reshape them to chosen rather than given ends. The risk is that the aberration is not merely aberrational, but historical reality itself, and the crisis not superficial and temporary but profound; and that the value-structure which at the level of the ideological project had apparently guaranteed that these things were in this sense limited, has in fact lost even that residual power. Even what it demonises may in actuality be on the agenda of history.

And so on. We might almost be reading, in the event, not so much an underwriting of sovereign power as its radical critique, a formation which strives tragically to remember – rather than actively to forget – the oppressed and the dispossessed, those whose identity was never confirmed by property, nor their reality by rank. A way even of thinking history as other than the story of sovereignty: as that at the very least of the failure of power always uninterruptedly to function; and at most of other possibilities, of a history which is not written under the aegis of the sovereign but in the practice of ordinary resistance and the struggle for change.

Except of course that this would risk a kind of nostalgia too. To be sure, if, in the event, the power of the king is no longer spectacular, the sovereign is not able to be dramatised, and the signifiers *and the signification* of the sovereignty the text sets out to underwrite cannot adhere or cohere, then representation as an ascertainable means of securing – not neutral, but politically effective – truths is vitiated. But in fact, whatever forces are 'liberated' in the political crisis of representation, the ultimate gesture of the tragic text is to achieve – as much no doubt by default as by design – a 'compromise formation' between the project of closure and the critical event. At neither the level of sovereign representation, nor at that of the sovereign represented, does sovereignty entirely break down.

At the level of representation it is necessary to contend with the fact that it is hierarchisation rather than polysemy in the structuration of the discourses of the Shakespearean text which can be observed at work in the relations between the project, the event and the compromise into which they are eventually forced. Relations between the ideological project and the 'dramatic' event are not even and symmetrical ones, as if a diffident historical indifference marked the neutrality and transcendence of the Shakespearean text. And nor can they be thought – as some have attempted recently to do – as a polysemous productivity, as if some universalised theory of language as meaning, always differing from and subverting itself, could continue to be blind to the historical, if conjunctural, forces which serve only too firmly to fix and sediment meanings, often in very terrifying – and sometimes in liberatory – ways. In the theatre of discourse which is the Shakespearean tragic text, there is neither deconstuctive anarchy nor liberal-democratic equality among the contending drives and depredations. Rather, there is an uneasy balance of forces normally and normatively – but sometimes in a fragile, quizzical and barely constrained manner – organised in the general figure of hierarchy under the overarching master-discourse of the project. But that project, under pressure from the subaltern discourses and figures, swerves from its unrealisable goal of full closure into the eventual formation of compromise. Or rather, it is 'permanently' compromised in this way, for the 'ultimate gesture' is not so much an episode in the dramatic narrative of the text as a figural modality of its complex discursive formation throughout. And in so far as endings, partial closures, are achieved, and the project remains the master-discourse, the relations between that drive to closure and the 'resistances' it encounters are observable by default – as what we might call, borrowing a phrase from physics, 'virtual effects' – and not by any positive depiction of what the text seeks not to represent, but to destroy. 'Compromise' in this sense is a misleading formulation: there is no genial seeing of the other point of view, but a historically determinate pattern of powers, and of obstacles to the total and Absolute regime of that power. Historical blockage might be a better metaphor.

This holds good at the level of the represented too. It would be fine, no doubt, to be able to reappropriate Shakespeare from the toils of conservative humanist criticism by seeing his texts as simply misread to its own purposes by that tradition, when in reality they are quite radical. But the case remains that while other 'voices' *are* at work – the felt pathos of the dispossessed and the thought need to modernise, to name but the two most historically significant – it is as traces rather than alternatives that they are able to be grasped. Because the discourse of the sovereign project and the forces to which in virtual form the depredation of the event responds are in *historical* and not merely intellectual conflict, they are to varying degrees and in varying formations prohibitive of each other. Hence the symbolic options are limited: the drive to closure of the project in a return to the presence of the *status quo ante*; or the devastation, meaninglessness and totalisation of loss which the event, if not recuperated, risks inaugurating. We also know, of course, that the further alternative perspective of a positive and fundamental social transformation, which we would have to call revolutionary, was on the 'real-historical' agenda. Of these 'options', the first proves impossible, the second unacceptable, and the third unthinkable. The result is stalemate in the tragic text.

But it is a stalemate legitimated and 'saved' for 'meaningfulness', by compromise. Incapable of fully satisfactory closure, the discourse of the project swerves away from impossible restoration to the downbeat affect of an Albany or even a Fortinbras. It is remarkable how 'compromise' – for which, of course, British political society, if not the alleged 'national temperament', is famous – in fact means, in the great tradition of the ruling class, force. Or it issues in the overdetermined, restorational but also invasively pacificatory ending of *Macbeth*. Central rule is re-invested, but stripped of symbolic efficacy and affective compulsion, as in each case a proximate and pertinent materialisation of motivation and reward impinges, as secular nexus supplants the representation of erstwhile bonds of obligation. The ruling form of power is preserved, but sovereignty is foreshortened and decathected. Differently in each of the texts, with a different degree and form of 'resolution' in each case, a 'middle course' is taken between devastation, breakdown, void, erasure – the total negativity of the play's inability to conceive the demise of sovereignty in any way other than as catastrophe – and the drive to maintain that sovereignty at any price: lest, presumably, the unthinkably revolutionary be let into dramatic reality. Even as it seeks to fashion a restoration of legitimacy in the only way in which it can conceive it, the text is constrained to admit the force of invasion; and yet it veers away from the logic of the distintegration of its own sovereign discourse, even as it strains to relegitimate the symbols and the signifiers of that power. The cost is usually very great, but the compromise is just able to prevent the tragedy of crisis turning into the open-ended drama of revolution. The text can be neither faultessly conservative, because it is impossible to produce presence in the past, nor can it be progressive, because it fears the future. The king and modernity don't mix; still less do sovereign authority and the landless poor – the entire majority of the population we might as well remember. Certainly the dispossessed, the forces of madness and displacement, are not to inherit the earth. And modernity is held at bay for a little while longer.

The – dialectical – structure of project, event and – not synthesis, but – compromise, poses a particular problem of reading. In part it is the problem of reading violence – in as much as it is the wound of the missing, the virtual effect that has to be deciphered. But this is then also a problem of reading the historicity of a formation which is, as it were, hollow, which does not speak in 'its own voice', but in the transactions among the forces contending in it. In other words it is a question of trying to understand history, or what has passed for history, as a formation constituted in and of the virtual – and not so virtual – effects of violence. These problems are one and the same.

If on occasion a linkage has been made between violence on the one hand and memory on the other, it has usually consisted in figuring history as repression. But from my point of view, more important is the more rarely noted violence of recall. The connection has not often been established, however, within the forms, or with the intensity, of the Shakespearean tragic text. In the twentieth century the risk of theory, and even of theoreticism, has been run, whether the link is made by some interior articulation of each to the other when regarded as psychological – or even neurological – functions, or by some philosophical or grammatological thematic of writing and violence. These are indeed contexts. But in the Shakespearean formation, rather than a scientistic account of the functioning of the psyche or the brain of the individual, or an otherwise philosophically abstract and anthropologically somewhat universalistic liaison, we are led to consider a dramatically articulated *deployment*, which demands, if not a social and historical account of this association, at least a diagnosis of the historicity and sociality of the deployment itself. Not of course that the generation of such an analysis is much assisted by the project of the Shakespearean high tragic text, which as usual tends to obscure rather than elucidate the historical rootedness of its own drives and negotiations. It is impossible not to see, however, that there is an insistent proximity, even an imbrication, of the 'themes' of memory and violence which has to begin to be thought through in cultural and social terms as an *historical* horizon of the text's representational formation. For, despite the nostalgic lament for a lost wholeness that underpins the Shakespearean deployment of these themes – and, stronger than lament, a structural deployment of minatory nostalgia as a discursive weapon – it is clear that a society that loses its memory is inevitably engaged in violence. Reciprocally, a society that is shot through with violence either loses its memory, or is caught up in a problematisation of memory which tends to suggest that the order and continuity that memory at the sovereign level offers apparently to preserve, are themselves in fact violences and forgettings.

If, on the one hand, loss of memory is offered, as it is in *Hamlet*, as a diagnosis of domination, it is because without historical difference there can be no sign of change but only the eternal present of the fixity of tyranny, and memory has to be held up against the power which will dominate the present in the name of timeless similarity, even if in the event of the text similarity is impossible, as we have seen. On the other, it is important to see how a control of the past (on any of the models available, from official rewriting to 'innocent' tradition), is one of power's means of domination. Official memory – 'History' or tradition – is not only a strategy and effect of present power, but is continuous with and underpins the violence of domination; memory is not thus the antidote of systemic violence, but part of it. It takes, of course, a lot of excavation to see this latter dimension built deep into the Shakespearean formation, for if *Macbeth* contemplates *violent* 'solutions', it is not on the basis of the king representing absolute violence, but rather the opposite: an – entirely fictional – benignity to which violence offers its threat. Sovereign – particularly sacred – symbolic discourse functions to secure a particular kind of historical domination, not merely by force but indeed also by legitimation in discourse and symbology. But in any case, the former, the violence of sovereignty itself, is utterly occluded by the text, especially when the sacred registers of the legitimating symbology are at issue. At least, that is the project and the ideology which the text struggles to sustain. Whichever way it goes, memory and violence are linked, and linked on the level of the political organisation of the social.

But if the Shakespearean text represents and thematises violence, it is also *involved* in it. It not only deals representationally with, but even formulates, direct power and the indirect effects of power. We have seen how the locus of *applied* power moves in the course of the tragedies from embodied sovereignty to violent practice, and how the tragedies themselves participate in a more general movement of the textual relocation of violence from the situation in the Histories where the threat is dominantly external, although there is also internal conflict, to the tragic representation of total crisis, which is in both an immediate and a supplementary way inlaid with the threat of violence from abroad, and from within. Both are signs of invasion. In the course of the work the weighting of the locations of offered and applied violence alters, and becomes ever more nakedly the sign of the breakdown of sovereignty and of the 'internal' forces ranged against its erstwhile and imagined completeness. But it is clear that in the tragic text violence is, in addition to armed might or physical confrontation, something in the structure of the representation itself. Even for the surface level of the discourse of the project, the crisis is, as we have seen, profound, and effects dislocations at many levels. If in *Macbeth* a king is murdered, no less is time convulsed; or if in *Hamlet* common doubt afflicts the present legitimacy, so too is vitiated the ability to remember and narrate; in *Lear* sovereign decay is unthinkable without multiple disruptions in relationship, identity, and even the symbolic formation of the land itself. But there is also the very formation of the text to contend with, which puts into play both the project and the oblique underside of the sovereign narrative. Almost independent of, but in a sense masked by, the 'positive' representations of violence and their 'official' deprecation, is the persistent sense that there 'must be' domination. This is never challenged by the tragic text as a positivity, even if the extant forms of domination are thrown into implicit crisis and the new ones feared and rejected.

Throughout there is a pervasive violence in the most 'unconscious' of the texts' representational strategies. In *Lear*, the text which I have taken as foundational here, there is a violence in the depopulation of the land. But nobody – no character – depopulates the land, there is no campaign of forced evacuation that is part of the event or narrative of the drama. And yet the land is unquestionably and unquestionedly empty of all but the handful of noble characters and their various retainers. And similarly *Hamlet* rarely opens out beyond the isolated scene of the court. Or again, if memory is an issue in *Hamlet* and violence part of the fabric of *Macbeth*, is it not, despite the positivity of

the representation of history as noble history, the 'common' people –
even if they are, in passing, compassionately remembered by
aristocrats – who have been 'forgotten', and against whom the
violence of this – and any other – tyranny must have been massively
and dominantly directed? The plays invest non-representational
violence of their own in this forgetting. What I have called the depth
of field first allows the popular absence, and then allows for it not to
be focused on to any insistent degree.

In this amnesia of representation the Shakespearean text is one of
power, even if it charts, wittingly and willingly or not, historical
disturbance – and even a certain transitionality – in the forms,
directions, strategies and class-content of power. But of course,
because of the way in which the function of literary representation
has been established and sedimented, to press the point further
would be to engage a thoroughly Shakespearean mixture of
patronage and sentimentality by which 'the people' do, of course,
appear, but in minor roles as – when not a dangerous mob – servants,
messengers, and soldiers, clowns and players; or are referred to, with
some emotional but not exactly metaphysical charge, in the register
of pathos. If there is a discourse of the people, it is cast in the
externality that will speak of poverty and wretchedness certainly, but
of an object 'over there' nonetheless. Or if interiorised, then by a mad
king, as something more remarkable than the routine condition of the
poor; an awakening for Lear, maybe, but a sustaining of the
systematic blindness of *Lear* nonetheless.

Explicitly or not, then, positively or by traces, the Shakespearean text
is marked by violent contestation, particularly in the extent to which it
is either able to protect its sovereign desire against the depredation of
the event, or conversely must admit its demise. But even as it then
also strives to occlude this very ambivalence, perhaps we can glimpse,
in the oscillations it is possible to register between these contradictory drives, a form in which its historicity shows through?

In the first place, given the degree of failure the tragic text
encounters in attempting to make its audience present at the display
of power – witness the depredation, the displacements and blockages
– the risk is run of another violence: that the inability to give charisma
to the dominant forms might lead to the admission of ideas

dangerously above the station of those who – present instead at the spectacle of their betters' slaughtering each other in the course of a naked struggle for power – should otherwise have been recruited to submissiveness if not submission. But then the fundamental structuration of the tragedy seems to exist to ensure that revolutionary, popular violence is not one of the lessons that could be taken positively from that theatre out into the wider 'society': we need only remark how subversive or revolutionary violence is consistently demonised, while ruling-class violence – both as structural privilege and deployed, even physical, force – receives the mystificatory label of metaphysical and secular-historical 'order'; and is represented as, say, 'majesty'. To 'critical' approval. The Shakespearean assumption that the king is the prophylaxis against violence and his demise its admission is, of course, the reverse of the truth, happily concealing in an absolute silence the extent to which 'the king', or – to put it in a less historicist way – sovereignty, power, *is* violence, in body and fact. But the tragic project – and indeed, the retrospective 'tradition' which apparently finds it so useful to think that it has been engendered by 'Shakespeare', 'England', 'history', or even (this time rightly) by tradition – promulgates the inexorable truth that domination is natural and even benign.

But if the Shakespearean tragic project has contributed powerfully in the formation of the culture of the English-speaking 'world' to this mystification, the interpretative question, then, is whether it is possible, or even worthwhile, to disentangle from this dominant fantasy of symbols without violence – sovereignty with sacred charge but endowed with nothing so vulgar as political power – the political and historical significance of the difficulty the Shakespearean text has, in the depredation of the event, of dramatising the political and representational axiom of the benignity of sovereign violence. For in a strange way, to the extent that the Shakespearean text can see the old *as old* – and this accounts, despite the nostalgia or in alliance with it, for a lot of the critical recognisability of Shakespeare – it has already moved beyond that fantasy into a kind of modernity. After all, there is no grace in self-appointment: Macbeth is not Duncan, Claudius isn't the elder Hamlet, and Lear is not himself. This is not, after all, a medieval text, and certainly not coherently a feudal one. Indeed, it is, instead, itself even part of the periodisation by which it is possible to talk in these terms. For if the tragic text is – by virtue of its deepest historical, rather than formal, definition – transitional, it must be reasonable to expect some ambivalence, not just in its formation but in its positive representations. It is, for example, not impossible to read the way in which in Shakespeare 'sacred' kingship has also entered the ambit of secular modernity, because the sacred – having to be defended, rather than being fundamentally pre-given – has already become a *cult* of monarchy. There is an important sense, thus, in which Shakespeare is a secular, or even a 'modern', writer in as much as his text uses the sacred functionally, in an image of the 'social' world which is already, by dint of this functionality, 'demystified'. Secularity and function only become issues when 'modern' ideologies are already ascendant.

But yet again, however, if the Shakespearean text is engaged in a secular politics in despite of itself, the consequences of this may be – as distinct from the thesis of a critical reading against the grain of the project – an antithetical sense in which the disorder of crisis is conceded by the text in order to secure its most conservative positions at a deeper level. In the unlikeness of the king to himself, and in much of the pathos, say, of the king becoming like a beggar (as distinct from that of the condition of original beggars, who were always-already merely 'themselves'), it claws back some of its secular demystification. By laying some of the responsibility for the crisis at the feet of the king, but granting him most of the pathos in the ensuing event – not least that of the reduction to mortality – an overblown and unsustainable monarchist case is avoided, in order to secure the more subliminally and coercively a dramatic argument for the inescapability of domination, or 'sovereignty' in the extended sense. If it gives some ground to the demystification of sacred monarchy, it is in order to secure the wider purchase of its deepest commitment to fixed order at the level of the political.

In the complexity of these feints and double-feints, what has been under discussion is not so much the play texts, merely and empirically, but the repetition of a number of ideological positions – and their disfunction – that amount to something like a structure, certainly the formation, of tragedy. Or to be absolutely accurate: the formation of tragedy is the precise ensemble of what the text can show and what it is constrained not to represent.

In other words, the question of history, and of *historical transformation*, is averted. In particular it is deflected into themes of personal commemoration, and only in certain subaltern forms does collective-memory-against-power surface. In the name of the need to remember the past, something politically important transpires. But then again, this is articulated by and in a text which will eventually come down more on the side of the security of rule which trades on forgetting, than on that of the deployment of memory against power, which can thus only cry out for the right telling in a fragile, dying breath. At the same time the counter-story of a violence that might have to be used in the pursuit of liberation is coded as the blasphemous slaughter of the sovereign, even if the sacredness of sovereign majesty can reside textually in nothing but its assertion as a protectively-constituted metaphysic.

And yet even so, there are supplementary senses in which the formation of tragedy, constituted as it is in the unquestionable violence of history, may turn out to be – certainly in historical, and perhaps even in suasive or ethical registers – critical.

We have been habituated to regarding 'Shakespeare' as a body of texts, a cultural phenomenon, that has been historically constituted not only as a major transcription of the immediately pre-revolutionary, early modern moment, but also as one then central to the tradition of what has subsequently counted as official History. I have been concerned, however, to argue that it is not the positive historicism of the represented, but the historicity of the representation, in Shakespearean tragedy, on which we should focus in order to address the real problematicity of the problem of reading history.

The field of forces whose contestation marks the Shakespearean texts, and the tensions and compromises engendered between them, eventually design not so much a plenitude as a form of lack, a rent in the seamless closure of the representation of history, by way of which – the wager of my reading is – a profounder historicity shows through. It is a historicity – as distinct from a positive history – inscribed in the tragic hollowing of the doubleness of project and event, the compromise discourse, the nostalgia of traces, the demonisation and deracinations, the possibility and impossibility of representation; or, in short, the crisis of the tragic text.

It isn't just that dispossession, displacement, disidentity, compromise, bad memory, violence, demonisation and destroyed time are in the positive sense what history is made of – although this is so – but also that in the difference between the hollowing and the self-appointed fullness of the tradition, the ethic of historicity can be heard to insist.

Historicity, here, is the sign – invaded, to be sure – of the possibility, need and inescapability, of history. It is almost even the value of the value of the sign of history. The historicism of Shakespeare's history is radically inadequate, as we have seen; but the insistence of history in the tragic text – even history as forgetting – is like a memory that comes unbidden. It is what signals, even in the unpropitious reaction of the Shakespearean project, the need to lift, in order to make possible the future, the dead weight of both official history, and traditional forgetting – that undifferentiated story, told in the alleged present about the so-called past.

For very survival we shall have to remember history, and remember the forgetting of history; in the name of the historicity of the undetermined future.

2

NIETZSCHE'S CATTLE

Today we are being invited again, if not induced or compelled, to live like Nietzsche's cattle. 'Consider the cattle, grazing as they pass you by: they do not know what is meant by yesterday or today, they leap about, eat, rest, digest, leap about again, and so from morn till night and from day to day, fettered to the moment and its pleasure or displeasure, and thus neither melancholy or bored.' Nietzsche judged the cattle to be happy because they lacked a sense of history. Dwelling without any apprehension of a past or future, and still less any sense of the temporal complexity of the present – Nietzsche's cattle are not, in this, alone – they inhabit instead eternal and uncritical presence.

And now again, in one or two forms, we are being offered this condition of brutal happiness. Either history has been traduced as one of the meta-narratives towards which, now, nothing but a famous incredulity is due; or, substantively, as the *fin de siècle*, if not millenarian theme of the end of history gathers force, the real process itself is adjudged to have come to an end.

Homologously, our choice is also between two 'possibilities'. Is our happiness, our cow-like happiness, to be one of undifferentiated plenitude, or highly differentiated (that is, in practice, undifferentiated) dispersal?

As far as the individual is concerned – the Western individual anyway – these two forms of happiness are on offer in and as the posthistorical condition. One involves the bucolic pastoral of disidentity, the forms of fragmentation and dispersal of the self which defuse both its centrality and its centredness, and thus dislocates it from any conceivable historical burden of responsibility either for the past or the future. The other involves a certain reinstallation of the self, as in a sense self-invented, imaged, styled, even replicated. Self-made, or apparently so, these selves are the site of intensities and even ethics, but again hardly susceptible of what Nietzsche called the 'historical sense'.

The first of these figures, disidentity and fragmentation, has itself a history, although it is one which is difficult to write. A great deal has depended historically, in bourgeois Western modernity, on the fashioning in early modernity of the punctual autonomous self as the centre of value and 'sociality', even if this was no more than a set of appearances, a 'lived ideology' rather than a real historical entity. The ethical and political centre of freedom, but the object of discipline and subjection, the modern individual, or 'Man', as an essential identity has dominated Western thought. But if the story goes – and I have told part of it – that this self was once invented, instituted, and constituted, it is also said that it has subsequently, rather recently, fragmented. The death of the author, the death of the subject.

We could ask when the assault on identity began, and what its cause was. With Freud, with the Bolshevik revolution (with any of the historical revolutions?), with nineteenth-century science, with the computer, with God's *various* deaths? Multi-national technologism? The atomic bomb? There are various stories which attempt to locate the breakdown of self-hood in the loss of community or even loss of touch with the land.

The multiplicity of the answers that seem to offer themselves as possible explanations for the evident reversal of the centering of strategies in the individual which doubtless began in the Renaissance, attests to the complexity and the totality of the crisis of identity itself. And equally we are dealing with something systematic, or at least systemic, rather than anything which can be resolved, as is so often the case, into either peculiar or general subjective experience. From alienation to existential *angst*, this tradition will not do any longer. Not that there isn't an experience of crisis: the experience of a loss of identity is acutely attested in Western literature and philosophy. But problems of interpretation remain. We cannot rest with the experience, because of the systematicity. And again, what is it that experiences the lack of identity? Is that not, in troubled modern form, itself a kind of identity? 'Postmodern' experience is actually the opposite of experience in that it tends to disorientate the subject born into modern (humanist) assumptions and practices – still the cultural and ideological dominant of the West – and undermine any concept of the stability or unity of a subject able to have experience in the first place. Delirium is a name which has not altogether happily been given to this dual interference in the experiential and conceptual fields; one which now, however, enjoys a range of reference that is useful if not always too precise.

But perhaps to ask the question of origin and cause, when and why did this begin, is not to be *historical enough*. Much has been written already, in one way or another, about the character of modernity and its crisis. But to put the question in the form of origin and cause is secretly to assume stable and personal identity as a norm, and to investigate the regrettable loss of it. I wonder whether the more radically historical gesture is not to ask the question of this question, and begin to refuse the normality of identity, both ethically and epistemologically, and embrace resolutely non-identity as the project: or rather, not non-identity, for this falls within the old trap, but jettison the problematic altogether (without actually advocating the politics of a longing for death, which is where the alien and normal forms of the modern-postmodern dynamic tend, as so many have sensed).

Thus one of the persistent and central problems with this history of identity is, of course, that as soon as the punctual and self-possessed individual appeared on the stage of history, so did his opposite, the dispersed and fragmented disidentical, alienated, critical persona whose *existenz* consisted at best in an unstable play of masks and guises. Descartes, as in so much else, emblematises the problematic. In one sense he is the author of the self; in another sense, the Cartesian subject is already deeply divided in and from itself. It is not only separated from its body, but also from that self which it utters as self at every moment that it confirms its self-hood by self-pronunciation.

This problem of the originary duality of the modern subject may be focused in the question of whether reflection is critical or narcissistic. In Descartes these two turn into each other: the discourse of criticism is the discourse of the self. If reflection is to be critical and not self-sealingly narcissistic (and therefore complacent), that must be because one knows that the self in question is not a substance and not therefore reflectable, but an ensemble of discourses and practices. At most – and this is the best that can be said about Descartes – it is a narrative, or rather a narration. The point is that Cartesian 'criticism' pre-empts reflexivity (even as it apparently promotes it) by building it into the centre which is the self. In this it forms an unholy alliance with wider puritan emphases on 'self-possession', where the self as property and the self-control of the self against transgressive dynamics which range from intoxication to passion and beyond, reproduce and enforce the disciplinary ideology of integrity.

The other problem, for those who want an undialectical history of the individual, is, of course, that along with the centred self, we should also have to encounter not just his opposite – for every Descartes, a Freud – but a whole series of his others, who never made it far enough into the charmed circle to be alienated from it. They are of course another story.

The tension between the punctuality of the modern individual and its contrapuntal fragmentation in critical or pathological complexity if not dispersal, is not perhaps as radical a paradox as at first it seems. For the Cartesian figure, if critical – and it isn't really, in any radical senses of the word – is also utterly individualistic nonetheless. We should be clear that if this is the form of happiness which is again on offer today in some newly re-styled form, it is quite continuous with the denial of other forms of identity which the original individual of modernity was constructed to forestall. For all the thematics of the fragmented or dispersed self (whether that dispersal is thought as a generalised condition or as an historical event) the evident attractions of delirium remain individualistic. At least the task of thinking through the collective forms of disidentity is posed; and posed, one would hope, historically and strategically.

The other model of happy individuality is the reinstalled, intensified self. After the historical death of the subject – which is probably in reality a modernist theme – there is today a rebirth of the individual, if not quite as a subject or a centre, at least as a sort of field, a bounded if permeable intensity. It is possible to sense this new self-hood all around us.

This new subject, which given that modernist death, we probably ought to call the *post mortem* self, but which I shall call the postmodern self, is in some ways newly punctual, even if it does not share the reaches of rational self-possession, critical reflection and puritan discipline by which the 'classical' modern subject was constructed.

Its subordination is more occluded still.

It is, or is designed to be, post-historical in Nietzsche's bovine sense, the happy subject of consumption, whether dimly aware that shopping is now a definitive and intransitive activity, or a node in some network of sensory – or when it comes to pay, electronic – 'information'. This condition, this delirium, this 'obscene ecstasy of communication' is the happy post-historicity of contemporary desire.

The postmodern self is a kind of hybrid of the punctual selfhood of classical modernity and the fragmented identity of modernism. With the former it shares that absolute individualism and some of the capacity for self-invention which went along with the modern subject's wider industrial desire, although the capacity for self-fashioning is now, because precisely not historical in its scope, largely a matter of style and image. It also has something of the modern subject's role as ethical centre: in as much as a whole classical structure of political, social, legal and aesthetic law was apparently built up around the classical individual, today, at least in much of the theoretical literature, a similar thing is happening. (I say 'apparently' because, of course, the structure of capitalism was never in fact built around the individual in this way: on the contrary, the individual was fashioned for it.) But where, in the classical case, the value of the individual was essential, in the contemporary self, which is also the target of a whole superstructure of 'values', it is nonetheless a wholly impersonal phenomenon. Probably still a subject, but in fact hardly a self, the new individual thus doesn't share with the classical subject the capacity for anguished alienation which often characterised its more critical moment. Where the classical self was capable of acute – often introspective – negativity, if the postmodern self is disfunctional or negative, it will be in the form of obscene ecstacy, anomie, delirium, or oceanic plenitudinousness of a dark kind. In these respects it then shares something with the modernist fragmentation of the self, the other term of the hybridisation. If in late modernity – to accept, for the sake of argument, the modernist story – the centre of self-hood cannot and does not hold, whether it is Marx or Freud, Nietzsche or Ford (as I suspect), who is 'responsible', that dimension of the dialectic of the modern individual grows over (at least, again, in the theoretical literature) from alienation to fragmentation, or better to ironic self-division. The Baudelairean moment, heroic in a modern sense, has latterly become the retrospective emblem of this, a kind of archetype of the ironic insertion of the modern self into modern life. The postmodern self articulates something of this fragmentation, but not in an ironic mode: there is no irony in the condition of this self (not least because there is held to be no history or historicity in it either), but a loose binding of surges of capacity or disaffection. Rather than integrity or fragmentation, or the ironic tension between them which characterised the modern self, the postmodern self is a miasmic unity or a miasmic dispersal. It hardly matters which. There is aesthetic definition to be sure; the postmodern self shares this with modernism. But it is a definition of a new depthlessness which elides critical distance of any kind, producing a single plane of experience or reality with which its 'life' is continuous. And if the modern subject was once at a distance from the body, in the transposition of the new form there insists what we might call, reformulating Kantorowitz, the 'least body' of electronic information, and delirium. And 'we, postmoderns', 'know' in our bodies what 'least' means.

In all of this it is unhistorical and indeed 'happy'.

I have begun to call this condition by the name which might as well be mentioned explicitly as that of the host at this pastoral, or at least the name it takes for itself: postmodernism. Or is it postmodernity? It is in any case a name which would need careful analysis, if the likely benefit in historical clarity were judged to be worth the effort. Two distinctions would have to be made, one between postmodernism and post-modernity, and the other within the historicity of the postmodern. In the first case it would be more than important, of course, not to fall into the trap of nominalism and confuse the discussion of words with the discussion of concepts (it isn't clear whether any 'things' are at stake). It often appears that one person's modernism is another's postmodernism, and *vice versa*. This potential for confusion is likely to remain so long as postmodernism – taking this here to mean the variety of discourses which 'name' the condition of the present as postmodernity – continues to refuse to clarify its own theoretical status, or until someone takes it seriously enough to sustain the burden of doing this work on its behalf (for, despite the industrial scale of the secondary literature, this remains undone).

For my own part, the distinction between postmodernity and

postmodernism, if at all useful, lies in my sense that it is possible to have more sympathy with the former, as a descriptive historical name for the present conjuncture, than it is with the velleities of much of what passes for the latter. But this raises within the idea of the postmodern the important historical problem of periodisation, and whether it is a quantitative 'definition' of the crisis of late capital that is evoked in 'postmodernity' – a chronological and perhaps even an historical period – or whether the postmodern is a qualitative category, describing a distinct moment of any given conjuncture, including some past ones. The 'question' of names notwithstanding, are we to think 'the postmodern' as indeed a new era, or as a component dimension of the present (and arguably therefore a dimension of earlier presents)? Has history moved, since 'the Renaissance', through phases of early and then full modernity, and on into postmodernity; that is, in other words, into, through and out of history? Or are modernity and postmodernity moments, in the component sense, of any historical conjuncture (at least since it has been possible to think of now as modern), so that all presents – even those which from our point of view lie in the past, or indeed the future – would have, in their own simultaneity, their constituent modern and postmodern dimensions and temporalities?

In reality this question is probably more urgent as it relates to modernity and the modern. However, for expository reasons, I use the term 'postmodernity' and 'the postmodern' here in a provisional, descriptive version of the period sense. The real rhythms of bourgeois modernity – from the early modern to date – seem to me more connected with the self-revolutionisation of capitalism as an increasingly global system, and with revolutionary challenges to that system: in this sense there definitely are new current developments in the strategies and effects of late capital, perhaps very tellingly in the 'culturisation' of its self-representation. These are of course, *pace* postmodernism, historical developments. I say this without prejudice to the discussion of whether 'the modern project' has either been superceded or indeed remains incomplete. This seems to me a wholly culturalist question. Postmodernism itself does not and cannot resolve, or even satisfactorily address, the historical question, in as much as it is avowedly post-historical and cannot – almost by definition – clarify its own historical status.

This is one of the reasons why it has little sense of crisis, beyond

crisis of representation, because it cannot cogently address any continuum or totality, let alone any more localised entities – despite
postmodernism's commitment to the local – *capable of being in crisis*.
Rather than a sense of historical crisis, the present conjuncture is
thus transcoded by postmodernism as a seamless new *condition*.
Postmodernism thus abolishes history, not just thematically or
ideologically, but structurally also, in the very structure of its –
postmodernism's – formation. In this sense it is deprived of any real
historical grounding, in as much as it is impossible – and this impossibility is indeed thematised by postmodernism – to specify the conditions of the condition.

The erasure of the representation of the historical present as crisis
in this transcoding of the present, the aversion of the possibility of this
critical thought – despite the otherwise breathless radicalism of postmodernism – has, of course, its overt and veiled political significance
and, arguably, a political purpose: I shall return to this shortly.

Among writers who embrace the term and the concept of the
postmodern there is considerable variety between the degrees to
which the 'condition' represents new opportunities for critical action
at one end of the scale, through what might best be regarded as a kind
of twentieth-century revision of Engels' sense that freedom is the
recognition of necessity which non-evaluatively acknowledges the
displacement of erstwhile ontological or epistemological guarantees
(real or imagined), to those who regard the postmodern as new and
more powerful oppression, a further denaturing of human and humane objectives. But in each case, the historicity of postmodernity, as
it is evoked by postmodernism, consists instead in a suspension, a
timeless absence of historicity.

In part this is aesthetic 'effect'. The autonomisation of the aesthetic
under modernism turns into a totalistic revenge on the alienation and
marginalisation of elite art, by which in postmodernity the whole of
reality becomes part of the aesthetic and is 'acculturated'. There is a
simultaneous over-dramatisation and under-dramatisation of the
postmodern: all is 'spectacle', but lacking both objective essence and
– allegedly – a controlling gaze, without epistemological certainty or
ontological grounding (and certainly none susceptible of representation), the reality which would otherwise have to be thought as

historical becomes simulacral. Here there is, in comparison with many earlier historical and cultural conjunctures, a certain sense of the first time as tragedy and the second time as farce.

The enigmatic minimalism of postmodern fiction sets one of the agendas for the localisation of the dialectic of intensity and flattened coherence of affect (although not of thought, where coherence is not postmodernism's strong suit) which brackets the larger structures of historical time or social formation. The short story is even experiencing a renaissance but in a paradoxical form: it is no longer a story, and indeed narrative more widely is cancelled as part of the dehistoricisation of the present.

The celebration of machine intelligence sets another agenda, in the 'existential' short-circuiting of what it fondly imagines to be 'historical' time afforded by a 'world' of instant information. The machines may now be intelligent, but this will hardly be a human property: inability to distinguish the critique of humanism from the mechanisation of people, will not delay the 'cultural' universalisation of the machine, not as physic but as metaphysic. Engaged, it is held, in *circulation*, but in no sense 'social'; with effects to be sure, but nothing so 'willed' as *political* power; neutral in the sense of that postmodern impersonality. Of course there is nothing about machine-use, or its uncritical celebration, that is either politically or socially neutral, but when all the words we write or say are recorded on disc and stored on the moon, who will much longer be able to contemplate the interruption of this delirium, this 'obscene ecstacy of communication', in the name of a social or political objection? Indeed, the critique of the metaphysics of presence – otherwise a postmodernist theme – will soon look like a dated modernism. Postmodernity, with information machines as its – metaphysical – emblem, is figured by postmodernism as a seamless if unbounded presence in the edgeless present of instantaneity, simultaneity, depthlessness, and groundlessness. A suitable habitat for Nietzsche's cattle.

Postmodernism is wedded to the notion of representation which nonetheless cannot represent. It is arresting to observe how in its simulacral aesthetics and its fetishised, disarticulated desire, there is a double decorporealisation at work. Where the liked and the likened – both at origin bodily – become utterly weightless. The 'time' of postmodernism has no 'body'.

The bodilessness of contemporary historicism is thus appropriate.

Despite having no 'time-sense', no history, postmodernism is an historicism – to use a word which has become current, but whose concept has a considerable history that has not been allowed to impinge significantly on the currency. At the theoretical level historicism was theorised a long time ago as the reduction of history to a single inner principle, whether that principle was figured as willed or objective, providential or blind, pragmatic or teleological. And whether the form of the principle is unitary or dialectical, it is the determinate reduction (which may be a logical reduction or itself 'historical') that turns history into abstraction. To reject historicism in this sense is not of course to deny that history is interpretable; it is merely to reject the inherent simplicity (even in the form of contradiction) of that interpretability. It is certainly to reject the idea that the ground of the possibility of interpretation is that history itself operates as a discursive or logical figure, as idealism old and new, positive and deconstructive, perennially claims.

Happy as it would make us to believe that history is intelligible because it is in principle like our interpretations of it, or that history has to be like we think it is because otherwise we would not be the kinds of historical beings who think that history is as we think it is – the anthropic principle translated into the social sciences in its weak and its strong forms – this is no less absurd than to displace our ethical axioms, philosophical principles or political desires into history and claim that it will inevitably take us where we want to go.

A more empirical – and empiricist – version of historicism involves an interpretative flattening which ultimately refuses historical intelligibility as such. Whether an epistemologically naturalist (and politically pragmatic) acceptance of the facts as they appear to be, or a more sophisticated and discursive (although epistemologically pragmatic) refusal to generate properly theoretical statements about historical intelligibility, the result is normally a passive (or perhaps unconsciously willing) acceptance of, and even an identification with, the underlying assumptions, political goals and current dominance of whoever or whatever is capable of giving an authoritative and perhaps also pleasing account of 'history'.

Sometimes these historicisms are even persuasive, but the net result is the same. History becomes one-dimensional. Either infinitely interpretable or inexorably unnegotiable in its principle, history becomes de-historicised.

On the surface postmodernism looks nothing like historicism because its sense of the intelligibility of the past, the present or the future is so groundless, so localised, so minimally speculative that it could hardly be said to engage 'history' at all. And, of course, it claims that history, like God, is dead. Even when in literary and cultural studies postmodernism deals with primary materials from the past, its refusal of interpretative grounding makes its historical claims weak ones at best.

But for all its refusal of either totalised explanation or of meta-narrative (and its frequent confusion of the two), postmodernism stands accused of historicism on precisely these grounds. Its dispersal of the real through the refraction of representation, for example, becomes a sort of essentialisation and centralisation of postmodernity around a thus totalised inner principle. The dialectic of identity and difference is not escaped – especially not at the theoretical or methodological level, and still less as a hermeneutic or philosophical theme – by substituting one for the other. The same can be said of each of postmodernism's other main motifs to the extent that they are each or together held to sum up the present. The pluralisation of difference, also held to be projectively celebratory and at the same time to relieve postmodernism of the burdensome need of cogent social or historical thought, similarly comes to occupy the discursive position and to play the rhetorical role of the totality, in as much as it is held to be the homogeneous general principle of post-modernity. Nor is the problem evaded by the refusal to make general statements about the theory of history with which postmodernist interpretative strategies operate: as if we were incapable of reading the theory in the practice, whether it is declared or not.

On both the theoretical and the empirical counts then, postmodernism is a reductive historicism. Either it projects into the present (and usually globalises and eternalises as well) the essential principle of non-essentiality (while exempting its own interpretative discourse from what would otherwise be an ensuing totalised unintelligibility), or it gambols like Nietzsche's cattle among the superfices of the appearances, the representations which do not represent (except of course when they have to be summoned as exemplars for, or anecdotes about, a condition or a state of affairs, an interpretation or a theory, which will be differed, or deferred, but not yet).

And in both cases it has much in common – uncannily – with the more familiar form of historicism called tradition, which is also wholly committed to the fulfillment of the present. Whether it is in the form of tradition as such, or pastiche 'heritage,' or even official and respectable historiography, all too often the contemporary organisation and valorising of apparently historical material participates in a circularity by which the construction of the past by the present legitimates the present that can then construct the past. Of course it is far too abstract to speak in this way of 'the past' and 'the present': there were and are real social forces which contend for the past and present (and the future). Historicism, especially in the form of tradition, governs the story of history as it is told by the victors. The historicist substitution of tradition for history elides those social forces and their contestation; at best it victimises by representation those whose continued subordination the telling of the traditional narrative exists to secure. Dissembling a common descent and a shared background, tradition is historicist but not historical, and precisely suppresses and excludes other histories, which is its *raison d'être*. But in a sense, of course, tradition is only too historical, in that it has gained a certain sedimentation through imposition over time which makes it *now* a part of the history of the present. Despite official views to the contrary, this is not how societies remember, but how they forget.

Because postmodernism is an historicism, it has no memory: or, if it 'remembers', it does so in order to forget. I have already invoked the incredulity towards meta-narratives – 'history' prominent among them – and the end of history with which postmodernism defines much of its 'theoretical' profile in this area. In that sense it is simply prepared to forget. To let the past disappear into the past, and at best to thematise the impossibility of usefully knowing the past. More 'radically' it simply declares history over, and the matter of historicity is at a stroke cancelled. More widely, 'cultural postmodernism' participates in ending history even if in the form of 'remembering' it. The pseudo-classicism, the twee pastiche retro, the hard-edged *nostalgia* of its architecture may stand emblematically for its forgetful historicism. In as much as pastiche in particular is not a critical trope, postmodernism is again not essentially different in this respect from the more traditional 'historical' form of 'tradition'. Both are committed to an intense or casual remembering in the present not only of something which may never have happened in the past, but with the definite purpose of forgetting what did. The legitimation of what is the dominant in the present is thus underwritten by this form of active forgetting, which, is the pseudo-memory of historicism. In some forms – academic ones at least – a very full remembering of past conjunctures may fulfil this amnesiac function.

But if there is a problematic of remembering and forgetting in postmodernism, there is nothing new about this. It was there at the tragic inscription of the beginning of the modern, and it is there in the peculiar tension of Nietzsche's text between the positive and negative valencies of the historical sense: 'This, precisely, is the proposition the reader is invited to meditate upon: *the unhistorical and the historical are necessary in equal measure for the health of an individual, of a people and of a culture*'. But it is most importantly, saliently and persistently there in the Marxist 'tradition' (which is, of course, nothing of the sort).

If Marx, in a famous formulation, seems wholly committed to the revolution abandoning 'the tradition of all the dead generations' which 'weighs like a nightmare on the brains of the living', Walter Benjamin, on the other hand, the worst part of a century later, will valorise the 'tradition of the oppressed'. If Marx will 'let the dead bury their dead', for Benjamin, *'even the dead* will not be safe from the enemy if he wins'. If Marx's 'social revolution of the nineteenth century cannot draw its poetry from the past, but only from the future', Benjamin's 'angel of history' has his face to the past, as 'the storm ... blowing from Paradise' nonetheless drives him 'into the future to which his back is turned, as the pile of debris before him grows skyward.'

But even if seemingly at odds, point for point, over the value of memory and the image of the future (and I shall return to this issue later), Marx and Benjamin nonetheless thus share what is necessarily critical, or diacritical, in the representation of history. Despite the apparent clarity of the break from the 'spirits of the past' which Marx recommends, his figuration of historical time is inherently complex. As well as a movement of demystification, stripping away 'all superstition in regard to the past', history – and historical action – is a play of representations and repetitions – 'the first time as tragedy, the second as farce' – of costumes and disguises, illusions and scripts, which are inherited from history but which, if they may mock or haunt the present, can also provide, among the involutions of the phases and moments of the historical process Marx addresses, its most compelling idiom: 'the awakening of the dead in those revolutions served the purpose of glorifying the new struggles, not of parodying the old; of magnifying the given task in imagination, not of fleeing from its solution in reality; of finding once more the spirit of revolution, not of making its ghost walk about again.' And no more is Benjamin's sense of the historical present either temporally punctual or intrinsically simple. Albeit infused with 'the presence of the now', the time of history is not an homogeneous, empty time, but one 'blasted out of the continuum of history', galvanised by the memory that 'flashes up at a moment of danger', and layered with other historical imperatives and dynamics than those either of the monovalent social democracy or the violently historicist fascism against which he struggled.

Within and between these texts, with their different levels and forms of temporality, there is a complexity in the figuration of history which defies temporal reduction or univocal narration. Indeed, Benjamin's text is important here precisely because it is an intervention against historicism in the allegorical name of a nuanced, dialectical and historical materialism, where the differentiation between a radical historicity on the one hand, and the flattened temporality and reactionary politics of historicism on the other, is crucial. In all historicisms – theoretical, cultural, traditional and academic – the amnesiac function is in fact a double one: the forgetting of the past (often in the form, as I have suggested, of selective 'remembering'), but also the forgetting of historicity as such.

Historicism – in any of its positivist, postmodernist and traditionalist forms – organises the past for its own purposes. There is some variety as to the amount of 'resistance' the past offers to this will to pacify it: at one end of the scale positivism will claim simply to record the past in all its neutral facticity, while at the other some of the more 'radical' forms of postmodernism even claim simply to construct it *tout court.*

But in the theoretical or empirical dimensions which I evoked above, the historical sense has thus nothing to do with historicism, for all the conceptual slackness of the current tendency to speak of any discourse that pays attention to history as 'historicist'. Or indeed as nostalgic, on the basis, presumably, of the peculiar assumption that a reference to history is necessarily a reference to the past. Whereas historicism is the systematic and systemic deployment of a 'history' which is not historical but rather history flattened into a-temporality – either in the instantaneous postmodernist present, or in a simplified, dehistoricised past – a properly radical, anti-historicist historicity, on the other hand, moves back and forth between past and present in movements of recognition and of differentiation, especially if the 'history' addressed is on the threshold of the modern. It operates a kind of parallax by which the legitimating circularity of the dominant historical discourse is interrupted in a dialectical movement between the history of the present and the difference of the past. In ultimate epistemological senses it may have to exercise some scepticism about its own groundedness, but this is quite different from beginning in a programmatic way from that lack of foundation. But it need not fear – as historicism must (or would if it had a properly historical sense) – that in the objective of a full historicisation it will commit itself to regressive perspectives, as if general statements about the structure and transformation of history which are not rooted for their 'truth', nor important for their critical yield, in a single *and particular* historical moment inevitably carried with them a burden of reaction. On the contrary, the complexity of its sense of the historicity of history disemburdens it of that dead weight of the apparent past in order that it may remember.

Most important for a radical historicity – and for the understanding of the radical historicity of history – is its grasp of the present, the historicity of the present.

Hegelians once thought the totality in very complete forms, to be sure. But today it is difficult to instantiate the totalisation of interpretation or structure in quite the absolute form that postmodernism – its own totalisation of the postmodern aside – affects to discover. On the contrary, it is, rather, the received historicism that suggests that if we theorise the present we tend to take the contemporary moment to be a punctual and self-present unit of time, which is not the case with the formations at stake here in the Marxist tradition. Certainly, Benjamin's now is not the non-time of postmodern, post-historical, 'time' because it is a temporality shot through, inlaid, layered with other times, with past and future temporalities; a complex historical time rather than simple, singular, non-historical time of historicism. It is another kind of time. Neither the undifferentiated duration of tyranny or plenitude, nor the linear time of teleology or nostalgia – in which, variously, the present belongs in its value and to all intents and purposes in its reality, to the past – in Benjamin's figuration of historical time, the past is that disturbing, critical irruption into the present that even if it fans the spark of hope, also signals the present state of emergency. Compared with this – tragic – hollowing of the present, any present, postmodernist historicism *fills* the present with indifferent difference, with anecdotal similitudes, with non-representational reflections, with refusals of explanation that leave facticity in place, when they do not underwrite things as they are by refreshing the historicism which in its turn sustains the appearances of the present. Tradition commits itself to this task in more straightforward ways.

The postmodernist rejection of history is, of course, in veiled or overt ways an assault on Marxist and other forms of radical, historical, thought. But in the form, predictably enough, of travesty. Rather than as a totalised unity, radical critique has repeatedly thought and articulated the moment, not as a self-identical punctuality but as both part of a diachronic process and also as a synchronic structure or *ensemble* of forces, whose meaning and being lie not in its discrete self-presence and self-sufficiency but in its relations of difference with the other diachronic contexts. The moment is not, thus, a reified instant or instance, but a *critical* term, which is unstable, non-self-identical, open. Engaged in processes of becoming and unbecoming, in a *dispositif* of tactics and strategy, the apparently self-identical instant, event or entity, is actually the critical mark of struggle. Social and political relations – usually of confrontation – are encoded in the historical 'moment': we should not regard historical moments as *items* of social and political 'interest' as does the historicist 'ethic'. In contrast to sweeping rejections of history, it makes a difference which history we are talking about. What is the conceptualisation of history in play? What is its conception of temporal dispersal, teleological patterning, sequential and structural components and determinations? What forces are admitted to be part of it, what are its dimensions, what lies outside it? Whose history is it? What political and ideological purposes does it formulate and serve? What is its gender? Once these questions, and others like them, begin to be formulated, singular and banal formulations like '*the* end of history' start to break down: there are some histories which should be brought to an end as swiftly as possible. There are others which have hardly begun.

In any case, it is quite clear from the complexity of the diacritical figurations of historical time in which history has been inscribed by oppositional thinkers, that it has not been conceived as the kind of meta-narrative which the postmodernist 'argument' alleges. On the contrary, in fact. The variety of such figurations, Marxist and otherwise, suggests a far more complex and more internally diverse analysis of historical time than postmodernism allows. Gramsci's important sense of hegemonies and counter-hegemonies of the conjuncture, for example, or Althusser's formulation of contradiction and overdetermination as key formations in historical process – a theorisation coupled in Althusser's work of course, with a systematic critique of an unacceptable historicism in the Marxist tradition itself – are both instances from within that tradition where history is certainly not understood either as simply linear or recognisably narrative. Or again, to choose examples from outside Marxism, and even critical of it, positions as diverse as that disclosed in the vocabulary of the emergent, the dominant and the residual, or in that of the 'history of the present', each suggest the *inherent* structural complexity with which historical time has been conceptualised, even recently, in radical thought.

Or, to return to the Marxist text itself, is there not something importantly dialectical articulated in the striking, if sometimes enigmatic, remarks about the anatomy of man being – in a deliberate reversal of the historicist order of derivation – the key to the anatomy of the ape; or in the necessary difference between the order of presentation of historical categories and the historical order of their emergence? Are these not also instances of the diachronicity that characterises radical conceptions of historical time, rather than the monotemporality of historicism? This dialectic of differentiality is perhaps best evoked by another famous formulation of Marx's, that it was only possible to generate in thought an abstract concept of labour after labour had in reality become abstract. Whether or not this insight is in itself true, the 'philosophy of history' on which it is founded is signal: it effects a reading-strategy that situates interpretation within the history it seeks to read and situates it as one critically at odds with its history, even as it seeks to read it. The dialectical hinge of critical distance is here opened within the historical sense itself, and is articulated to the complex temporality of history and historical discourse alike. Unlike the pessimistic totalism which links the historical process and the historical knowledge of that process in a sealed and reciprocally sustaining form in, for example, some of Foucault's accounts of historicity, here the necessarily historical character of knowledge and the critical address to history are mutual and differential, diacritical rather than totalised.

In these figurations of historical time and of historicity, history begins to look less like the narrative that postmodernism mistakenly assaults, but rather – if one were thus to demand a literary genre as the appropriate metaphor – like tragedy. Certainly Marx thought of history as by turns tragedy and farce; Walter Benjamin, as more a tragic, although no less differentiated, process. And their formulations of the complexity of historicity as the interaction of past, present and future temporalities resembles a tragic formation, with its distinctive problematic of spatial and temporal – historical and 'social' – displacement, violence and forgetting. In this sense, tragedy, either as a genre or a concept, is likely to be more historical than much history. Where histories tend toward either the replication of some dominant story which seeks to justify and legitimate whatever is in actuality dominant, or protest against the dominant *on its ground*, tragedy, on the other hand, discloses the problematicity – the unforeclosed character, and thus the critical and diacritical value – of the historical.

But if history resembles tragedy in the complexity of its temporalities, it is also tragic in the extent to which it consists in violent depredation. Although the state of emergency is usually occluded by the dominant historicism: this, after all, is its purpose. Certainly there is a bourgeois nostalgia in the breathlessness with which post-modernism notices and celebrates the rapid transformations of now, the vertiginous sensations of dissolution and disorientation which it takes to be the characteristic experience of contemporary life. But in fact the normal experience of the vast majority of the population of the world has been for centuries that of unstable, turbulent uncertainty, as individuals, families, communities and even entire societies, nations, peoples, have been tossed about, transformed, and not infrequently simply destroyed by 'vertiginous' change. In this respect the nostalgia of the postmodernists for a time when everything was settled is wonderful. The ignorance – who knows how innocent it is? – which thinks of change as novelty has been well-schooled. But the impertinence with which the oppressed masses are instructed not to be afraid of change is chilling. Postmodernist and traditionalist historicisms 'conspire' together to achieve – not least in the erasure of historicity – the elision from history of the ongoing crisis which history actually is. Because both seek to produce dehistoricised, homogenous time, the ongoing state of emergency is occluded, as are those for whom it is the rule rather than the exception, for whom 'invasion' is a daily lot. Both are systems of denial, removing from history the domination which they support and hide.

For if history is more like tragedy than like narrative, this in turn raises the crucial question: for whom is history tragic? It is necessary to say here clearly what – or who – it is that historicism actively forgets. Or rather it isn't, in the sense that quite outside official histories are all the others who were never admitted into history, as historicism's history exists in order to secure that very exclusion and subordination. The others are another story, although it is they, or we, to whom history dominantly happens.

Thus it may turn out that if, conversely, we are to rethink the historicity of history, we may have to think history in quite another way, as Benjamin suggested. We may have to brush history 'against the grain', to think the underside of what we have been told by the victors, to trace occlusion in 'the real'. In this sense even what is often seen as Nietzsche's call to 'forget' (in as much as he, 'like' Marx, measures the burden of the past), is conversely a call for critical history: a rejection of the past as it has been officially constituted and then passed off as history – or more usually as natural tradition, as the sign not of change but of stasis.

This radical historicity entails the inhabitation of more than one time, with complex memory, in as full as possible a recognition of the violence that is entailed in this 'condition': the recognition of the violence which is revealed as history, together with the sedimented, ongoing violence of the dominant historicism; the violence of having to wrest sense back from facticity which that violent history consolidates as the truth and the criteria of truth; and the violence which might have ethically to be used against 'history' as it has been constituted.

If Benjamin would have the fragments blasted out of the continuum, the apocalyptic tone of his language ran historically only slightly ahead of the technological means of its realisation. The demonisation of those who in opposition contemplate but the minutest fraction of such violence is, naturally, total.

But it has never proved easy to keep memory free of the seductive continuities of tradition, or of the allure of the secular discontinuities whose contemporary form postmodernism names. Indeed, to challenge the tradition of the discourse of power in the name of memory might seem paradoxical. If memory were to be deployed against power how would this not be a nostalgic complicity with the control of the past?

The answer doubtless entails the recognition that history – or, to avoid the confusion here of very different things, historicity – is actually the name of difference and not of the relentless sameness of all historicisms. Memory is not individual, nor the sign of invasion but of sociality. But nor is it the sign of indiscriminate difference: critique, if it is radical, is always situated, and *inevitably* social. This is evident not least in the converse. Some curiosity in our condition once turned memory into mourning (or its impossibility) and now, even more threateningly, offers to turn history into nostalgia. Loss of memory has been consistently concomitant with domination. But if history can be figured as haunting, not all mnemonic analysis – which, as analysis prompted by memory, is not to be confused with historicist analysis of the dead past – is relevant in that way: rather, it is the analysis of domination now prompted by memory. Still less is mnemonic resistance backward-looking, despite the wind that is blowing from Paradise.

There are some things that simply cannot be said, not because their outrage consists in that they are forbidden, or even offensive, but because they test the limits of discourse as the historical and ideological sedimentation of received and contested cultural practice. History, in the sense of the historicist dominant, is the process of the prevention of their articulation. The counter-task is to put historicity as the critical investigation, and even perhaps the experience, of transgressive limit to work, in a general politics of historical transformation.

It is not only or simply a problem of elocution, but also one of practice, the practice of making the future. For although enslaved ancestors may be a surer prompt than liberated grandchildren, nor, on the other hand, should a radical history attempt to be a kind of retrieval of the past, even if this were possible. There are senses in which the past must be protected, for if the enemy is victorious not even the dead will be safe, but there is no recovery. Restitution cannot be made to the oppressed, and a radical historicity should not risk becoming involved in compensating for that in which it bears no responsibility. For if history from below is something that has to be done rather than contemplated, perhaps this provides in its way a non-epistemological sense of the authenticity of history. Rather than critical or speculative thought concerning the possibility of providing epistemological guarantees for knowledge, it offers the formation of the project of freedom in its practicality. Or at least the horizon of the real. Freud pointed out that reality kills you in the end. But this formulation appeals ultimately and implicitly to an indifferent naturalism. It is necessary to put back into the discourse of reality the historical and social forces which in many circumstances short of 'natural' death do the killing, or impose a life which is hardly worth the living.

Perhaps the delirium of now can function as effectively for liberation as it currently does in the legitimation of historicist domination (for 'uncannily', it is those who pronounce the end of history who have most in common with a repressive historicism, the termination of the medium of transformation being the installation of closure)? But I for one remain unconvinced. Postmodernism 'represents' a certain breakdown, but does it represent that breakdown in ways which tend to unlock the historical blockage or to confirm it? To be sure there are no general answers, but one thing is clear: not to ask the question of historicity is to become complicit with systems of domination terrifying in their scope and intensity. For in contradistinction to the theme of postmodernist dispersal of difference, it is important to diagnose the dependence of domination on, and the historical fabrication by domination of, powerful metaphors, powerful practices and powerful metaphorical practices – some of them literary – of fixity, including the metaphorisation of the necessity of fixity. This is far too little understood by forms of analysis which will celebrate the delirium and neglect any account whatsoever, not of the undone, but of the done. It is important to reckon not only how identity slips but also how it seems not to (and how, in that 'seeming', there is not simply an illusion but real power and coercive effectivity). A radical historicity would indeed entail a difference, difference from domination. Putting due caution around the *problematic* of repression and liberation should not be allowed to function as a substitute for solving the problems, practical and discursive, of freedom. Freedom conceived like this may turn out to be, not the conceptual trap that Foucault identified, but the matter of real historical constitution he analysed. Freedom can be coercive; but coercion can never be freedom.

But if, on the one hand, cow-like happiness prevails, we should not be allured into thinking that history might yet be a comedy. If comedies have happy endings, there is no way in which bovine history can be comic. In as much as the pastoral of historicism has no diacritical historical sense, it has thus no displacement. There can be no end to plenitude.

But if it turns out, on the other hand, that forms of temporal displacement will have, after all, to serve as the figurations of our historical, critical consciousness, neither will it be possible to think history as closure.

If we think then of the Benjaminian model of the strange diacritic

– tricritic – of temporal displacement, then perhaps our model will make history tragic. But again not because it ends badly, but because history, like tragedy, does not end. Or, at least, it could *merely* end. Whereas there is no fulfilling, no plenitude towards which history is tending which could count as its full closure, there are certainly forces of termination at work. But even they are at work in the potentially transformable field of possibility which is the poetry of the future.

It is not necessary to instate your historical discourse in the fragility, or even the power, of the voices of ghosts, to be convinced that without history we die.

DOCUMENTATION: A BIBLIOGRAPHICAL NOTE

The main works consulted, and all of those cited or referred to throughout this volume, are listed in the consolidated bibliography at the end, including books and articles which have provided in one way or another the bibliographical background to *Signs of Invasion*. The following are some principal references.

The information of the absolute

The reference on p. 11 to the complexity of Cordelia's access to 'empowered speech' draws on Jonathan Goldberg's 'Shakespearean inscriptions' (1985); the theme returns on subsequent pages. My discussion 'elsewhere' of new subjection (p. 14) is in *The Tremulous Private Body* (Barker 1984 and forthcoming 1994); further references to this work are made on p. 17 and elsewhere below. The slippage of meaning from itself on p. 15 *et seq.* invokes a general context of deconstructive accounts of textuality. This issue is taken up again at various points below: see the discussion of Ophelia's language on pp. 43–4; see also 'In the wars of Truth', below, for a critique of 'slippage'. On p. 16, there seems to be a faint echo of Adorno in the phrase 'negative dialectic': I hope so; Adorno (1990). The references to languages and concepts of nature, and to Edmund as a Hobbesian figure, on p. 17, are to Danby (1961). The contrast between spectacle and confinement on p. 24 refers, of course, to Foucault's hypotheses in *Discipline and Punish* (1977). The idea on p. 27 that *Lear* might be a formal comedy, owes something to Michael Long's *The Unnatural Scene* (1976). On p. 30, and elsewhere throughout the volume, Raymond Williams's terminology of 'dominant', 'residual', and 'emergent' is invoked; see Williams 1977, esp. Ch. II.8. 'Deconsecration' on p. 31 and cognate ideas elsewhere draw on Franco Morretti's seminal essay on Shakespearean tragedy; see Morretti 1988. My comments on pp. 31–2 concerning the 'geo-political' figurations in *Hamlet* are indebted to a conversation with Gordon Brotherston. The 'difficult matter of writing', on p. 34 and *passim* (e.g. 'the problematic of writing' on p. 56), draws, of course, on Derrida, especially his good early work in *Of Grammatology* (1976) and *Writing and Difference* (1978). The 'considerable debate' referred to on p. 48 is discussed much more fully below: see in particular 'A wilderness of tigers.' For the notion of 'radical tragedy' mentioned on p. 49 see Dollimore (1984). 'Crisis of representation' (p. 56) is a common phrase these days; but Fredric Jameson's use of it in his Foreword to Lyotard 1984, is important, and relevant here and below. The phrase 'killing of the king' (p. 60) cannot help but evoke Maynard Mack (1973). For 'most body' on p. 60 and 'least body' on p. 98, see Foucault's use of Kantorowitz in *Discipline and Punish* (1977, pp. 28–9). Connections between submissiveness and subversion (p. 65) have characterised New Historicist discussions of Shakespeare; see in particular Goldberg 1985; and see below, Part Two, for further discussion of such figurations of 'power'. Behind the discussion on p. 74 and *passim* of patriotic nationalism lies in particular the renewed currency of Tillyard's *Elizabethan World Picture* (1972). 'Signifying nothing' on p. 80 refers obliquely to Malcolm Evans's book of that name, (1986). The references on p. 85 are to the early, neurological, Freud, and to Derrida. The phrase 'display of power' on p. 88 hints at a more explicit critique below of Leonard Tennenhouse's *Power on Display* (1986) in particular, and New Historicist exhibitionism in general; see 'A wilderness of tigers'. Quotations from Shakespeare are from the Arden editions; details are given in the bibliography.

Nietzsche's cattle

On p. 93 'Incredulity towards meta-narratives' and the 'end of history' are references to Lyotard (1984) and Fukuyama (1989); both are taken up again below; see especially 'Tragedy and the Ends of History'. 'Intensities', also on p. 93, invokes Jameson's seminal 'Postmodernism, or the cultural logic of late capitalism' (1984); this essay is also obliquely cited on p. 96 and *passim*, and explicitly so in the last essay of this volume. 'The death of the author' (p. 94) is Roland Barthes's famous idea; the disappearance of the subject, 'Man', Foucault's (1974). The 'obscene ecstasy of communication' on pp. 97 and 101 cites Baudrillard's essay (1985). 'Self-fashioning' (p. 97) of course evokes Greenblatt's 1980 text in particular, and this New Historicist preoccupation in general: both are taken up in more detail below (see especially 'A wilderness of tigers'). For an engaging account of ironic Baudelairean modernity (pp. 97–8), see Berman 1983. As to whether postmodernity is a qualitative category (p. 99), Peter Osborne asks a similar question of modernity; see Osborne 1992. The references to tragedy and farce on p. 101, are derived, of course, from the opening of Marx's *18th Brumaire* (1970), the text which is then taken up again on pp. 105ff., and in the last essay below; the 'critique of the metaphysics of presence' is again Derrida's project; see (1976) especially. Louis Althusser's critique of historicism (esp. 1970) lies partly behind p. 102. The text by Nietzsche quoted on pp. 93 and 105 and referred to on p. 111 is 'On the uses and disadvantages of history for life' (1983). On pp. 105ff., Walter Benjamin is quoted from his 'Theses on the philosophy of history' (1973). 'The history of the present' is Foucault's well-known phrase (1977). The anatomy of the ape, and related discussion (pp. 109ff.) is from Marx's *Grundrisse* (1973).

Part Two

VIOLENCE AND INTERPRETATION

1

IN THE WARS OF TRUTH

Violence, true knowledge
and power in Milton and Hobbes

I believe that it is not to the great model of signs and language [*la langue*] that reference should be made, but to war and battle. The history which bears and determines us is war-like, not language-like. Relations of power, not relations of sense. History has no 'sense', which is not to say that it is absurd or incoherent. On the contrary, it is intelligible and should be able to be analysed down to the slightest detail: but according to the intelligibility of struggles, of strategies and tactics.

Michel Foucault, 'Truth and Power'

I philosophize only in *terror* ...

Jacques Derrida, *Writing and Difference*

I

The texts I shall be addressing, Milton's *Areopagitica* and, all too briefly for such a monument, Hobbes's *Leviathan*, clearly have the Civil War as their historical context, each concerned, even if in rather different ways, with|the pressingly contemporary question of power, with the form and function of the state, and with the problems (thrown up in the last analysis by the revolutionary struggle itself) of, particularly, the production, circulation and control of discourse. But it is appropriate first to reflect on what sort of relationship between writing and history will be implicitly at work in my own text, and in particular to try to specify something of the theoretical profile of my approach to our topic of literature, or as I prefer, discourse, and the Civil War, or revolution.*

*The text is that of a lecture, and its spoken idiom has been retained. It was delivered to the conference 'Warre is all the Worlde About: Literature and the English Civil War' which was held at the University of Southampton in April 1987. Some opening remarks, and the last phrase or two, are prompted by the theme and occasion of that conference.

It was given in an earlier form to the annual conference of the Australia and New

The invitation to relocate these texts in the political – and as we now know, decisively historical – engagements of their day seems inescapable for any analysis tempted to claim a certain materialism for itself. And with such a project, expressed in these general terms, I have, of course, no quarrel. On the contrary, to do anything else would seem to me an intellectual and political dereliction of some proportion. But even to begin to put matters in the language of text and context is perhaps unwittingly to summon up a form of the historical study of writing which, while not without its own radical history and potential, may be too easily content with an empiricism of the 'text-and-background' kind: one which in the very attempt to return to a real history texts hypostatised by the traditional fragmentation of the academic disciplines and the inherent and sys-tematic tendency of the disciplines to idealise their own materials, nonetheless retains a foregrounding of literature in a way which remains quite acceptable to the methodological assumptions – although often not the explicit politics – of traditional study. The limit case is the move too directly to history 'itself', which in reversing the received hierarchy leaves it in place. I am at least as concerned, however, to challenge such assumptions as I am with appropriating them. Perhaps this sounds as if I simply eschew what have been called 'real historical' positions? Sceptical as I am about the pursuit of history 'itself', I think the matter of historicity is a little more compli-cated than that.

In practice my aim is to combine some description, in Milton and Hobbes, of the tropes of true discourse or Truth and the warlike violence with which they are associated, with some reflection on the theory of discourse today. But in the combination I hope – by a kind of dialectical parallax – to avoid two strategies which seem to offer a way out of the text-and-background trap, but do so only at the cost of other problems presenting themselves. They are the twin phenomena of what is sometimes called 'historicism' on the one hand, and 'theoreticism' on the other, errors, in my view, as much political as theoretical or methodological. They are both very much

Zealand Association for Medieval and Renaissance Studies which took place at the University of Melbourne, August 1986.

Versions of 'In the wars of Truth' have appeared in print in *Southern Review* (Barker 1987), and in *Literature and the English Civil War* (1990) edited by Thomas Healy and Jonathan Sawday. It has been revised again for publication here.

available today, and in very clear form in modern Renaissance and seventeenth-century studies; we have only to think of the contemporary map of such studies, and perhaps especially, although by no means exclusively, of the vital work that is being done in the United States, to see them powerfully at work. An academic movement of increasing popularity, even authority, announces itself more or less unashamedly to be a new historicism; while few critical schools can have been more assiduous in their espousal of 'theory' – sometimes to the point of ostentatious formalism – than Deconstruction.

Where for an older historicism the background provided at least a chronological locality and at best an explanatory ground, for the new variety, refusing the metaphor of foreground and background and emphasising the historicity of the texts themselves, the erstwhile 'background' becomes a network of discourses and symbolic practices, parallel, analogous or even intercalated with the textual materials under discussion. In its best versions the New Historicism possesses an impressive, although sometimes fetishised, scholarship which has considerably widened the scope of texts normally thought relevant, an advanced, theoretically-informed conceptual framework, and a pertinent insistence that it is cultural production and cultural power that should really be at stake. It is possible to have much sympathy with this insistence, but also a number of reservations about the politics of the characteristic New Historicist model of slippage and cultural containment. It seems to me that there are dangers in the approach of appearing to seek out what is oppositional or resistant in the text while actually incorporating that into the functioning of the culture at large – whatever that is – and so producing what amounts to a spectatorial passivity in respect of power. Within and among the discourses in play there are seen to be slippages and discontinuities to which older historicisms were far from alert, but these are often resolved in practice into a higher functional unity behind a tendency for history to be grasped – anti-empirically, but in my view rather simply – as other texts. At worst the anecdote is raised to a methodological level. And if the incorporation is pressed beyond the 'merely' methodological and theoretical (there is after all no such thing as theory or method which does not entail or imply a politics, however highly coded), a price presumably has to be paid. Certainly when slippage becomes 'subversion' – a key word for such studies, and one which has its uses, to be sure – the conceptual language of

New Historicism risks familiarity with discourses on the right that seek to empower and legitimate domination by a deviant rather than oppositional naming of those who resist its effects. Even on the left, subversion may be a poor name or a poor thing where in reality revolutionary perspectives are either meant or needed. At the very least I should want to measure what real distance there is (and there is some) between the demonisation of subversion in order to justify and maintain domination, and the ultimate lack – inherent in the incorporation of subversion into power – of a thoroughgoing critique of domination. I suspect that the latter tends at best to offer the political effect of leaving everything as it is, when it doesn't actually debilitate the very idea of opposition in the name of all subversion being a necessary condition of the functioning of power as such. The result is often, in the name of studying at least the poetics of power, a practical denial of the fact and poignancy of domination, substituting notions of circulation for those of oppression, anxiety for terror.

But if New Historicism is in any sense new, this must partly be because it is willing to attend to history again 'after' the resolutely anti-historical cast of theoreticism in its by now familiar deconstructionist form. Characterised by a tendency to identify in the texts of the Renaissance and the seventeenth century the linguistic phenomena and rhetorical practices which are essentially those of its own contemporary modernism or postmodernism (it is not always clear which), deconstruction, in the name often of engaging the *aporias* where cultural authority is not at one with itself, can also threaten a debilitating fatalism; either in the complacent form of the play of textual power (where it is not mere play in the weak sense) being seen to be egregiously self-subverting and therefore in need of no transformation other than that which it works upon itself by virtue of its nature as textuality; or by way of the pessimistic and radical scepticism that will interminably question as metaphysical all positive strategies. Its political limitations lie in its circularity, in precisely the theoreticism that in reducing all not simply to language but to a theory of the text tends to mistake the problem for the solution, seeing difference as ultimately endemic rather than fully critical.

In practice the boundaries between historicist and theoreticist approaches are not distinct. On the contrary, and despite their logical and philosophical incompatibility with each other, they are frequently combined. The New Historicism has little hesitation in adopting to its own uses a variety of post-modernist interpretative strategies, although usually without thinking through in conceptual terms the problems raised by the historical character – even the historical time – of such strategies themselves. And deconstructive readers, while analysing avowedly historical texts, seem equally well able in effect to abolish historical difference in the name of generalised textuality, without perceiving any problem of theory or method. A certain Foucault and a certain Derrida gazing into the mirror of each other's eyes. With, I imagine, some incomprehension.

What, then, is to be done? As a contribution to the formulation of a strategy in respect of all this I wish to offer the following exploration of a different way of approaching the relationship between writing and the 'Civil War', one which will involve discourse or writing and the war in a certain interiority with each other. While, in particular, I want to evade the received hierarchisation of literature and background, I don't in any sense wish, in the name of either 'circulation' or 'the play of the text', to lose sight of other hierarchisations of discourse, whose description should continue to allow the discussion and apprehension of the (traces of) structures and practices of domination and resistance.

I hope this will become plain in the process of more concrete analysis, to which I shall now turn.

II

In terms of contextualisation *Areopagitica* is not, of course, without its own pointers as to the correct background against which it ought to be set. Passages like the following suggest the immediacy of the Civil War as the significant environment of discourse:

Behold now this vast City: a city of refuge, the mansion house of liberty, encompassed and surrounded with His protection; the shop of war hath not there more anvils and hammers waking, to fashion out the plates and instruments of armed Justice in defence of beleaguered Truth, than there be pens and heads there, sitting by their studious lamps, musing, searching, revolving new notions and ideas wherewith to present, as with their homage and their fealty, the approaching Reformation: others as fast reading, trying all things, assenting to the force of reason and convincement. (Milton 1958, p. 177)

In the light of this invocation of the city at war, a certain kind of historicism might well attempt to dislocate Milton's text from its traditional setting, whether that be, say, a place in the history of English prose style or in the universality of some discussion of supposedly fundamental rights and liberties, and refer it to the immediate context of the Civil War as the real ground, or at least the most politically interesting content, of its representations.

But this is not the kind of locatedness I wish to examine here, preferring over too swift a resort to the text's evocation of a real London embattled by Royalist forces, the less empirical address to context inherent in the passage's association with each other of the figurations of warfare and of discursive practice. Counter to traditionally liberal versions of the relative value of violence on the one hand, and on the other what Milton would have called 'literature' (although we have since come to use the term in a narrow and impoverished sense), here the material preparation for battle and the forging of the ideological weapons of the approaching Reformation (or as we might say, this time in a richer idiom, the coming revolution) run parallel to each other. If the armouries and the munitions factories are self-evidently necessary for the advancement of Justice in defence of Truth, no less so, in the rhetoric of Milton's argument for free debate unhindered by licensing, is the discursive struggle, itself mobilising, significantly enough, the 'force' of reason and convincement. It is this association of discourse and violence, as likes rather than opposites, which will become the main thematic component of what I have to say.

The powerfully warlike character of discourse strikes an early and key note in Milton's text. In a famous passage usually taken to be a rhetorical sop to the parliamentary supporters of a reinstituted censorship replacing that of the Crown which had fallen together with the abolition of Star Chamber, Milton grants the need for a police of discourse in terms that infuse the latter with a dangerous criminality and a potential for militant, transgressive if not actually rebellious, violence:

I deny not, but that it is of greatest concernment in the Church and Commonwealth, to have a vigilant eye how books demean themselves as well as men; and thereafter to confine, imprison, and do sharpest justice on them as malefactors. For books are not absolutely dead things, but do contain a potency of life in them to be as active as that soul was whose progeny they are; nay, they do preserve as in a vial the purest efficacy and extraction of that living intellect that bred them. I know they are as lively, and as vigorously productive, as those fabulous dragon's teeth; and being sown up and down, may chance to spring up armed men. (p. 149)

The necessity is conceded of Church and State regarding books as potential malefactors and suborning them to a justice that is seen clearly as state power, even if, as it later becomes clear, Milton intends this action to be after the event of transgression, contrary to the Star Chamber practice of pre-publication licensing. And the positive – vigorous and productive – danger represented by books, the dragon's teeth that spring up armed men, can be measured in the extremism of its antidote as the passage turns rhetorically back on itself to emphasise the value of books – in an anti-humanism not of the theoretical kind – above the value of individual men, or even life itself:

And yet, on the other hand, unless wariness be used, as good almost kill a man as kill a good book. Who kills a man kills a reasonable creature, God's image; but he who destroys a good book, kills reason itself, kills the image of God, as it were in the eye. Many a man lives a burden to the earth; but a good book is the precious life-blood of a master spirit, embalmed and treasured up on purpose to a life beyond life. 'Tis true, no age can restore a life, whereof perhaps there is no great loss; and revolutions of ages do not oft recover the loss of a rejected truth, for the want of which whole nations fare the worse. (pp. 149–50)

Together with the casual disposal of the many who are a burden to the earth, the remarkable insistence of this language of killing, blood and death, connected with a significantly bodily discourse of 'progeny', 'the potency of life' and the notion of literary production as 'breeding', escalates to the point where only mass slaughter will have the required rhetorical effect:

We should be wary therefore what persecutions we raise against the living labours of public men, how we spill that seasoned life of man, preserved and stored up in books; since we see a kind of homicide may thus be committed, sometimes a martyrdom, and if it extend to the whole impression, a kind of massacre; whereof the execution ends not in the slaying of an elemental life, but strikes at that ethereal and fifth essence, the breath of reason itself, slays an immortality rather than a life. (p. 150)

The massacre envisaged reaches out to a death beyond death, to the decease of immortality itself. These early passages are shot through with a violence of, or against, discursive practice that offers little to ideal accounts of writing as expression, transcription or aesthetic value. Discourse and violence go, implicitly and explicitly, together in this text, whether one be the object of the other, or, rather, its active perpetrator. We are more or less forced to encounter in the very language of the text a conception of discourse as struggle and battle, in contradistinction to so many texts, or so many readings, which will neutralise the political register of textuality in the name either of some anodyne 'meaning', or, to pick up the language of one of my epigraphs, 'sense'.

But if discourse, and above all true discourse, is inlaid with violence, it is important to notice however the discrepancy among the forms of this imbrication. There are principally two quite differently inflected figurations of Truth in *Areopagitica* and I shall briefly describe the positivity of each of them. The first is of true discourse as a warrior. In the following passage, for example, the militancy of the personification of Truth enables a series of military metaphors for what would otherwise be conceivable only as the ideal (non-)practice of discourse:

And though all the winds of doctrine were let loose to play upon the earth, so Truth be in the field, we do injuriously, by licensing and prohibiting, to misdoubt her strength. Let her and Falsehood grapple; who ever knew Truth put to the worse, in a free and open encounter? Her confuting is the best and surest suppressing .... When a man hath been labouring the hardest labour in the deep mines of knowledge; hath furnished out his findings in all their equipage; drawn forth his reasons as it were a battle ranged; scattered and defeated all objections in his way; calls out his adversary into the plain, offers him the advantage of wind and sun, if he please, only that he may try the matter by dint of argument: for his opponents then to skulk, to lay ambushments, to keep a narrow bridge of licensing where the challenger should pass, though it be valour enough in soldiership, is but weakness and cowardice in the wars of Truth. (p. 181)

The extraordinary extension of the military metaphor – amounting to something like prose conceit – and the detail of its internal differenti-ation, between, say, the honourable encounter in open battle as against the skulking unworthiness of guerrilla tactics, again contains a charge of force which outpaces normal assessments of discourse as in some sense the opposite of violence. Discursive practice is here distinctly practice, and practice of a very practical kind. The strength, the sureness of her victory, carries over from the figuration of Truth as a warrior in the field of war grappling with Falsehood, into the account of learning as battle in such a way as to construct what is valued in the practice of knowledge as not so much the knowledge itself but its deployment. The argument here is again one for open debate rather than pre-emptive licensing: but the discourse is one of strategy and tactics in – precisely – the wars of truth.

Although it is men who do the labouring in 'the deep mines of knowledge', (and knowledge is at once abstract and a matter of deployment), Truth in this passage, and others like it, is personified and personified as a woman. The same gendering, which I shall return to below, also inflects the other principal figuration of Truth at work in *Areopagitica*, where true discourse is figured not as a militant activist, the subject of a certain force, but in its potential for becoming the object-victim of a definite violence. In contrast to the image of Truth who is 'strong next to the Almighty', who 'needs no policies, nor strategems, nor licensings to make her victorious' for 'those are the shifts and the defences that error uses against her power' (p. 181), there is another insistent set of references not to an heroic Truth in triumph over the forces of the adversary falsehood, but rather to 'those disseuered pieces which are yet wanting to the body of Truth' (p. 176). For example:

Tru[th] indeed came once into the world with her Divine Master, and was a perfect shape most glorious to look on: but when He ascended, and His Apostles after Him were laid asleep, then straight arose a wicked race of deceivers, who, as the story goes of the Egyptian Typhoon with his conspirators, how they dealt with the good Osiris, took the virgin Truth, hewed her lovely form into a thousand pieces, and scattered them to the four winds. From that time ever since, the sad friends of Truth, such as durst appear, imitating the careful search that Isis made for the mangled body of Osiris, went up and down gathering up limb by limb, still as they could find them. We have not yet found them all, Lords and Commons, nor ever shall do, till her Master's second coming; He shall bring together every joint and member, and shall mould them into an immortal feature of loveliness and perfection. (p. 175)

This, of course, is one of the passages that are usually thought of as arguments for religious toleration .... But in any case I am less concerned here with the notion that the truth may consist of separate elements the total of which is in the possession of no single person or group, (a similar idea is conveyed elsewhere in the allegory of the building of the Temple, where the discrepancy of form and substance but ultimate 'goodly and graceful symmetry' (p. 178) among its component parts also serves to evoke an argument against any imperious assumption of a monopoly on Truth), than with what is manifested in the trope of truth as a mangled body, where two things are important: that it is a trope of the body, and that it is a dismembered and female body which is at stake. Although this is, as it were, a 'positive' figuration, Truth, in this version, is the absent object – victimised cruelly in the torn and scattered corporeality of 'joint and member', 'limb by limb' – of what is elsewhere described as 'one general and brotherly search' (p. 177) but whose gender and corporal disruption give a new inflection to such otherwise unremarkable idioms. Would 'we' (whoever that is) be any the 'less knowing, less eagerly pursuing of the truth' (p. 180) if the precise character of what we are enjoined to pursue were at every moment as explicit as it is here? Perhaps it will not be stretching the point to suggest that what I shall soon call an economy of truth is equally an erotics of the figurations of truth? Certainly when we are invited not merely to 'do our obsequies to the torn body of our martyred saint' (p. 175), but to 'See the ingenuity of Truth, who, when she gets a free and willing hand, opens herself faster than the pace of method and discourse can overtake her' (p. 161), it is hard not to sense a certain sexual charging in the metaphor, even if there is no hint of rape here. And the gentleness of the search at one moment, or that ardour of the pursuit at another, is surely over-determined by the violence that has already been done elsewhere to the object of these desires.

But this is apparently paradoxical because against this violence of the body, the phrase 'method and discourse' ought to bring to mind that other great seventeenth-century philosopher of the truth, Descartes, who thought, or thought that he thought, that the only way to a truthful certainty was by, precisely, method and discourse. Is there not a tension between the scientistic procedure of discourse and method which is depassionated (to recall an ugly word) and disembodied, and the investment of sexual violence in the Miltonic figuration of Truth-as-victim? It is not that Milton is antipathetic to procedure, to 'method and discourse'. On the contrary there is that persistent emphasis on reason, especially as the measured exercise of judgement by the individual, which is intellectually cognate with Cartesian method, and theologically coherent with an albeit Protestant emphasis on the unmediated activity of the individual conscience in contradistinction to ecclesiastical – or at this stage in Milton's thinking, episcopal – authority which Descartes would have been able nontheless to recognise. But in the figures I have been discussing here there is a sense of truth having an availability which outstrips discourse and method, which offers a faster access by different, somehow more transcendental but at the same time more bodily means. And the crucial point is that these means are articulated in a metaphor which is specificially sexually inflected.

At one level Brian Easlea's account of the gendering both of Nature and of scientific enquiry in the seventeenth century may help to reduce this tension, and in any case provides an essential context for the Miltonic use of apparently conventional metaphor by which truth becomes figured as a sexually available woman opening herself to male entry (see Easlea 1983). Easlea detects in the discourses of the 'scientific revolution' of the period an insistent complex of metaphors for nature as veiled but penetrable woman and for the masculinity of knowledge which enters her mystery, which he is able to trace through to the epistemo-erotics of the production and use of nuclear weapons. Easlea's account of the masculinity of bourgeois scientific discourse would suggest that the procedures of reason and those at work so far in the Miltonic text may not be that distant from each other. There is indeed a sexual charging in both, even if reason dominantly represses its own bodily violence (if it is not actually constituted by that repression), while in the figures of Truth as object-woman, or even as female militant, the violence, the corporeality and the desire of true discourse remain more overt. But nonetheless the forms do differ from each other, and differ in the mode of their different representational weighting of the sexed violence of true discourse on the one hand and impersonal and bodiless method on the other. There is clearly a more than problematic dimension to the text when the drive towards the invisible because intellectual – and from the point of view of power, systemic – mastery of 'nature' inaugurated in the Cartesian initiative, and the positive figuration of embodied Truth whether militant or victimised, negotiate uneasily and unknown to each other. And there is much more to be said here, particularly concerning precise political interpretation of the different figurations of Truth, and their historical locations in a pattern of what, using a language with which I am not entirely happy, I would have to call residual and emergent components of the text.

Much more could be said here, but for the moment however, having established, albeit only descriptively, that Milton's figurations of Truth or true discourse are variable and varied within a text that eroticises even its abstractions, I want to move on now at another level to abstraction itself and suggest that in addition to these two positive tropes that I have been discussing – Truth as militant warrior, Truth as pursued victim – there is indeed a third discourse of the Truth which, for reasons that I shall explain, can only be referred to loosely as figuration. In fact it consists in a systemic organisation of the place, function and supports of true discourse that does belong properly on the Cartesian threshold of emergent modernity; I have discussed aspects of this formation elsewhere, and will rehearse only briefly here the outline of that earlier argument (see Barker 1984, pp. 41–52 and *passim*). The discussion addressed the constitution of the historical structure which gives the basis to that well-known Althusserian *double entendre* by which, according to Althusser's theorisation of the subjection of the concrete individual, the subject conceived in the philosophical or psychological register is also, implicitly and inescapably, the subject of a definite regime – both, I would want to suggest, in the narrowly political sense and in the Foucauldian understanding of a regime of discourse (see Althusser 1971). In arguing for the shift in the moment of censorship from pre-publication licensing to post-publication intervention by the state, Milton begins to construct, in design at least, the lineaments of the modern situation in which the great caesura between the public and the private is inscribed in the general form of social organisation, and the private citizen is constituted in reason and judgement as a self-policing entity, free in the sense of being free to transgress and to be punished for transgression, but unfree by virtue of its pre-constitution in docility. Now, this structure cannot be positively figured. Precisely in as much as it is a structure or a structuration it escapes positive depiction, and precisely because of this achieves its power. It organises, almost pre-cognitively, true discourse as that uttered by a properly self-disciplined subject, in whom the erstwhile authorisation of state licensing has been internalised and transformed into a quasi-critical, quasi-psychological restraint. This structure, as I have indicated, is different in kind from the positive depictions of truth which I have been discussing, but it is also at odds with them in terms of its political and historical strategy. The essential political sobriety, and above all the incorporeality, of this structural principle of true discourse sits very uneasily with truth as militant combatant – with its amalgam of classical amazon, renaissance republicanism and puritan valour – and is hardly more consonant with truth as eroticised but mutilated victim. Disappearing from the view of figuration is an ever more powerfully coercive, invisible – inscribed – domination infiltrated behind the text's otherwise more politically overt discursive figures.

There is an important argument to be had about whether the power of this process is a result of the difference between structure and metaphor, between the politics of organisation and that of positively figured discourse. It would probably be an argument tending not to celebrate the literary as narrowly and traditionally received; and certainly one whose historical basis would have to be in a very full discussion of a general movement in the seventeenth century from performance to text. But that being for the present assumed, the two positive figurations of Truth – taken together with the systemic framework I have just invoked – do turn the text into a quite complex and dynamic economy of truth. The tropes of true discourse do not exactly circulate (as the fashionable word has it) in the text, but certainly they take discrepant forms and positions within the text's organisation of various sets of eroticised relations among its uttering subject or subjects, the reading subject, the overt and virtual addressees, objective thirds, and so on. Indeed, the critique of writing could be taken still further in order to think the text not as a univocal tract but as something more like a *theatre* of discourses and positionalities. But in any case, what we encounter here is the mode of the text's lack of complete resolution into the modern regime of discourse that it nonetheless prefigures. A bourgeois text it is, and in its structure tends towards a post-revolutionary discursivity of apparently depoliticised private utterance. But it contains still – at least in the Truth-as-militant trope – a revolutionary figuration of true discourse not yet willing to surrender itself to private obscurity. And equally (at the risk of attracting the charge of a romanticisation of an older, fuller corporeality than our own), is there not, in the other positive figuration of Truth, a sign, even in its condition of victimisation, of a

certain bodily excess over structure, if not actually the site of a resistance? Not – and this is a reply to romance – that it is now possible to
'side' with one or the other, as if a 'return' to these discursive events were
available; or, even if it were, that it would be appropriate to identify
with an early bourgeois heroism of the truth – and still less with the
mutilation and dismemberment of women – as models of appropriate political and epistemological value. I take it that the point of
historical study is not such 'nostalgia', whether formal or positive: as
if even a full body (which would have to be regarded as wholly imaginary
in any case) could somehow stand against the system of subjection
emerging here. The point is rather to deploy what could be called the
parallax of historical difference which will want to apprehend *at the
same time* the 'slippage' in the text as an arena of struggle among
different figurations and strategies, and also the degree of ideological
fixation that secures this instability by tactics of hierarchisation and
writing in a degree of stasis (even if that stasis turns out to be located
only in the sedimented tradition of subsequently dominant
discourses and readings). The text is not a monolith, nor is it a free
indeterminacy, but rather a precise, and precisely historical, event.
But if the event secures a dominant, it is not without traces of the
violence of its institution (or even in some cases glimpses, however
utopian, of alternative possibilities) remaining a trouble to it. It is that
potential for the discovery of a limit to the dominant that both
constitutes and makes valuable for us the historicity of the text.

I shall return to these ideas at the end.

III

I want to turn now to another text in which tropes of war and truth are
imbricated with each other, and one also pre-eminently a police of
discourse. The composition of Hobbes's *Leviathan* spans the revolutionary period and in that sense is contemporary with *Areopagitica*. It too,
is not without its own – although curiously attenuated – gesture to
the war as its context. Milton's references to the war are explicit, and
Hobbes too, while for the main part apparently far less topical and
immediately conjunctural in his preoccupations, is nonetheless
prepared to define the purpose of his work in *Leviathan* as the
avoidance of the kind of conflict in which his compatriots are currently engaged. His conclusion states at last a project:

And thus I have brought to an end my Discourse of Civill and Ecclesi-
asticall Government, occasioned by the disorders of the present time,
without partiality, without application, and without other designe, than to
set before mens eyes the mutuall Relation between Protection and
Obedience; of which the condition of Humane Nature, and the Laws
Divine, (both Naturall and Positive) require an inviolable observation.
(Hobbes 1981, p. 728)

But the attenuation of the contextual placing is somehow typical of
the discourse if not of Thomas Hobbes, at least of the persona that
utters the text. The disclaimer of direct interest in the war that
nonetheless occasions the text acutely reflects in content and tone
that mixture of intellectual arrogance and timourousness in the face
both of constituted authority in particular, and all external conditions
in general, that otherwise permeates the work. The relative abstraction of 'the mutuall Relation between Protection and Obedience', of
natural and positive laws which require an inviolable observation,
both reveals and disavows the political objectives of a text at once
wholly committed to domination, yet simultaneously couched in
terms that tempt me to designate the text and its author-function
paranoic to a degree: Hobbes is pre-eminently the philosopher of,
and in, terror.

If only in respect of these different degrees and kinds of self-
contextualisation it is clear that in turning from *Areopagitica* to
Leviathan, we are dealing with texts apparently very different in kind.
And in contradistinction to the 'slippage' I have illustrated in the
Miltonic text, *Leviathan* is normally regarded as enjoying a very high
degree of closure indeed. But the closure of the text is not as total as is
usually thought, and I shall try to demonstrate this by identifying a
certain fissuring of its apparently monolithic and absolute character.
At the risk of some reduction, the discussion will concentrate on one
well-known area of what is technically a very complex theory,
although one not particularly obscure in its political objectives: I have
in mind the famous discussion in Chapter Thirteen of the state of
nature as a state of war, and the issues it raises in respect of power
and the power of true discourse.

It is of course commonplace to remark that Hobbes's account of
the state of nature (its speculative archaism on the one hand and its
appeal to contemporary America on the other notwithstanding) depends equally if implicitly on the immediate environment of the Civil

War and less directly but probably more profoundly on the extant social conditions of revolutionary and pre-revolutionary England in general. Not surprisingly then, Chapter Thirteen is in at least two important ways the linchpin of the theorisation of power. Most frequently noticed is the manner in which Hobbes's description of the state of nature picks up the theory of desire from Chapter Eleven in order to legitimate dominion as the overcoming of its own founding naturalism. Because, the deadly but not unfamiliar logic goes, desire is like this:

Nor can a man any more live, whose Desires are at an end, than he, whose Senses and Imagination are at a stand. Felicity is a continuall progresse of the desire, from one object to another; the attaining of the former, being still but the way to the later. The cause whereof is, That the object of mans desire, is not to enjoy once onely, and for one instant of time; but to assure for ever, the way of his future desire ...

So that in the first place, I put for a generall inclination of all mankind, a perpetuall and restlesse desire of Power after power, that ceaseth onely in Death ... (pp. 160–1)

Nature is therefore like this:

Hereby it is manifest, that during the time men live without a common Power to keep them all in awe, they are in that condition which is called Warre; and such a warre, as is of every man, against every man. For Warre, consisteth not in Battell onely, or in the act of fighting; but in a tract of time, wherein the Will to contend by Battell is sufficiently known: and therefore the notion of *Time*, is to be considered in the nature of Warre; as it is in the nature of Weather. For as the nature of Foule weather, lyeth not in a showre or two of rain; but in an inclination thereto of many dayes together: So the nature of War, consisteth not in actuall fighting; but in the known disposition thereto, during all the time there is no assurance to the contrary. All other time is Peace. (pp. 185–6)

And the only way of securing that peace, of abating the natural war engendered by desire, is indeed the constitution of a sovereign power keeping all in awe. I shall return to that sovereignty later.

But the other reason why this area of Hobbes is fundamental, and this is less usually commented on in relation to 'the nature of War', is the significance of what apparently escapes, or at least stands outside, the system of desire and power. In Chapter Thirteen it is science; or rather 'that skill of proceeding upon generall, and infallible rules, called Science' is used to stand for what Hobbes calls 'the arts grounded upon words', and which he insists on 'setting aside' from the faculties and capacities which in general men have naturally and more or less equally (p. 183). The setting aside is important because it does indeed tend to disengage science and, if we take Hobbes at the letter of his text here, all discursive practice, from the formations of power and desire. The most graphic, and the one which Hobbes takes to be the most politically neutral version possible of this improbable but necessary strategy that seeks to construct a discursive space where interest and power are held to be least at stake, is the example of geometry:

... the doctrine of Right and Wrong, is perpetually disputed, both by the Pen and the Sword: Whereas the doctrine of Lines, and Figures, is not so; because men care not, in that subject what be truth, as a thing that crosses no mans ambition, profit, or lust. For I doubt not, but if it had been a thing contrary to any mans right of dominion, or to the interest of men that have dominion, *That the three Angles of a Triangle should be equall to two Angles of a Square*; that doctrine should have been, if not disputed, yet by the burning of all books of Geometry, suppressed, as farre as he whom it concerned was able. (p. 166)

The segregation of geometry (standing here for science in a much broader sense, closer to rational discourse as such), to a place outside sociality and the desires and dominions in which it consists, is both essential to Hobbes's analysis and at the same time, as I shall show below, 'subversive' of it. Given the two epistemic models offered by Foucault in the passage I have quoted as an epigraph – the model of language on the one hand and the intelligibility of struggles on the other – it would seem obvious that despite its thematics of war and objective of domination, Hobbes's discourse appeals wholly to the former, to a manipulation of what Foucault calls the great model of signs and language. *Leviathan* begins not with a discussion of power or right, but with a theory of discourse, of signs and representation, which only subsequently provides the foundation for the emphasis on proper definitions and, ultimately, the language of contract, which are then central to Hobbes's account of power and language alike. The effect of this sequence from representation to the propriety of the submissive contract under which the members of any given society supposedly agree together to establish a power over themselves, is that of an ever-pre-constitution of a – highly political – 'truth' concealed in the very structure of what counts as 'sense' or 'intelligibility' itself. The fabulous contract itself is then subsequent to and consequent upon the language in which it can be conceived and framed: the discourse which is outside power constitutes an absolute power. It is not simply that mathematical and geometrical science (or the deployments of Hobbes's own reasoning, which he would have be of a similar order) represent but another mode of discourse from that either of the natural passions or of the laws of any duly-constituted commonwealth after the event of its constitution (for these are then explicitly the discourse of the sovereign power and need have no reason in them), but rather that the science of the text, in its very character as that discourse which is not involved in power, tends implicitly thus ever to pre-empt the possibility of civil conflict, because such would entail an unthinkable falling away from true language and even from language itself. I have mentioned how the persona of the utterance disassociates itself from faction, from explicit political engagement, but this can now be read not merely as a psychology effect, or even in this case a censorship effect. It is simply impossible to discourse properly or truthfully and rebel.

This contrasts markedly with the positive figurations of Truth in Milton. If there we saw an interiority to each other of truth and violence, or to put it at its weakest, a parallel between the warlikeness of discourse and the warlikeness of the war itself, in Hobbes true discourse is wholly a shore against civil war. The implicitude (if there is such a word) of this in Hobbes is analogous, rather, with what in Milton I have called the 'systemic', the *regime* of discourse, and similarly produces a coercive theoretical-juridical or power effect by writerly structuration. In Hobbes, with the exception of one major qualification that I shall come to, truth is not figured, personified or embodied, and not then also caught up in the drama of political and gender violence. This is not because his text is 'philosophical' rather than 'literary' – and how, precisely, would we characterise Milton's text in any case? – but because of the 'abstract' pre-givenness in proper language of inescapable, even 'involuntary' – or, as he says, 'inviolable' – obedience.

In Milton there are residual figurations of truth and war and an emergent structuration which dispenses with those figurations in favour of a more ineluctable, systemic domination. In the case of the Hobbesian non-figurative pre-constitution of obedience and truth, by contrast, we seem to be already wholly within structure, within an

abstract discourse, implicative and reasoned and in that sense politically unnegotiable. But there is, as I mentioned earlier, at least one
rent in this near-seamless, near-invisible closure. It involves that
paradoxical way in which truth and power, or the effectivity of truth in
power, are – in a fashion – embodied or 'figured' in the sense in which
I have been using the word, in the double person of the Sovereign
whose artificial rather than natural body is the Commonwealth itself.
Although it is not as rich in empirical detail, not as fully dramatised,
as say, the sacred person of the Shakespearean monarch, and if it is
figured, it is so in the abstract, non-depictive form seemingly
appropriate to philosophical and juridical discourse, the figure of the
Sovereign in *Leviathan* is nonetheless much closer to, say, 'The Lord's
annointed Temple' which in *Macbeth* 'Most sacrilegious Murther
hath broke ope' (II. iii. 66–7) than it is to the regime of discourse and
subjection we see emerging in *Areopagitica*. Or again, although the
symbolic register has been somewhat flattened since Shakespeare –
there is little finally that is both sacred and fundamental in Hobbes –
the paramount role in the polity of the monarch (which is how Hobbes
thinks of the Sovereign in all of his routine appellations and inadvertent examples, despite the fact that theoretically, if half-heartedly, he
allows for the possibility of other forms of sovereignty, democratic,
aristocratic or oligarchic), belongs more to the erstwhile fantasy of a
full kingship than to the implicative manipulation of true discourse
that characterises the dominant strategy of Hobbes's text itself.

The matter is complicated. For the Sovereign has a very curious
textual existence in *Leviathan*, double not only in body of course, but
in positionality with respect to the Commonwealth. This has almost
nothing to do with any sacred mystery of the royal person, so much as
a slippage in the theory itself. Or rather, since it is not ultimately a
philosophical critique of Hobbes I am conducting, in the textual
deployment of the theory. The problem is that the Sovereign is both
inside and outside the Commonwealth. Like science, which is set
aside from interest and conflict and yet yields the true discourse that
legitimates power, the Sovereign is outside of sociality as such. But if
discourse is in its most fundamental sense contractual and
subjecting, the Sovereign, with whom in Hobbes it is axiomatically
impossible to make a contract, is not subjected and the war continues. The Sovereign remains in a state of nature in respect of other
sovereigns and their commonwealths, but also in respect of its own,

carrying, in effect, the war that sovereignty is designed to quell into the commonwealth itself (an act, by the way, of aggression against its own body which is strictly unthinkable in Hobbes because of the primitive and fundamental right of self-defence, to which I shall return in a moment). Or, unless mediated by the textual no-place to which are consigned the trueness of true language and all that goes with it in Hobbes's 'great model of signs' (empowering as it ought the dominion of the Sovereign and the ever-pre-constitutedness of obedience), war and nature and the commonwealth are actually internal to each other. Language doesn't succeed as a prophylaxis against violence and desire, and the whole system breaks down under its own absurdity, as peace becomes war and war peace.

This critical, unstable slipping of the categories around the duplicity of the figure of the Sovereign is instanced again in the impossibility of Hobbes fully theorising the prohibition of resistance to sovereign power, which is otherwise one of the text's major objectives. The one natural right reserved to the subject, the only one which is inalienable in Hobbes, which cannot be contracted away and for the alienation of which there simply cannot be therefore any true sign or discourse, is that of self-preservation. This is famously never reconciled in Hobbes in the discussion of punishment, where the power of the Sovereign comes up against the limit of the subject's right to resist. In fact it would even be possible to fabricate from Hobbes's account of the subject a theory – a somewhat individualistic one, no doubt – of revolution, a theory which would be consonant with Hobbes's general position on nature and power, but quite at odds with his project of obedience. Hobbes is simply and symptomatically evasive and eventually silent on the question of resistance to punishment, because it represents a sign of profound contradiction where the inalienable nature on which his theory is founded there confronts itself as an opposite. If the Sovereign carries the war into the commonwealth by violence against his subjects then in such a case the individual must resist by nature. But if such resistance is not naturally given then the theory which empowered the Sovereign in the first place is fatally flawed. The problem is that Hobbes doesn't really have a model of subjection at his disposal, which is clear enough from the way in which private belief or mere opinion in Hobbes remain truly private, an ineffable, unconstituted area where dominion does not run. And this in turn is because, as I suppose

Foucault would have said, he hasn't – he has no desire to – cut off the king's head *in theory*. Or rather, another way of putting it, his text hasn't become writerly or written enough. The violence of nature fails to be contained by the very theorisation of sovereignty it was supposed to underwrite. The slippage is in the terror, by which, through a whole series of points of fracture in the Hobbesian text where implicitude fails quite to achieve an adequate dispersal of power throughout the system, domination remains the external offer of the threat of a performable violence, rather than, as Hobbes would rather have had it, the inevitable and 'acceptable' correlative of true discourse.

IV

I began by drawing attention to what I see as problems in the nature of contextualisation and in the dilemma offered by the notions of textual indeterminacy, of slippage, limitless semiosis, free circulation or play on the one hand and the closure of historicisation on the other. This needs, I think to be brought into contact with the seventeenth century's own movement from transactions of discourse and violence to the essentially ideal epistemological models that we dominantly inherit, but in respect of which Foucault's reference to the intelligibility of struggles should offer a kind of critical limit. It should also prompt some discussion of whether it wouldn't be better to attempt to evade altogether this binary opposition given in theory in favour of an emphasis on the degree to which patterns of closure and slippage are themselves textually intrinsic and, above all, historically determinate and historically variable. I have tried to offer contemporary examples in Milton and Hobbes where different degrees of closure or of slippage and fracture correspond to the texts' different political strategies, among which definite organisations of both hierarchisation and play are detectable. The main traditions of reading have – no doubt for ideological reasons – preferred the dominant discourses of these texts at the expense of what in them tends to 'subvert' the hierarchy. That is understandable of course. But only if the subversion is not in fact 'contained' (in the sense of forming a constitutive moment of what it apparently subverts), but rather remains in the historical time of the text unreconciled with and even critical of the dominating discursive strategies. The aggravation of that precision of difference would seem much to the point if under newer forms of reading it is indeed criticism in which we are interested.

Finally, having apparently eschewed earlier what have been called real-historical positions, I would like now to emphasise what in fact I take to be the 'real-world' character of the understanding of discourse I am trying to elaborate. Just as my sense of the right context is not that which appeals to the empirical content of the text's representations, but rather to the problematic of representation itself, so my sense of the 'real-worldness' of discursive practice is linked entirely to its political function. In fact it is as much from the texts of the seventeenth century, where we can detect a movement from figurations of true discourse as political action to writerly and epistemic structures of a coercive truth, as from contemporary theory, that I gain, by that parallax effect of historical difference, an understanding of discourse as anything but ideal transcription. On the contrary, there is quite a strong, and fully political sense, which it would be well to infuse into our discourse today – even our academic and literary discourse – of powerful *inscription*, of real things thus at stake: positions being marked out, enabled or prevented, and advances, even victories, being gained. Or not.

And after all, it matters which, in as much as 'Warre' – and not just the war of epistemology – truly is 'all the world about'.

2

A WILDERNESS OF TIGERS

Titus Andronicus, *anthropology*
*and the occlusion of violence**

To articulate the past historically does not mean to recognise it 'the way it really was' (Ranke). It means to seize hold of a memory as it flashes up at a moment of danger. Historical materialism wishes to retain that image of the past which unexpectedly appears to man singled out by history at a moment of danger. The danger affects both the content of the tradition and its receivers. The same threat hangs over both: that of becoming a tool of the ruling classes. In every era the attempt must be made anew to wrest tradition away from the conformism that is about to overpower it. The Messiah comes not only as the redeemer, he comes as the subduer of Antichrist. Only that historian will have the gift of fanning the spark of hope in the past who is firmly convinced that *even the dead* will not be safe from the enemy if he wins. And this enemy has not ceased to be victorious.

Walter Benjamin, 'Theses on the Philosophy of History'

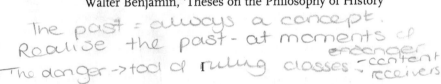

Judging from the early incidence of human sacrifice or from the prominence that it gives to an act of cannibalism, it could be argued that *Titus Andronicus* represents Rome as a primitive society. This impression persists in the host of related, accessory ways in which the text not only displays the beliefs and practices of the ancient

---

*A first version of this critique of the contemporary culturalism was presented under the title 'Thick Description: the Theoretical Politics of the New Historicism, or, 'Turtles all the Way Down" to the Sixth International Conference on Literary Theory, 'American Visions, Visions of America: New Directions in Culture and Literature' at the University of Hong Kong, December 1988. The constellation of that material with a reading of the anthropologism of the Shakespearean text in general – and that of *Titus Andronicus* in particular – began with the preparation of a lecture for the Symposium 'wisemans threasure' which was held at the University of Alabama, Tuscaloosa, in October 1990. An excerpted version of the present essay appears under the title 'Treasures of Culture: *Titus Andronicus* and Death by Hanging', in the volume based on the Alabama symposium, *The Production of English Renaissance Culture*, edited by David Lee Miller, Sharon O'Dair and Harold Weber.

culture but displays them as 'marked' behaviour in a manner which signifies its primitive character, from such large scale practices as the habit of enslaving captives taken in war (and the attending spectacles of triumph and tribute with which the play begins), to details like the fetishisation of bodily emissions, especially tears, blood and breath, which the text so frequently notices. Equally, the formal production of the representation of Roman society is also 'marked'. One of the play's editors remarks the way in which 'ceremonies provide an almost uninterrupted series of spectacles' (Waith 1984, p. 58); the sense of the depicted society being shot through by ceremonial and rite is itself conveyed in the ceremonial character of the depiction.[1] Thus, although the Rome of *Titus Andronicus* is not a pre-literate society as most cultures which are designated 'primitive' are held to be, and not in that sense prehistoric, it is nonetheless clear, whether one looks at the depicted behaviour itself or at the form of the marking, that the play foregrounds ritual practices, ceremonial spectacle, and the charging of the sacred by fetishism and taboo, in a way fully reminiscent of the representation of that undeveloped, native, ancient, indigenous condition which the various discourses of anthropology have insistently called primitive: the Rome of *Titus Andronicus* is a society organised by the signs of the primitive.

This is perhaps most clear if we consider its representation of the treatment of the dead. Early in Act I comes Titus's entry into Rome after his victory over the Goths. Captured Goths, including their queen Tamora, and her three sons, along with her lover Aaron, a moor in her entourage, are led in formal triumph into the city. But it

[1] The quotation continues by enumerating the 'spectacles'; I cite it more fully here as further evidence of the 'ceremonial' representation of Rome: '... the confrontation of Saturninus and Bassianus, the entrance of Titus drawn in a chariot in a procession which is both triumph and funeral, the sacrifice of Alabarbus following the unsuccessful intercession of Tamora, the burial of Titus' sons, the election of an emperor, preparations for a wedding, the burial of Mutius after the successful intercession of his uncle and brothers and the seeming reconciliation of the Andronici with Saturninus and Tamora. Another procession and another unsuccessful intercession mark the opening of the first scene of the third act, which closes as the Andronici formally vow revenge and file out, carrying the severed hand and heads. The most spectacular of the remaining ceremonies are the shooting of arrows with messages to the gods; the masque-like visitation of Tamora and her sons disguised as Revenge, Rape, Murder; the final banquet; and the election of Lucius as emperor to restore order in Rome. We know that for at least one viewer at the private performance in 1596 the "*monstre*", or spectacle, was worth more than the "*sujet*" ...' (Waith 1984, pp. 58-9).

is also a funeral procession to the ancestral tomb of the Andronici, where the remains of an unspecified number of Titus's sons killed in the war are buried, and where later in the act another son, Mutius, slain by Titus himself, is also interred. The disposal of the sons' remains is considered 'burial amongst their ancestors' (I. i. 84),[2] a rite which unless properly observed will leave them 'unburied yet,/ To hover on the dreadful shore of Styx?' (I. i. 87–8). To ensure that 'the shadows be not unappeas'd' (I. i. 100) a human sacrifice is needed and their living brothers demand Tamora's eldest son Alarbus for the purpose, 'That we may hew his limbs, and on a pile/ Ad manes fratrum sacrifice his flesh' (I. i. 97–8). The sacrifice – 'Our Roman rites' – is 'perform'd' and 'Alarbus's limbs are lopp'd', his 'entrails feed the sacrificing fire,/ Whose smoke like incense doth perfume the sky' (I. i. 143–5). One would hardly need look further for evidence of a typically primitive account of the sacred incarnate in a material, indeed corporeal, ritual of sacrificial propitiation of the unseen spirits of the dead. With the further addition only of their sister Lavinia's 'tributary tears' (I. i. 159), the dead brothers are then interred in 'peace and honour' (I. i. 156).

The significance of these rites and practices, what I am calling their 'marking', is then underlined by the burial of Mutius. At first Titus denies him interral in the ancestral tomb: 'Traitors, away! he rests not in this tomb:/ This monument five hundred years hath stood,/ Which I have sumptuously re-edified:/ Here none but soldiers and Rome's servitors/ Repose in fame' (I. i. 349–53). These terms – the allegation of treachery, the invocation of half a millenium of ancestral tradition and military service, the warding or protection of the elaborately maintained monument from pollution or abuse – are, of course, heavily charged. But so are those of the intercession of his paternal uncle and his brothers for proper funeral, intercession which depends upon naming the transgression of the self-same senses of honour, virtue, and nobility which would be offered if the rite were denied. The rhetorical *summa* of their counter-invocation of the con-stitutive pieties consists in citing what turn out to be the most charged categories of all: 'Thou art a Roman; be not barbarous' (I. i. 388). Titus concedes and, the 'impiety' (I. i. 355) avoided, Mutius's 'bones' are laid in the tomb until the ritual can be in proper course completed by the decoration of the monument with 'trophies' (I. i. 388).

[2] All quotations are from the Arden edition, ed. J. C. Maxwell (Shakespeare, 1968).

The play gives considerable detail of Rome's mortuary practices, from its custom of tomb burial to the monumentalism of its funerary architecture, from the importance of propitiatory sacrifice (and the role of olfactory sensation in its appeasement rituals), to the habit of decorating male graves with war goods, etc. But beyond mortuary practice itself we also learn much of the significance of its funeral rites as instances of the wider ideological formations and social structures of the culture. Its funerals not only disclose ideational patterns, such as the belief in *post mortem* survival, that are apparently central to Roman society, but also articulate in important ways its kinship structure, especially the bonding of male siblings, living and dead, and the importance of male ancestral lineation. In other words, if we cast the eye of a certain anthropology over the Rome of *Titus Andronicus*, we would learn a great deal that would be convenient to the expectations we would thus arouse. It would be quite possible to derive from the text insights into what Rome means by peace, and how it uses familiar names; we could describe the significance of consecration or expiation, and that of the act of kneeling or of raising the voice; we could establish the lexicon of its warriors' honour code, or write the grammar of the metonyms and synecdoches it uses to speak of corpses, and so on. Read thus, the text discloses much of what would be necessary to what we might indeed call a positive anthropology, or at least a descriptive ethnography, of this primitive Rome, from the inner structure of its metaphysics to the cultural texture of its daily life.

Something crucial, however, is disclosed in that invocation of the notion of 'the barbarous' as an antithetical or exclusive category when compared with what it is to be 'a Roman'. Its importance lies in the sense that beyond – or perhaps within – the cultural positivity I have been describing there are underlying forms of categorial and representational organisation in *Titus Andronicus* which disclose an anthropology that is properly-speaking *structural*. It is valuable in this context to compare the elaborate and elaborated senses of the 'culture' of Rome, especially as it is embedded in the funeral rites of Act I, with the mortuary treatment of Aaron, and more especially of Tamora, with which the play ends. Where the proper burial of the slain Andronici at the beginning provides the signs of culture, and its neglect risks barbarism, the killing of Aaron and the disposal of the remains of Tamora are very differently coded. The last scene of the play leaves Titus, Lavinia, the emperor Saturninus and Tamora dead, with Aaron captive to Titus's son Lucius, who, now in command of the victorious Gothic army, accedes to power in Rome. It is Lucius who pronounces the final 'settlement'. First Aaron is sentenced: 'Set him breast-deep in earth and famish him;/ There let him stand and rave and cry for food./ If any one relieves or pities him,/ For the offence he dies' (V. iii. 179–82). The contrast between this and the treatment of the Roman dead is marked: 'Some loving friends convey the emperor hence,/ And give him burial in his father's grave./ My father and Lavinia shall forthwith/ Be closed in our household monument' (V. iii. 191–4). But the contrast is greater still when this is compared in turn with Lucius's orders for the disposal of the remains of Tamora, which provide the last lines of the play: 'As for that ravenous tiger, Tamora,/ No funeral rite, nor man in mourning weed,/ No mournful bell shall ring her burial;/ But throw her forth to beasts and birds to prey' (V. iii. 195–8). While the Roman corpses will be assumed or re-assumed, with proper ritual, into the order of culture, Aaron is planted in the earth in a kind of vivid parody of pious burial, by which he will be made to 'rave and cry' like an animal for food. He will not grow; there will be no further culture for him. And the body of Tamora, a 'ravenous tiger' (l. 195) whose 'life was beastly' (l. 199), is merely thrown away, her waste corpse is symbolically jettisoned 'forth' from the order of culture into that of nature, from the human world into that of the beasts, from society into the wilderness, or into whatever it is that is outside, and constituted in opposition to, Rome.[3]

The text is thus bracketed by elaborate funeral ritual on the one hand, and its marked lack for those who are not of Rome on the other: rites are counterposed to waste. This contrast represents the formation of an 'anthropological' structure which is rehearsed over and over again in the play. As distinct from the 'positive' description of the custom and belief of the world of the play, it establishes, rather, a boundary between behaviour and belief that is marked as being within the community, and that which is not. To one side of the boundary lies

---

[3]It is worth remarking the frequency with which imputations of bestiality occur in the language of the demonisation of Tamora; in particular she is several times called a tiger, here and at II. iii. 142. (Aaron is a 'ravenous tiger' at V.iii.5.) Associated with this is Tamora twice being referred to as Semiramis, at II.i.22 and at II. iii. 118 where she is 'Semiramis, nay, barbarous Tamora'. The beautiful and the lustful alien conjured by the invocation of the mythical Assyrian queen articulate with the bestial and barbarous in the Goth Tamora.

culture, and to the other lies either unmarked behaviour, or behaviour which is marked as the determinate 'other' of culture.

This boundary is constituted in and by *Titus Andronicus* in two principal ways: by mutually exclusive, mutually defining categorial antitheses, and by a bipolar topographical distinction. In the former case the contrastive construction of the civilised is achieved in the counterdistinction with behaviour which is not human, for example, or simply by the deployment of the explicit language of barbarism (itself bringing with it of course a ready-formed, and very ancient 'anthropology'). A language of monstrousness and bestiality, of the inhuman and the less than human, reinforces and reciprocally constitutes the civil which is itself thus mapped to the human as such. Examples among others are V. ii. 177 where Chiron and Demetrius, the sons of Tamora who rape and mutilate Lavinia, are called 'Inhuman traitors', and V. iii. 14 where Aaron is called 'inhuman dog'; at II. iii. 78 and V. iii. 4 Aaron is called a 'barbarous Moor', at II. iii. 118, as we have noted, Tamora is 'barbarous Tamora', and at V. i. 97 Lucius speaking to Aaron refers to Chiron and Demetrius as 'barbarous beastly villains like thyself'. And so on. Except in the minatory case of Titus noted above, these words are not used of Romans. While in the latter case, the text elaborates a highly-charged topography by which the city is marked – tautologically – as the place of civilisation, whereas that which lies outside it is the place of the barbarous or of the barbarian. Rome is, of course, archetypically 'the City', a notion powerfully sedimented in the tradition of the West, and one which contributes to the politico-anthropological structure of *Titus Andronicus* which designates the place beyond the boundaries of the city as the place of the Goths, the vandals and barbarians who are not Roman. One of the main acts of the play's extravagant violence, the rape and mutilation of Lavinia by Tamora's sons, takes place in the woods beyond the gates: the place of Roman civility is by definition Rome, the place of Gothic barbarism is by mutual constitution not-Rome, the wilderness outside.[4]

[4]For the purposes of approaching the main matter I am of course simplifying the way in which such 'anthropological' structures actually work (although not necessarily the way they appear to work in Shakespeare and in *Titus Andronicus* particularly). For an illuminating discussion of the way in which 'boundaries of community are often created by accusing those outside the boundary of the very practice on which the integrity of that community is founded' see Hulme (1986), p. 85 and *passim*, who is in turn drawing on Arens (1979). A cognate idea is developed later in this paper; see below, pp. 193–4.

If Rome is *the* place of civility as such, by which, for example, the idea of banishment as a punishment, like that of Lucius in Act III Scene I, depends for its sanction on the degradation and danger offered by expulsion beyond the limits of the city, it is thus also important to remark the way in which the crossing (if not the transgression) – or its confusion, about which I shall say more below – serves to reinforce it. The miscegenation between Tamora and Aaron, for example, serves such a purpose in as much as by being demonised by the text, it is marked as a practice whose negativity resides in the mixing of what should properly be separate, and thus the more strongly delineates – rather than subverts – the original and constitutive structure of separation. And it is with this in mind that I have emphasised the parodic 'burial' of Aaron, and the treatment of Tamora's body as detritus. Not least do they figure and connote that marking of the boundaries of the culture which has been elucidated in an exemplary way in the work of Mary Douglas on pollution and taboo, and in particular on the significance of dirt, filth or refuse in the constitution of the community by the delineation of its limits and the warding off of the 'formlessness', as she puts it, that lies beyond the frontiers of the community. If dirt, as Douglas famously defines it, is 'matter out of place', then Aaron the Moor and Tamora the queen of the Goths are, *in Rome*, examples of the matter of such ritual pollution: a defilement cleansed by their final removal from the city to the true place and condition of dirt without.[5]

In the reading, then, which, with some detachment, I have been outlining, two connected but slightly differently weighted anthropo-logical perspectives are at work. One involves the observation of the cultural marking in *Titus Andronicus* of the ritual customs, religious pieties, metaphysical convictions and ideological norms, as well as the societal and familial structures of Roman society as it is represented by the play. This is a marking which makes Rome appear a 'primitive' society in as much as the text's representations are made of the stuff that anthropology, or its practical support, ethnographic fieldwork, investigates when it interrogates primitive societies, in particular the belief-structures of traditional societies as they are revealed embedded in ritual and in senses of pollution or taboo, and

[5]For Douglas's work on pollution and taboo see especially her *Purity and Danger* (1984); Chapters 6, 7 and 8, on 'Powers and Dangers', 'External Boundaries' and 'Internal Lines' are particularly relevant here.

the structures of kinship and authority. But this positive anthropology of the forms of meaningful organisation that define, order and
sustain the physical and the metaphysical worlds, plays an important
part in the text not least in as much as it is articulated with the second
and more important anthropology which involves the circumscription
of culture. At the first level the emphases on 'marked behaviour',
whose foregrounding in the play I have highlighted, are signs of
culture, signs that Rome has, in the way that 'primitive' societies do,
a culture. I have emphasised the funerary which, in terms of the
positivity of the processes of a culture, is doubtless highly valorised.
But it is not, therefore, an entirely arbitrary instance here, for the
pieties and tabooings with which these cultural practices are charged
then act, at a second level, as markers of civility *vis à vis* a
countervailing barbarism. This then engages signs not of cultural
primitivism but a-cultural or anti-cultural savagery, so that at the
second level, the other sense in which the play can be seen to engage
an anthropological perspective involves the manner in which the
marked practices of the depicted world are themselves representations structured in such a way as to *constitute* an 'anthropology'. In
forming, in other words, the boundary between civility and humanity
on the one hand and that which is not civil and human on the other,
the play enacts an anthropology, rather than simply providing a depiction of Roman society as one which is of anthropological interest, or
defining its own interest in Rome as principally an anthropological one.

Thus if I began with the sense that Rome is represented as a
primitive society, it is now important to see how in another sense it is
not primitive at all. If I have indicated how what I called above a
descriptive ethnography or a positive anthropology is possible, I have
suggested that the world of *Titus Andronicus*, and especially its Rome,
is certainly not constituted by the 'positivity' of these materials alone.
Rather, or in addition, it is the 'structure' of oppositions established
between these marked terms and what they are not that is culturally
constitutive. Thus, my opening formulation notwithstanding, the
world of *Titus Andronicus* is in fact only 'primitive' in the special, and
ambiguous, sense which the anthropological perspective has so
frequently, if not systematically, committed itself to: the primitive
resides at once in those societies which have – studiable – culture and
in those which have none, those which in being savage or *sauvage* are
beyond and outside culture.

If the primitive is both the site of 'culture' and the absence of culture, then the marking of the primitive in the representation of Rome in *Titus Andronicus* is doubly formed. If the world of the play looks at first glance primitive, this disposition is subsumed by the way in which that marking is then co-ordinated categorially and topographically within the second, structural anthropology of bipolar civility and barbarism. Primitivism in the sense of the savage is expelled beyond the signs of the civil, and where once precisely these signs had seemed 'primitive' in the cultural sense, now they appear as the very presence of culture.

For the moment then, one can speak, in these co-ordinated senses, of *Titus Andronicus* as an 'anthropology', or at least of the 'anthropologism' of the way in which it gives us a primitive world, but in a manner committed to describing the boundary, and the structure of the boundary, of its culture. This delineation, constructed by the constituting of the categories of the civilised and the barbarous, is itself constitutive of the anthropological perspective as such, both in the broad sense that this marking goes back, it seems, to the beginning of the West and *its* 'anthropologism', but also in the sense that anthropology – in more restricted, recent and even technical, academic and professional senses – is, arguably, constituted by the very concept of 'culture', and one arguably so constructed.

II

There are no doubt plausibilities – and perhaps some interpretative verity – in the readings I have outlined of the primitivism of the depiction of Rome, and then the more sophisticated, although not altogether unfamiliar, sense of a Shakespearean structural anthropology. But my intention was more to rehearse such possible readings than to advocate them. I wish rather to examine what might be at stake in such a literary 'anthropology', and it is the role of anthropology in criticism, especially cultural anthropology, to which I now turn.

There is nothing wholly novel about work on Shakespeare which is in one sense or another interdisciplinary.[6] But it is in the work of the

---

[6]At junctures, albeit literary ones, of, variously, sociology, popular history, anthropology and literary criticism itself, one thinks of studies in recent decades as

1980s that one can detect a pronounced anthropological trend in Renaissance studies, to the extent that I take it that anyone who has followed the development of this work has had to become familiar at least to some extent with the use of anthropological categories in the interpretation of sixteenth and seventeenth-century texts. Indeed, the very notion of Renaissance 'culture', with which I began and which is, in some evident and some subterranean senses, the critical object of what I have to say at the theoretical level, has recently become very fully inflected by anthropological thought. This is not least due to the fact that cultural anthropology has been a very important influence on the so-called New Historicism, which has occupied in turn a prominent, if not dominant, position in the field. Stephen Greenblatt's seminal *Renaissance Self-Fashioning*, the founding text in many ways of the New Historicism, cites such anthropological writers as Clifford Geertz, James Boon, Mary Douglas, Jean Duvignaud, Paul Rabinow, Victor Turner and others in an explicit recognition of the influence of their work, and in particular that of their shared 'conviction that men [sic] are born "unfinished animals", that the facts of life are less artless than they look' (1980, p. 4), a conviction which is in turn central to cultural anthropology itself.[7] But if there is an overt and acknowledged influence, there are also senses, some of which I shall try to elucidate shortly, in which cultural anthropology sets a kind of hidden agenda for New Historicist criticism, or at least acquires that effect when it is appropriated by the New Historicism, an effect with not altogether satisfactory political results.

I approach these issues – via an anecdotal connection perhaps – through the brief, remarkable Epilogue to *Renaissance Self-Fashioning*, in which Greenblatt describes his now well-known encounter on a flight

---

different as Danby's work in the 1940s on *Lear*, that of C. L. Barber on festive comedy in the 1950s, or of a text like Michael Long's *The Unnatural Scene*, published in 1973.

[7] I focus the discussion on Greenblatt because his work has been the most influential, not least on other New Historicists. A more wide-ranging account of the New Historicism would also notice the work of among others Jonathan Goldberg, Stephen Orgel, Steven Mullaney, and in particular an important series of articles by Louis Adrian Montrose whose 'The Purpose of Playing: Reflections on a Shakespearean Anthropology' (1980) is especially relevant here. Jean E. Howard offers an excellently lucid critical discussion in her 'The New Historicism in Renaissance Studies' (1986); other useful texts in this regard are Cohen (1987), Montrose (1986), Porter (1988) and Wayne (1987). Veeser (1989) is a worthwhile anthology of essays on and by New Historicist critics. See also Hall and Abbas (eds) *Literature and Anthropology* (1986).

from Baltimore to Boston with a man travelling to visit his sick son who had lost, Greenblatt says, both the will to live and the power of speech. Anxious that he would be unable to understand his son, the man turns to Greenblatt and asks him to pronounce some phrases soundlessly so that he can practise lip-reading. The words he chooses are 'I want to die, I want to die'. Greenblatt balks at this eerie invitation, and in the course of relating his reasons for doing so, uses the incident to prompt, among other things, the re-citation of central issues of the book. It ends: 'I was aware', he says 'in a manner more forceful than anything my academic research had brought home to me, of the extent to which my identity and the words I utter coincide, the extent to which I want to form my own sentences or to choose for myself those moments in which I will recite someone else's. ... To be asked, even by an isolated, needy individual to perform lines that were not my own, that violated my sense of my own desires, was intolerable' (p. 256). But the Epilogue also evokes the transformation of the project of *Renaissance Self-Fashioning* in the course of the book's development. Having set out 'to understand the role of human autonomy in the construction of identity' (p. 256), and believing not only that it was 'the very hallmark of the Renaissance that middle-class and aristocratic males began to feel that they possessed ... shaping power over their lives' but also that 'this power and the freedom it implied [was] an important element in my own sense of myself', Greenblatt recounts the way in which as the work progressed he

perceived that fashioning oneself and being fashioned by cultural institutions – family, religion, state – were inseparably intertwined. In all my texts and documents, there were, so far as I could tell, no moments of pure, unfettered subjectivity; indeed, the human subject itself began to seem remarkably unfree, the ideological product of the relations of power in a particular society. (p. 256)

Remarking that the book as written 'reflects these perceptions ... in a manner more tentative, more ironic than ... originally intended' *(ibid.)*, he ends *Self-Fashioning*, however, with the ambiguities and ambivalences in his representation of the relation between autonomy and determination intact:

... in our culture to abandon self-fashioning is to abandon the craving for freedom, and to let go of one's stubborn hold upon selfhood, even selfhood conceived as a fiction, is to die. As for myself, I have related this brief story of my encounter with the distraught father on the plane because I want to bear witness at the close to my overwhelming need to sustain the illusion that I am the principal maker of my own identity. (p. 257)

To be sure, this might be thought of as more tiresomely ambivalent than teasingly ambiguous. But pre-reflectively the incident recounted is doubtless itself rich with cultural meaning, susceptible of interpretation at numerous mythic, psychic and literary levels, and disclosing much of the society inscribed in it, from the engendering of its paranoia to the airmobility of – some – of its academics ('salaried, middle-class shamen' as Greenblatt calls them elsewhere (1988, p. 1)). And beyond this, important issues are raised by the Epilogue, and the book it represents, not least among them being the sense at work in it of cultural power, to which I shall return presently.

But for the moment I am particularly interested in what we might think of as the text within the text, the book, in other words, on which Greenblatt was trying to concentrate when he was distracted by the father. It was of course Clifford Geertz's *The Interpretation of Cultures*, and it is more than instructive to turn back to this text for much of the methodological and some of the political agenda of the New Historicism, the appropriation of which from cultural anthropology I am concerned to excavate. The key section of Geertz's text in this respect is the opening theoretical essay, 'Thick description: towards an interpretive theory of culture' (Geertz 1973), the very title of which supplies in turn key terms for the anthropology whose method and objectives it elucidates and which are carried over – more or less transformed – into New Historicism: viz, that *culture* is indeed the central concern, that it is an *interpretative* practice which is needed, and that the appropriate method will be *descriptive*.

That Geertz regards the concept of culture as at the centre of anthropology is clear enough: he speaks of it as the concept 'around which the whole discipline of anthropology arose, and whose domination that discipline has been increasingly concerned to limit, specify, focus, and contain' (Geertz 1973, p. 4). But along with the centrality he also notes the extant variety, instability and even confusion of the concept, citing eleven various and often discrepant or incompatible definitions of, and four metaphors for, culture in the twenty-seven pages of a textbook chapter on the concept.[8] In contrast

[8] I.e. Clyde Kluckhohn's *Mirror for Man*, cited in Geertz 1973, pp. 4–5.

to this apparent confusion, Geertz then offers a definition of his own sense of culture: 'The concept of culture I espouse ... is essentially a semiotic one. Believing, with Max Weber, that man is an animal suspended in webs of significance he himself has spun, I take culture to be those webs ...' (p. 5). In the same semiotic vein, culture is later defined as 'interworked systems of construable signs' (p. 14) and again – appealing to inscription in a way which prefigures New Historicism's own use of metaphors of writing, and of representation more widely, as cultural and quasi-sociological concepts – Geertz describes the ethnographic enterprise as 'like trying to read (in the sense of 'construct a reading of') a manuscript – foreign, faded, full of ellipses, incoherences, suspicious emendations, and tendatious commentaries, but written not in conventionalized graphs of sound but in transient examples of shaped behavior' (Geertz 1973, p. 10).

Inevitably the nature of ethnographic inquiry is closely linked to the conception of the culture to be observed. If culture is conceived of as 'a multiplicity of complex conceptual structures, many of them superimposed upon or knotted into one another, which are at once strange, irregular and inexplicit, and which [the ethnographer] must contrive somehow first to grasp and then to render ...' (p. 10), then 'Right down at the factual base, the hard rock, insofar as there is any, of the whole enterprise, we are already explicating: and worse, explicating explications' (p. 9). In the light, thus, of the inexplicit but nonetheless semiotic manner of culture, Geertz takes the modality of its apprehension by ethnography to be not that of 'an experimental science in search of a law but an interpretive one in search of a meaning, ... construing social expressions on their surface enigmatical' (p. 5). Indeed, so central is this conception of cultural understanding to Geertz's theory of ethnography that he counts among the three or four key characteristics of 'ethnographic description' the insistence that it is 'interpretive' and that 'what it is interpretive of is the flow of social discourse' (p. 200), to the extent that not only are 'anthropological writings ... themselves interpretations, and second and third order ones to boot' but they may even be 'fictions, in the sense that they are "something made", "something fashioned"' (p. 15).

But Geertz cites this, 'the original meaning of *fictiō*?', to suggest – without to my mind anything like adequate inspection of the problems raised thereby – that anthropological interpretations are not thus 'false, unfactual, or merely "as if" thought experiments' (p. 15). For these interpretative and 'made' senses of ethnographic writing notwith-standing, Geertz also believes that the appropriate way to carry out what he calls by a favoured term the 'appraisal' (p. 16) of the 'piled-up structures of inference and implication through which an ethno-grapher is continually trying to pick his [sic] way' (p. 7), is 'an elaborate venture in … "thick description"', a notion he borrows, of course, from Gilbert Ryle (p. 6). Believing that 'it is not in our interest to bleach human behavior' (p. 17) in the manner, he believes, of more systematic or more systematising sociologies, Geertz dwells rather on 'the immediacies thick description presents' (p. 25), the 'sensible actuality' (p. 23), 'complex specifics' and 'small, but very densely textured facts' (p. 28) which derive from 'exceedingly extended aquaintance with extremely small matters' (p. 21). By contrast with what would otherwise be, in his estimation, the abstract presentation of 'symmetrical crystals of significance, purified of the material complexity in which they were located' (p. 20), thick description, as Geertz under-stands and recommends it, attends to 'behavior,' and attends 'with some exactness, because it is through the flow of behavior – or more precisely, social action – that cultural forms find articulation' (p. 17). Thick description, the paramount method of anthropological reflection, is the localised, concrete, writing up – at once interpretative and also almost pre-analytic – of cultural material in its dense particularity.

There are other 'complex specifics' in Geertz's writing which there is not room to trace in every detail here. But it is possible to see clearly the marked similarities between the interpretative strategies of the New Historicism and Geertz's account of ethnographic interpreta-tion. 'Sorting out the structures of signification', as he somewhat casually puts it, is an activity which he likens explicitly to that of the literary critic (p. 9), and indeed when Greenblatt acknowledges in the passage cited above his indebtedness to the notion that man is born an unfinished animal, he goes on immediately to define the inter-pretative consequences of this for the – literary – instance of his own work in terms which are wholly reminiscent of Geertz. Greenblatt's view that 'particular cultures and the observers of these cultures are inevitably drawn to a metaphorical grasp of reality', and that 'anthro-pological interpretation must address itself less to the mechanics of customs and institutions than to the interpretive constructions the members of the society apply to their experiences', leads to the belief, cognate with Geertz's sense of the fictive nature of ethnographic writing, that a 'literary criticism that has affinities to this practice must be conscious of its own status as interpretation and intent upon understanding literature as a part of the system of signs that constitutes a given culture' (Greenblatt 1980, p. 4). The notion that a 'system of signs' *constitutes* a 'given culture' is, of course, more tendentious than the assertion itself is willing or able to admit. But it is perfectly in tune with the kind of consonance between Geertz and Greenblatt at work here, not least the central and shared ways in which the notion of culture they espouse has the effect of turning society more or less wholly into discourse. This slippage can be illustrated in Geertz when, for example, following Paul Ricoeur's idea of the 'inscription of action' (Geertz 1973, p. 19), he thinks the task of anthropological writing, thick description, as that of 'trying to rescue the "said" of [social] discourse' (p. 20),[9] which resonates in turn with a contention like Greenblatt's when, in regarding each of the literary texts he deals with as 'the focal point for converging lines of force in sixteenth-century culture', the consequence is that 'their significance for us is not that we may see *through* them to underlying and prior historical principles but rather that we may interpret the interplay of their symbolic structures with those perceivable in the careers of their authors and in the larger social world as constituting a single, complex process ... ' (Greenblatt 1980, pp. 5–6). While naturally no one today wishes to reduce texts to reflections of a social reality elsewhere, the extent to which it is appropriate to regard the social process – even that of the fashioning of selves – as 'single,' and one wholly constituted of the interplay of symbolic structures or located at the level

[9]Connected with the idea of the 'saidness' of culture is the view shared by Geertz and Greenblatt that culture is also 'public'. Geertz clearly believes not only in the textual nature of culture but also in the public nature of the cultural text (which is surprising in view of his commitment to particularity: in practice there is wide variety in the ways that different cultures regard the very notion of the 'public', if indeed they entertain such a notion in the first place). For Geertz, culture, 'this acted document ... is public ... [t]hough ideational, it does not exist in someone's head; though unphysical, it is not an occult entity' (Geertz 1973, p. 10), and again '[c]ulture is public because meaning is' (p. 12). An equivalent passage in Greenblatt reads as follows:

Social actions are themselves always embedded in systems of public signification, always grasped, even by their makers, in acts of interpretation, while the words that con-stitute the works of literature that we discuss here are by their very nature the manifest assurance of a similar embeddedness. Language, like other sign systems, is a collective construction; our interpretive task must be to grasp more sensitively the consequences of this fact by investigating both the social presence to the world of the literary text and the social presence of the world in the literary text. (Greenblatt 1980, p. 5)

of Ricoeur's and Geertz's 'said', remains, for reasons which will be instanced below, highly questionable.

Among the most significant of the intellectual assumptions that the New Historicism shares with cultural anthropology, however, are those concerning the role of general theory in the practice of interpretation. As a result of his belief that thick description must deal in concrete actuality, Geertz comments in these terms on potential weaknesses in his own preferred approach: 'The besetting sin of interpretive approaches to anything – literature, dreams, symptoms, culture – is that they tend to resist, or to be permitted to resist, conceptual articulation and thus to escape systematic modes of assessment' (1973, p. 24). Although acknowledging that for 'a field of study which ... asserts itself to be a science, this just will not do', Geertz nonetheless insists that 'a number of characteristics of cultural interpretation ... make the theoretical development of it more than usually difficult', the first of which is 'the need for theory to stay rather closer to the ground than tends to be the case in sciences more able to give themselves over to imaginative abstraction. Only short flights of ratiocination', he continues, 'tend to be effective in anthropology; longer flights tend to drift off into logical dreams' and 'academic bemusements with formal symmetry' (ibid.).[10] Indeed, Geertz regards 'the essential task of theory' as being 'not to codify abstract regularities but to make thick description possible, not to generalize across cases but to generalize within them' (p. 26). This in turn is connected with the contention that

The major theoretical contributions not only lie in specific studies ... but they are very difficult to abstract from such studies and integrate into anything one might call 'culture theory' as such. Theoretical formulations hover so low over the interpretations they govern that they don't make much sense or hold much interest apart from them. This is so ... because, stated independently of their applications, they seem either commonplace or vacant. (p. 25)

In all of these formulations, Geertz is remarkably close to specifying what becomes in the event the practice of New Historicist interpretation: it is almost as if these reservations about the possibility of

[10]The passage continues: 'The whole point of the semiotic approach to culture is, as I have said, to aid us in gaining access to the conceptual world in which our subjects live so that we can, in some extended sense of the term, converse with them' (Geertz 1973, p. 24). This notion of conversation will be taken up below; see n. 54.

general theory come to govern the critical practice itself. In fact the incapacity or unwillingness to 'generalize across cases' has usually been matched by a reluctance even to 'generalize within them', exemplifying, in ways which are even even more reticent than Geertz himself, a theoretical localism which systematically declines to set out second-order accounts of the assumptions and methods which inform its analytic procedures. Relying instead on the resonant anecdote, the suggestive example, the surprising reference across unlike texts or the startling connection between lived and fictional practices, New Historicist interpretative strategy constitutes its thick descriptions, in exemplary Geertzian fashion, by deploying the local reading of specific material. The reading is normally performed in a critical language whose lexicon and strategy frequently suggest a more general purchase than is quite sustained by the particular material (even up to the level of very generalised claims about the whole culture), but whose theoretical formulations nonetheless 'hover low', as Geertz puts it, over the interpretations themselves. Greenblatt's New Historicism shares the sense with Geertz's ethnography that the interpretation of culture is necessarily both 'microscopic' (Geertz 1973, p. 21) and 'intrinsically incomplete' (ibid., p. 29). Writing in this case in his 1988 text Shakespearean Negotiations, Greenblatt remarks that the essays of which the book is composed enact a 'shift in attention' from 'the presumed center of the literary domain' to its 'borders', in order 'to try to track what can only be glimpsed, as it were, at the margins of the text'. The 'cost' of this, he continues, 'will be the satisfying illusion of a 'whole reading', the impression conveyed by powerful critics that had they but world enough and time, they could illuminate every corner of the text and knit together into a unified interpretive vision all of their discrete perceptions'. This catches well the sense endemic at least to the New Historicist claims (although these latter are not systematically made, and that is part of the problem) about its method stemming from a 'vision' which is 'necessarily more fragmentary' (Greenblatt 1988, p. 4). This 'vision', when it becomes critical practice, is typified by the New Historicist emphasis on the telling anecdote, or on the – unexplained – 'resonance and centrality' of particular authors and texts (Greenblatt 1980, p. 6) coupled to an equally typical ambivalence regarding the general applicability of any such reading. And this is, as we have seen, also Geertz's sense in turn of the particularity and the interminability of cultural interpretation.[11]

There is, of course, much that could be said about the *sociological* probity of Geertz's anthropology, and of Greenblatt's use of it. I shall return to these issues below. But having suggested how it is that Geertz's account of what culture is, and of how ethnography must explicate it, sets much of the methodological agenda for the New Historicism, I turn now to what I referred to above as a more implicit sense – although one which is no less decisive – of the way in which anthropology is appropriated, adapted and deployed by and in New Historicist positions and interpretations. For suggestive as the culturalist strategies are – and they are certainly more appealing than some more dogmatic and totalised accounts of the social structure and of how it may be understood and by whom – it is nonetheless important to apprehend how the 'groundlessness' of culture and cultural interpretation at work in Geertz leads to what in the critical practice of the New Historicism is a signal de-realisation of power in society, of its mechanisms and effects, and even of its representation. This is a fully political consequence.

Geertz sums up much of his sense of the semiotic, inscribed character of culture, and the interpretative and descriptive character of its ethnographic explication, in, appropriately enough, a suggestive, resonant anecdote:

There is an Indian story – at least I heard it as an Indian story – about an Englishman who, having been told that the world rested on a platform which rested on the back of an elephant which rested in turn on the back

---

[11]It is also worth remarking here how even the literary form of New Historicist analysis seems to be provided for in Geertz's writing: many have noted not only the prevalence of the essay form but its appropriateness to the kind of 'incomplete' interpretation undertaken. In Geertz the suitability of the form, which is connected with his scepticism about the utility or possibility of general theory, is more or less programmatic:

'the essay, whether of thirty pages or three hundred, has seemed the natural [sic] genre in which to present cultural interpretations and the theories sustaining them, and ... if one looks for systematic treatises in the field, one is so soon disappointed, the more so if one finds any. (Geertz 1973, p. 25)

This should be brought into contact with Jean Howard's concern about the institutionally assimilable character of the New Historicist 'reading' (see Howard 1986, p. 19).

of a turtle, asked (perhaps he was an ethnographer; it is the way they behave), what did the turtle rest on? Another turtle. And that turtle? 'Ah, Sahib, after that it is turtles all the way down.' (1973, pp. 28–9)

It is, of course, hard to parse the critical implications of this story precisely; that is part of the point. I for one prefer to read it as an instance of a 'native informant' satirically baiting the bafflement of the incomprehending Englishman. But when taken, as Geertz surely intends it, as being in some measure emblematic of at least the general tenor of cultural interpretation, it succeeds quite effectively nonetheless in suggesting important characteristics of the epistemological and ontological status of culture and cultural meaning as Geertz understands these. At the epistemological level, it appears, interpretation is interminable in principle, and in practice always incomplete. This keys in exactly with the senses cited above of the unfinished and even fragmentary nature of analysis in both Geertz and Greenblatt. While at the ontological level of the reality of the lived cultural forms, the reason for cultural meaning to be regarded as potentially inexhaustible seems to be that there is no 'ground', no foundation, no fundamental level of social reality at which interpretation stops, but rather 'turtles all the way down', as far, one assumes, as infinity. Despite the 'this-worldliness' of culture – whose ontological status, Geertz asserts, is that of rocks and dreams (1973, p. 10) – in the event there are no 'hard' structures, neither ontologic bedrock nor stop of meaning.

But the implication that there are no limit structures whatsoever, whether economic, political, social or, indeed, 'cultural', does not correspond to my, or as far as I can judge, to many people's senses of the perceived and felt fabric of social life, and to few formal sociologies either. Nor does it seem to match the internal, embedded ways in which cultures figure themselves to themselves and to others, which all seem to be about limits, boundaries and definitions, even when these are crossed.[12] Nor, as I shall show, does this sense of there being no limit to cultural interpretation correspond to the coercive

[12]Cf., for example, Mary Douglas's discussion of the way in which human or animal forms can provide an image of the 'idea of society' (Douglas 1984, p. 114ff.). If the boundary is permeable, it is nonetheless clearly demarcated, and if there are points of inarticulation, these too are functional to social articulation (p. 99 and *passim*).

pressures of actual social power, including what might be thought of as pressures and limitations on interpretation itself: even in the sphere of interpretation, power may entail the power to interpret, the power to control interpretation, the power to limit or canalise the power of others to interpret, or to deny them that power altogether. It is thus important to examine with particular attention the way in which power is figured when such a sense of culture and cultural interpretation is translated into critical practice.[13]

In the first instance I shall give two examples – descriptively, and without at this stage extensive comment – of the effects of the transformation of society into discourse as it is methodologically ingested by the concept of culture derived from Geertzian and related definitions, and to an extent legitimated by their invocation. In both examples the idea of culture includes the idea that there are indeed no hard or impermeable barriers, nor significant differences of onto-logical or epistemological status between apparently separate cultural phemonena; and certainly not between cultural production in the narrow sense – for our purposes this means the theatre – and culture in the wider sense, this latter embracing all other forms of social practice.

The first example is taken from one of the versions of Greenblatt's essay 'Invisible Bullets' (1985), an important text in as much as it incorporates, in the model of the function of Shakespeare's theatre as the production and containment of 'subversion', one of the most significant New Historicist figurations of power. In discussing the relation between theatrical performance and social process, Greenblatt offers this account of the problem:

Shakespeare's theatre was not isolated by its wooden walls, nor was it merely the passive reflector of social and ideological forces that lay entirely outside of it: rather the Elizabethan and Jacobean theatre was itself a *social event*. Drama, and artistic expression in general, is never perfectly self-contained and abstract, nor can it be derived satisfactorily from the subjective consciousness of an isolated creator. Collective actions, ritual gestures, paradigms of relationships, and shared images of authority penetrate the work of art, while conversely the socially overdetermined work of art, along with a multitude of other institutions

[13] The New Historicism has played an important part, of course, in popularising the idea that the question of power is indeed paramount, 'interpretatively' as well as 'politically'; for some, even in Renaissance studies, the concern was not wholly novel. Cf. Barker *et al.* (eds), *1642: Literature and Power in the Seventeenth Century* (1981).

and utterances, contributes to the formation, realignment, and transmission of social practices. (pp. 32–3)

A reciprocal relation between theatre and society here involves an interpenetration of each by the other. But the materials extant and the forces deemed to be at work are wholly – and significantly – culturalist in the manner of their expression. If the 'work of art' is not isolated from external forms and pressures, these latter are described as *inter alia* 'ritual gestures' and 'shared images'. While the 'socially determined work of art' in turn participates in the wider 'transmission of social practices' by taking its place among other, *ontologically undifferentiated*, 'institutions and utterances'. It is not easy to avoid the thought that a much sharper dialectic has been made to masquerade as reciprocity and integration here, as social practice is absorbed into culture.

This tends to be confirmed by the second example, which takes us closer to the figuration of power as such, and which is drawn, in order to widen the focus somewhat, from the work of another New Historicist critic, Leonard Tennenhouse, in his appropriately titled *Power on Display* (1986):

To the degree that the Renaissance theater performed a political function … we may assume Shakespeare's plays, unlike the written Shakespeare, were not enclosed within an aesthetic framework. They opened onto a larger arena of events and observed a transgeneric logic. In my account of Shakespeare's drama, then, stagecraft collaborates with statecraft in producing spectacles of power. The strategies of theater resembled those of the scaffold, as well as court performance, I am suggesting, in observing a common logic of figuration that both sustained and testified to the monarch's power … (p. 15).

The book is epigonous and the passage quoted follows Greenblatt closely. It too rejects the separation of cultural and other social practices, and in particular denies the enclosure of the theatre. But although, it is claimed, Shakespeare's plays were not confined within 'an aesthetic framework' (whatever that might mean), the wider social sphere – 'political function' – is nonetheless an *'arena'*, and the transgeneric logic which the theatre shares with other practices is that of a common *spectacularity*, and a 'shared logic of *figuration*'. There are a number of obscurities in the passage (in which it typifies the book from which it is taken), but what is clear, however, is that as the move is made from the separation of aesthetic and lived practices to senses of their common substance, two things happen simultaneously: the 'wider arena' of the other social practices with which the aesthetic, or narrowly cultural instances are homogenised, is identified as that of 'power'; while it is the language of the aesthetic which provides both the lexicon and the conceptual repertoire for thinking the thenceforward single domain of 'culture'. If society becomes simultaneously power and culture, then power becomes cultural, and its analysis, in Greenblatt's generic phrase, a 'cultural poetics'; or more specifically 'a poetics of Elizabethan power' which 'will prove inseparable, in crucial respects, from a poetics of the theatre' (Greenblatt 1985, p. 44).

In asserting, then, that it is power with which the theatre shares its spectacularity via a 'common logic of figuration', the passage from Tennenhouse is as much summary as it is crude or simplistic, and in its representation of power it is nothing more or less than orthodox. Theatricality functions in the New Historicism both substantially and formally, in as much as it is taken both to be constitutive, and also to provide the homology among the forms of the otherwise ostensibly various social practices and institutions it identifies and privileges. Tennenhouse's insistence on the theatricality of power is quite in tune, thus, with such meta-critical formulations as Greenblatt's '[t]heatricality then is not set over against power but is one of power's essential modes' (1985, p. 33), and is indeed wholly consonant, finally, with Greenblatt's – by now 'classical' – assertion in 'Invisible Bullets' of the theatricality of power in early modern England:

... this poetics [of Elizabethan power] ... is inseparably bound up with the figure of Queen Elizabeth, a ruler without a standing army, without a highly developed bureaucracy, without an extensive police force, a ruler whose power is constituted in theatrical celebrations of royal glory and theatrical violence visited upon the enemies of that glory ... Elizabethan power ... depends upon its privileged visibility. As in a theatre ... (1985, p. 44)

As in a theatre .... The implications of this remarkable passage and the interpretative stance it delineates are far-reaching. But we must first grant, in whatever perplexity, that it actually means what it says, as it passes seamlessly from a *poetics* to the substantive statement that Elizabethan power *is constituted in theatrical celebrations of royal glory and theatrical violence visited upon the enemies of that glory*. If it does mean what it says, it is the distillation and epitome of the entire process of assimilation I have been tracing through the New Historicist appropriation of cultural anthropology to precisely such a decisively culturalist figuration of political and social power as this.

III

The interpretative yield of the articulation of cultural anthropology with literary criticism might be expected to insist, surely, in the arena of the specific instance which plays such an important part in the articulation. Among the equivalences between cultural anthropology and the New Historicism that I have been describing it is, when it comes to the figuration of power, the homology of the spectacularity of the scaffold of punishment with that of the theatricality of the stage which provides both the half-hidden syntax of the general culturalisation of power, and also, in the scaffold of punishment itself, the graphic connecting instance, which is both specific and controlling, both an instantiation and a totalisation, of the wider paradigm. According to Tennenhouse's 'transgeneric logic', and he is not alone, there is an effective parity or conformation, as we have seen above, between the scaffold on which powerfully cultural playing took place and the scaffold on which a cultural power was played out,[14] for how else could the case for an inseparable poetics of Elizabethan power be made to cohere? But, returning to the reading of the particular Shakespearean text (which is, of course, where New Historicist essays largely begin and end, both in practice and in principle), if we read *Titus Andronicus* in the light of the theatricality of power, in Act IV Scene IV something strange happens. There is a violence unseen. Amid the spectacular brutalities and exotic theatrical barbarisms with which the play is otherwise laden, there is, by contrast, an instance of the representation of the exercise of power so undemonstrative and marginal that it has consistently escaped notice.

It begins in Act IV Scene III, a scene organised by Titus's conviction that the goddess of Justice has left earth and must be sought elsewhere, first below in 'Pluto's region' (IV.iii.13), and when she is reported not to be in hell either, among the empyreal gods above. It is

---

[14]Tennenhouse is drawing on Foucault of course, especially on the emphasis in *Discipline and Punish* (1977) on the 'spectacle of the scaffold'. It is not clear to me that among possible readings of Foucault's work this culturalisation of power is the happiest, if it is indeed possible. I address the matter again below; see pp. 200–1.

one of the scenes of Titus's real or assumed derangement, in the unhinged energy of which his associates are in any case caught up. Significantly, it is also one of the play's scenes of foregrounded theatrical spectacle: Titus, Marcus his brother, 'other Gentlemen', and the boy Lucius, grandson to Titus, prepare and shoot arrows with petitionary letters addressed to the gods attached to them. To Titus's mind they shoot the arrows into the heavens; according to Marcus they are launched into the court where 'We will afflict the emperor in his pride' (IV. iii. 62). At this point there enters, as it were unannounced and unprepared for, a 'Clown' who is himself on his way to petition the emperor Saturninus in a law suit. Having, it seems, a less elevated sense than Titus of what justice entails, and how judicial process works, he carries a basket of pigeons which he intends to offer the emperor as a bribe in the case, a matter of a brawl between his uncle and one of the emperor's men. Titus, affecting to regard the Clown as a messenger from heaven, demands an answer to his airborne petitions: ' ... Sirrah, what tidings ... / Shall I have justice? what says Jupiter?' (IV. iii. 77–8). The Clown's reply depends upon the representation of a linguistic and cultural miscommunication or equivocation. Lacking in any case a classical education – he is drawn not in the aesthetic register of Shakespeare's Roman vocabulary but in that of his English-rustic idiom – the Clown hears 'Jupiter' (or, in his non-elite diction, 'Jubiter') as the dialect-word 'gibbeter' and answers accordingly: 'Ho, the gibbet-maker? He says that he hath taken them down again, for the man must not be hang'd till the next week' (IV iii. 79–81). Or at least, not until the next scene. It is, of course, what we must be constrained to think of as a comic moment. There is at least a discrepancy, measured by a certain 'humour', between Titus's overblown, distract railing and madcap scheming, on the one hand, and what is represented as the only half-intended wit of the Clown's simplicities and misunderstandings on the other: 'Why, didst thou not come from heaven?' Titus asks incredulously; 'From heaven? alas, sir, I never came there. God forbid I should be so bold to press to heaven in my young days' is the Clown's ingenuous and, as it turns out unwittingly ironic reply. In a sequence which in this same vein both mocks and utilises the Clown's lack of sophistication, the scene then has Titus enlist him to carry a message on his behalf to the emperor in the form of an 'oration' or 'supplication'. Titus gives the Clown money for his 'charges' and promises him that, presenting the quickly-written message to the emperor along with his pigeons, he will 'have justice at his hands' (IV. iii. 96–7, 100–5). In an opaque passage Titus then asks the Clown for his knife and has Marcus wrap it in the petition.[15] The Clown is dispatched.[16]

But whatever laughter may have been produced in this scene – albeit nervous and uncomfortable laughter, like that which *Titus Andronicus* as a whole has both engendered and received – will seem perhaps less appropriate when in the next the Clown delivers his pigeons and Titus's oration to Saturninus. I reproduce the moment here in all its brevity:

Tam....
        How now, good fellow! would'st thou speak with us?
Clo.   Yea, forsooth, and your mistress-ship be emperial.
Tam.   Empress I am, but yonder sits the emperor.
Clo.   'Tis he. God and Saint Stephen give you godden. I have brought
        you a letter and a couple of pigeons here.
                                   [He reads the letter.
Sat.   Go, take him away, and hang him presently.
Clo.   How much money must I have?
Tam.   Come, sirrah, you must be hanged.
Clo.   Hang'd by'lady! then I have brought up a neck to a fair end.
                                             [Exit.
                                      (IV. iv. 39–49)

This moment is stunning. The Clown is simply taken away to execution. Without cause given. We can speculate that the written 'oration' the Clown delivers contains threats or curses, or that Saturninus

---

[15] See Maxwell's note to IV. iii. 115 (Shakespeare 1968, p. 95).

[16] The representation of the Clown is contained within that comic-grotesque stupidity, sometimes flecked with low cunning, in the light of which plebeian figures almost invariably appear in the high-cultural tradition, when not dangerous, or simply – normally – invisible. He is part of that Shakespearean vernacular by which non-elite, and especially peasant, figures are comic in as much as – circularly – rustics and other 'lower class' figures are, by definition of this mode of representation, figures of fun. Compare it with the 'comic closure' (Barker and Hulme 1985, p. 203) of Caliban's subplot in *The Tempest*. The Clown is not, of course, grotesque in exactly the same way as we have argued that Caliban is. At least he is not, as far as can be told from the text, physically demonised. He is nonetheless always-already 'safely' comic, like Caliban; and this is of course grotesque.

There is also, doubtless, comedy in the wit of the Clown's responses to the extravagantly mad, or feigned-mad Titus, although again it is a condescending humour: if there is some mockery of Titus, the Clown is not much more than an instrument of its expression, cloaked no doubt in the mode of Shakespeare's notedly 'affectionate' portrayal of his menials.

interprets the knife wrapped in it as a symbolic offer of violence. But the point is that *our* interpretations would remain speculative. The emperor's action in ordering the Clown's death is inexplicable. Unexplained in the literal sense that no overt reason for it is given (and this is important because it contributes to the uncanniness of the incident), it is also unjustified in other senses. Not only does it lack credence according to the positive norms of behaviour the play assumes, but equally it fails to conform to the protocols of the deviations from those norms which the play more prominently fore-grounds as the reality of Roman life: characters in *Titus Andronicus* may act 'barbarously', but their behaviour is rarely random or arbi-trary, on the contrary it is invariably *ad hominem* and selfishly pur-poseful. Here the rueful lack of protest in the Clown's last line, his last words – 'Hang'd by' lady! then I have brought up a neck to a fair end' (IV. iv. 49) – bespeaks an apparently cheerful acceptance, and equally cheerful incomprehension, of what is to be done to him. The poor are happy to be hanged by their betters. It is a well-known fact. Without his killing even being represented as an articulation of a Rome in general given over to the tyranny or savagery that maims the Andronici, the Clown, so evidently a dupe of Titus's, rather than a conspirator or accomplice, the Clown who heard, eerily perhaps, 'Jupiter' as 'gibbeter', thus dies on the gallows, 'dazed' we might imagine after the Wyatt poem, and 'with dreadful face'.[17]

And as a whole this brief episode remains entirely enigmatic and arbitrary. It is as if, running one's hand along a surface, something snags here. It is formally unmotivated in the sense of being aestheti-cally discrepant from the primitivism and the classicism of the rest of the play, and of lacking convincing preparation or legitimation in the thematic, narrative or hermeneutic codes of the text. It is inexplicable, as I have said, and never mentioned again. It is simply *there*: strange, *unheimlich*, and, I have found, haunting.

It pointed me to some historical research.

---

[17] The image seems compelling, if one imagines as I do, the contrast between the bizarre levity of the discourse of this moment and the reality of the death by strangulation with which it is but barely articulated. In Wyatt's poem, *Stond whoso list upon the slipper top*, of course, death 'grip'th right hard' him who is 'much known of other': this is clearly not the Clown's case.

IV

Unlike the Clown in *Titus Andronicus*, the majority of people who died on the gallows in early modern England were killed after convictions for felony sustained in the course of what is frequently called 'the administration of justice'. For this purpose lay magistrates, Justices of the Peace, sat in quarter sessions in each county hearing petty offences, while the superior provincial courts, presided over by a judge, were the Courts of Assize which heard the capital offences. England was divided into six assize 'Circuits', the South-Eastern or 'Home' Circuit, the Midland, Norfolk, Oxford, Northern and Western Circuits. Wales was divided into a further four. London and the so-called 'metropolitan' county of Middlesex were not included in the circuit system, having separate but equivalent courts to which I shall return below. Twice each year, usually in the Lent and Trinity vacations, two royal justices, empowered by commissions of oyer and terminer and of gaol delivery would 'ride' each of the circuits convening assize courts in appropriate towns in each county, hearing pleas and delivering the gaols of those who had been committed by the Justices of the Peace to await trial on more serious offences than could be dealt with by magistrates, and of those who had been arrested since the last quarter or assize sessions.

It happens that relatively full records survive for the Home Circuit, which consisted of the counties of Essex, Hertfordshire, Kent, Surrey and Sussex, as they do for the Middlesex sessions, and it is these which provide the basis for what I feel compelled to say – in a decidedly unanthropological way – about hanging in Elizabethan and Stuart England and Wales. Initially, setting aside considerations of the quality of justice, and other evaluative issues concerning the relation between Elizabethan and Stuart power and the mass of the people, this involves simply attempting to enumerate the instances of death by hanging (and other related causes) as a result of judgements in the assizes. In order to count the dead I have drawn very fully in the first instance on Professor J. S. Cockburn's painstaking work on the bundles of what have come to be called 'indictment' files (although their actual content is more varied) which comprise the main records of the Home Circuit Assizes in our period.[18]

---

[18]From 1975 to 1982 Professor Cockburn published the records of the Home Circuit in ten volumes, one for each of the circuit's constituent counties for each of the

According to these files it appears that in Essex, in the period 1559–1624,[19] of the 3,449 people indicted for felonies, 801 were sentenced to death. In Hertfordshire the figures are 1,291 and 320, respectively; in Kent they are 2,684 and 732; in Surrey, 2,872 and 623; and in Sussex, 1,435 and 352. Of a total of 11,731 people (10,107 men and 1,624 women) indicted in the five counties of the Home Circuit, 2,828 were sentenced to be hanged, 2,571 men and 257 women. This figure must be adjusted, however, to take account of the known pardons issued in the relevant period. The figures for the Home Circuit in the reign of Elizabeth are as follows: Essex, 105; Hertfordshire, 66; Kent, 148; Surrey, 120, and Sussex, 55. These numbers, which total 494, must then be adjusted to encompass the reign of James as well.[20] The resulting total is 729. When this figure is subtracted from the total of felons sentenced to death in the period it yields the number hanged as 2,099.

To this must be added, however, the numbers sentenced by Justices of the Peace. Although in theory the more serious offences should have been dealt with by the royal justices at the twice-yearly assizes, and in practice this was probably increasingly the pattern during the period, there is nevertheless sufficient evidence that the lay magistrates were also hanging felons at a considerable rate. Although the surviving records for quarter sessions are not, so far as I am aware, anything

reigns of Elizabeth and James. His introductory volume to the *Calendar of Assize Records* (Cockburn 1985) discusses the organisation and procedures of the assizes, and tabulates in summary form data distilled from the county volumes. I have reproduced many of those data here, sometimes without further acknowledgement; in most instances I have submitted them to further arithmetical or statistical processing, and occasionally I have interpolated information from other sources. Interpretation of the significance of the figures and of their likely reliability is either mine, or it is the work of either Cockburn or of other commentators, in which cases my indebtedness is noted accordingly. The same general principles govern my use below of John Cordy Jeaffreson's work on the records of the Middlesex Sessions and F.G. Emmison's work on the Essex county records. For information about the general operation of the assizes I have relied on Cockburn's history of these courts from 1558 to 1714 (Cockburn 1972).

[19] Following Cockburn's tables, these 65 whole years have been taken, for arithmetical and statistical purposes, as the numerical representation of the extent of the period under consideration, i.e. the reigns of Elizabeth I and James I. (Neither of these monarchs had the forethought to be born or to die at the exact beginning or the exact end of what we think of as the calendar year.)

[20] This figure is derived from Cockburn's. On the basis of his own data, Professor Cockburn appears to err when he gives the number pardoned as 495 in the body of his text (Cockburn 1985, p.128). The number of pardons for both reigns has been derived by averaging the Elizabethan figure for the years of that reign and multiplying it up for the 65 years of the two reigns.

like as full as for the Home Circuit assizes and for Middlesex, there are some telling exceptions. Fairly detailed records exist, for example, of the disposition of felons for both the quarter sessions and the assizes held in Devon between 1598 and 1639 (see Cockburn 1972, pp. 94–6). Where in this period the judges of assize are recorded as having had 511 people hanged, the Justices of the Peace were responsible for the execution of a further 109, or about another 20 *per cent* of the figure for the assizes. This excludes the 15 people recorded in the same documents as dead before judgement (not to mention the 1,600 who are recorded as having other forms of corporal punishment inflicted on them in the same Sessions in the same period). If it is at all statistically responsible to generalise from the Devon figures and from other instances where records of executions ordered by quarter sessions exist side by side with the figures from the equivalent assizes – and it should be remembered that Devon was not a populous part of the country compared with the Home Circuit, so any resulting distortion is like to be in the direction of underestimation – it appears that figures given above for executions in the Home Circuit should be increased by a fifth to account for the Justices of the Peace acting in lieu of assize judges. This would mean that the total of people hanged within the jurisdiction of the Home Circuit assizes during the years under consideration is not 2,099 but 2,518.

Turning now to the records for London and Middlesex, it is necessary no doubt to note the slightly different forms of the organisation and legal basis of the courts, which were nonetheless the metropolitan equivalents of the quarter sessions and assizes in the provincial counties.[21] But although the sessions of the peace held in London and in Middlesex were not, strictly speaking, quarter sessions, and nor were the superior courts strictly assizes, the general pattern, by which inferior courts and courts of first instance were presided over by lay justices while judges empowered by commissions of gaol delivery and oyer and terminer heard felony cases in superior courts, also held good in the metropolis and the metropolitan county. Middlesex justices sat at Westminster and elsewhere in the county, while London justices sat at Guildhall. Sessions of gaol delivery, however, were held for both Middlesex and London at the Old Bailey, which stood adjacent to Newgate, the principal prison for both the capital and the county.

[21] See Cockburn 1972, pp. 29–31; Jeaffreson 1972, pp. xx–xxvi.

In dealing, first, with Middlesex it is necessary to distinguish the kinds of records available. The most extensive material is the bundles of files known collectively as 'sessional rolls'.[22] But the Middlesex archives also contain a number of volumes of folio record books among which is a Gaol Delivery Register begun in the fifth year of James's reign. This was a record of the actual disposition of the cases of felons, rather than the more or less reliably annotated indictments and recognizances of the Sessional Rolls proper. The former records, amongst other things, actual executions, while the latter documents may contain such information if they have been annotated to that effect, or may only provide information from which such data can be, at best, inferred. Thus for my purposes the Gaol Delivery Register is in principle a far more accurate document than the sessional rolls themselves. John Cordy Jeaffreson's original analysis of this material suggests that in practice as well it was kept with great accuracy, at least for certain periods in the early seventeenth century. While during the last seven years of James's reign the Register was kept 'with a remissness that in certain passages wanted nothing of scandalous negligence' (Jeaffreson 1974, p. xvii), from the sixth to the fifteenth years of the reign it seems to have been 'kept with sufficient care and exactitude; and from the entries made in the folios during these years, one learns even to a unit how largely the criminal code of our ancestors was destructive of human life in one of the smallest of the English counties', as Jeaffreson puts it (p. xvii).

According to the Middlesex Gaol Delivery Register, in the ten years from 6 James to 15 James the numbers of people hanged were 55, 55, 52, 77, 46, 98, 84, 91, 71, and 75 respectively, a total of 704. On this evidence, then, at least 70·4 people on average were executed by hanging each year in the metropolitan county.[23] In the case of London, as distinct from Middlesex, the figures I present are calculated,

[22]The Middlesex records were investigated and described in the nineteenth century by John Cordy Jeaffreson at the instigation of the Middlesex County Records Society, who published his two volumes at Clerkenwell in 1886 and 1887 (Jeaffreson 1972 and 1974). They were re-published by the Greater London Council before its demise at the hands of a Conservative government. Jeaffreson's volumes, as well as analysing, in the strict sense, the material, print numerous documentary examples of indictments, coroners' inquests, recognizances, sessional orders, minutes, memoranda and other 'entries of record'; a systematic tabulation of the results of his search of the Middlesex records, giving numbers of indictments for various classes of crime, of convictions, grants of benefit of clergy, sentences, reprieves and numbers of felons at large, etc., for each of the reigns, is printed at the end of the second of these volumes.

or, to be precise, are only evidential in as much as they are estima-
tions based on the Middlesex records. I have followed Jeaffreson in
cautiously estimating the incidence of penal demise as at least no less
in the city and the liberties than in Middlesex, whose population was
probably significantly lower than that of London (see Jeaffreson 1974,
pp. xx–xxi). Therefore to the Middlesex figure of 70·4 executions a
year on average may be added a further 70·4 for the metropolis
itself.[24]

However, in enumerating the extent of the taking of life which the
records of the assizes and of the equivalent metropolitan courts
represent, it is important not to forget two other causes of death
besides executions by hanging: mortality resulting from the *peine
forte et dure*, and deaths *in prison* while captives were awaiting trial,
sentence, further investigation or other judicial procedure (gaol sentences as such were, of course, rare in the period).

A prisoner who refused to plead, or who entered a 'perverse' plea,
was subjected to the *peine*, which consisted of being pressed with
heavy weights until the captive either pleaded or died (Cockburn
1985, p. 72). A first taste of the penalty was applied in the courtroom
itself, and if the prisoner still refused to plead he or she was incarcer-
ated and the weights applied permanently, or at least until one or

---

[23]In giving this as the average annual figure (the equivalent total for the whole
period is 4,576), and in adducing and aggregating later not only numbers of executions
by hanging but also of 'related' deaths in Middlesex (execution by the *peine forte et dure*
and 'prison deaths' discussed below), I have thus decided to base my calculations and
extrapolations on the qualitatively best evidence available to me, i.e. on that of the ten
accurate years of the Stuart Gaol Delivery Register. In applying them to the whole
period I have accepted Jeaffreson's reasons for thinking that the generalisation of these
figures (and of those given below for executions by the *peine* in Middlesex) to the rest of
James's reign and to that of Elizabeth is not only statistically convenient but historically
probable; see Jeaffreson 1974, pp. xxi–xxii. In view of the principles of methodological
and numerical caution outlined below, however, I think it important to indicate that
the figures yielded by this apparently high-grade but chronologically limited record
differ from those which can be derived from the sessional rolls as such, which embrace
the entire period but are very imperfect both in their original comprehensiveness as
records of actual executions and also in their state of preservation. The latter figure is
somewhat lower than the former.

[24]As in the case of the Home Circuit, it is probable that lay justices in Middlesex
and London were also ordering executions despite the fact that felonies were supposed
to have been referred to the higher courts. Estimates for likely levels of such executions
in London and Middlesex, based on the adjustment already noted of the Home Circuit
figures in light of the records of the Devon Sessions, are given below along with the
aggregated figures, national estimates and projected modern equivalents.

other of the desired results was achieved.[25] It is incredible that anyone chose to endure this torment unto death rather than to plead, but some did; it is conceivable that they held out in order to protect their families from destitution, for to be executed in this way meant that the prisoner had not died a convicted felon, whose real property would have been forfeit to the Crown (the prisoner's 'moveables' were forfeit even under the *peine*) (Cockburn 1985, p. 72). According to the Home Circuit records at least 23 prisoners were killed in this manner during the two reigns, although this is a questionably low figure when compared with the 48 who, according to Cockburn, were ordered pressed to death at the Old Bailey in the same period (Cockburn 1985, p. 72 n. 135).[26]

According to the Gaol Delivery Register the figures for Middlesex were as follows. In the ten years from 6 James to 15 James, 6, 3, 6, 2, 1, 3, 5, 2, 1 and 3 people were pressed to death, a total of 32, and an annual average of 3·2. On the basis established above, these figures should be doubled to include the London jurisdictions, resulting in a total of 64 and an average of 6·4. The aggregate for deaths by the *peine* in Middlesex and London over the full period would be 416.

The *peine forte et dure* should properly be considered both a form of judicial torture and a method of execution.[27] But clearly it would not be wholly accurate to count those who otherwise died in prison – of natural causes – among the number executed. However, it is arguable that no death is the result of 'natural causes', or at least it cannot be known that a death is natural except in the context of a society which has achieved every possible condition for the prolongation of life. And even if to call a death 'premature' might be to engage the unfathomable metaphysics of a pre-destined span believed to have been allotted either to a given individual in particular or to humanity

---

[25]See Cockburn 1985, p. 72; but for a discussion of the distinction between the *peine* as a form of torture designed to extract a plea and a sentence imposed on conviction for refusing to plead, see Jeaffreson 1974, p. xix. Cf. n. 27 below.

[26]In fact, Jeaffreson's figures for the Old Bailey are higher than Cockburn suggests, but in any case I have resisted the temptation to adjust the Home Circuit figures to take account of the likely real level of executions by the *peine* that is suggested by comparison with the more reliable evidence of Jeaffreson's Middlesex hanging book, which I summarise immediately below.

[27]Cf. n. 25 above. According to Jeaffreson (1974, p. xix), the *peine* was certainly used in the later part of the seventeenth century as a form of torture designed to extract a plea as well as a sentence for 'standing mute' or failing to plead. The figures which I have given here for our period, based on Jeaffreson, are for convictions.

in general, it is nonetheless quite possible to establish under the conditions prevailing in given societies at given moments normal, or at least average, life expectancies. It is reasonable to assume that had they been at liberty, the deaths of those who succumbed in gaol to disease or starvation might not have occurred when they did, and in this sense are consequential upon the 'administration of justice' rather than on nature or destiny. As Cockburn puts it, '[g]aols in the early modern period were uniformly overcrowded and insanitary, and lengthy incarceration frequently proved the equivalent of a death sentence' (1985, p. 36). The so-called 'prison deaths' resulted mainly from what was known as 'gaol fever', which we call typhus; but deaths in gaol 'increased dramatically during periods of dearth' suggesting that malnutrition or starvation was also an important cause of penal fatality (Cockburn 1985, p. 36). In the scaled-up aggregate figures which I give below I have, of course, recorded 'prison deaths' separately from the totals for execution, but I have thought it appropriate to represent them nonetheless as numbers of people killed by the authorities.

Figures are available which indicate the number of those who died in prison on the Home Circuit in this way, as an indirect result of judicial process (see Cockburn 1985, pp. 145–71). They are as follows: Essex, 315 (including two suicides); Hertfordshire, 91; Kent, 243 (including three suicides), Surrey, 543 (one suicide), and Sussex 123 (including one suicide). In total, then, the records which survive count 1,315 men and women who died in prison on the Home Circuit between 1559 and 1625, of which at least 7 took their own lives.[28]

I am not aware of equivalent data to that of the Home Circuit for prison deaths in Middlesex or London. I have had therefore to derive estimated figures for these jurisdictions from likely equivalence with the Home Circuit. The ratio between the number of executions and

[28]With the exception of three who are unidentified, we know the names of all those who died in prison on the Home Circuit in the period. Indeed we know the names of a great many of the men and women the enumeration of whose deaths form the basis of the figures I am presenting. I cannot help comparing this with the fact of our knowledge of '162 real persons known to have attended playhouse performances' in 'Shakespeare's London' (see Gurr 1987, pp. xv and 191-204), and wondering about the different degrees of critical attention the two vastly disproportionate groups of 'real persons' have received ...

In two cases the Home Circuit records are annotated in ways which might indicate the social standing of the victims of prison death: one is marked 'gent.', another 'clerk'. We may assume that the rank of the other 1,313 who died was beneath notice.

the number of prison deaths on the Home Circuit is 1:0·52. I assume a similar ratio for Middlesex and for London. If this assumption is well-founded, then this would indicate that in addition to those who were executed by hanging or by the *peine*, a further 5,710·8 from Middlesex and London would have died in Newgate and the other metropolitan gaols during the period.[29]

I turn now to the estimation of national totals of deaths by hanging which resulted from sentencing in sessions, and, along with these figures, analogous estimates for executions by the *peine forte et dure* and for prison deaths will also be given. Although they are based on the detailed records which are available for the Home Circuit and for London and Middlesex, which I have discussed above, these must necessarily be calculated and estimated figures: equivalent data do not exist for the other English and Welsh circuits. The method adopted is that of calculating a figure for the remaining of English and Welsh circuits based on the data for the Home Circuit, and then adding to this the figures for London and Middlesex.

In order to estimate a total figure for the provincial jurisdictions it would seem appropriate, in view of the fact that that there were six English assize circuits and a further four in Wales, to multiply the Home Circuit figures by a factor of ten. However, even without the aid of anything like realistic demographic modelling or a scientific sociology of early modern penal victimisation, it is clear that such a multiplication would seriously inflate the figures. The Home Circuit was the most populous and wealthiest of the English circuits; the population of Wales was disproportionately tiny in comparison with that of England. In line therefore with the mathematical caution which I discuss below, I have in fact first derived a figure for England and then added to this a total figure for Wales based on the comparative sizes of their respective populations. To obtain a figure for England it would seem reasonable to multiply the Home Circuit figures by a factor of six as there were six English circuits in all. I have in fact multiplied by a factor of four: this is an arbitrary figure (although demographically reasonable), but certainly a cautious one, well below that suggested by the administrative form of the organisation of the

[29]The calculation is as follows. 2,518 executions on the Home Circuit (including those ordered by JP.s) stand in a ratio of 1:0·52 to 1,315 prison deaths. If the number of hangings in Middlesex and London (including the equivalent adjustment) is 10,982·4 (see below for the derivation of this figure), then the number of prison deaths – assuming a similar ratio – is 5,710·85.

assizes. The result of this calculation is as follows: if, as I have shown above, there were in the period 2,518 hangings on the Home Circuit (or an average of 38·7 each year), in the whole of provincial England there would have been 10,072 (or 154·95 each year). However, if the estimates given above for executions ordered by justices sitting in quarter sessions are to be trusted, this figure must be adjusted accordingly and becomes 12,086 for the period or 185·94 annually. A similar multiplication of the Home Circuit figures for executions by the *peine forte et dure* and for prison deaths, gives an estimated total of these kinds of fatalities for the English provincial circuits as a whole of 92 (or 1·41 each year) for the *peine* and 5,260 (80·92 annually) for deaths in prison.

The figures for Wales, which should be added to these totals, are based on D. C. Coleman's estimation of the populations of England and Wales in 1545 as 2·8 million and 0·25 million respectively (see Coleman 1977, p. 12). In other words, the population of the principality is 8·93 *per cent* of that of England. Assuming a similar statistical relation between population size and number of executions suggests a figure for executions in Wales during the period which is equivalent to that percentage of the English figure, i.e. 1,079·28 (or 16·60 on average each year).[30] The Welsh figures for deaths by the *peine* and for prison deaths have been derived from the estimated English figures in the same way. They are 8·21 deaths by pressing (or 0·13 on average each year), and 469·72 deaths in prison (7·23 each year).

The aggregate figures for the provincial circuits of England and Wales together which result from these calculations are as follows. During the whole period at least 13,165 people were put to death by hanging, 100·21 by the *peine*, and at least 5,729·72 died in prison. The average annual figures for each of these classes of fatality is 202·4, 1·54 and 88·15.

To these must be added the figures for Middlesex and for London. I have discussed the methods by which these were derived above; here it suffices to give them in summary form. It is estimated that in Middlesex at least 4,576 people were executed by hanging during the period, or, 70·4 on average each year. If, however, these figures are adjusted, on the basis noted earlier, to include likely numbers of

---

[30]These are the *adjusted* figures, taking account, according to the previously-stated principle, of likely numbers of executions ordered by Justices of the Peace: the estimates for the Assizes alone are one fifth lower, or 899·43 and 13·83 respectively.

executions ordered by lay justices, the resulting totals for the jurisdiction are 5,491·2 hanged over the entire period, or 84·48 on average every year. I have estimated that a further 208 men and women were executed by the *peine* in Middlesex (or 3·2 each year), while 2,855·4 (or 45·93 annually) died in gaol. Following Jeaffreson's suggestion, noted above, that numbers of executions in London may be conservatively estimated as equal to those of the metropolitan county, the figures which I have just given may be doubled in order to obtain aggregates for London and Middlesex together, i.e. at least 10,982·4 hangings during the whole period (or 168·96) each year, 416 executions by the *peine* (or 6·4 each year), and a further 5,710·8 (or 87·86 people annually) dying in prison.

Finally, estimated national totals for England and Wales including London and Middlesex are given by the addition of these aggregates. The resulting figures are as follows: 24,147·4 men and women hanged; 516·21 pressed to death, and 11,440·52 dead in gaol; or, on average at least 371·5 were put to death by hanging, 7·94 were killed by the *peine forte et dure* and a further 176 probably died in gaol in each and every one of the 65 years of the reigns of Elizabeth and James.

To give a sense of the extent of the slaughter[31] it is perhaps worth scaling these figures up to modern-day equivalents. One way in which this can be done is by a comparative analysis of population.[32] The early modern population of England and Wales, estimated by Coleman (1977, p.12) to be 4·085 million at the arbitrary but more or less mean date of 1603, is related to the modern population of England and Wales, which on 30 June 1989 stood at 50,562,000, in a ratio of 1:12·38 (See HMSO 1990, p.49). Multiplying the early modern figures for execution and related deaths accordingly would mean that if a similar proportion of the present day population were put to

---

[31] I have tried in this section of this paper not to allow the language to become too heightened. But the process of gleaning, extrapolating, adjusting and aggregating these figures – before even beginning to assess interpretatively their likely underestimation of the real scale of executions, (and still less to account for *that*) – was extremely unpleasant, and one which I found, moreover, morally and politically uneasy, especially in view of the ghastly irony of the fact that the higher the eventual figure proved, the stronger the overall case argued by this paper became. The counting often seemed more part of the problem than part of the answer, and it was only possible to do this work for short periods of time before the revulsion became too much. It was not possible to forget – which is what numbers often help us to do – that it is the untimely extinction of real lives which is enumerated in these figures.

[32] Although see n. 34 below.

death, at least 4,599·17 people on average would be executed as convicted felons each year, a further 98·29 would be pressed to death without plea, and 2,178·88 would die in gaol. A similar 'calculation' can be made for the modern United States.[33] The resulting figures are these: 22,383·88 executions by hanging each year, 478.39 executions by the *peine*, and 10,604 prison deaths.[34]

These figures, whether evidential or projected, are horrendous. But there are three kinds of reason for believing that they are radical underestimations of the numbers of people actually put to death, and that the aggregate figures should be very much higher than those given here (and might have been, as we shall see, even higher again). In the first place there are technical reasons to do with the nature of the records drawn on, their original quality and the state in which they have survived, along with methodological factors connected with the way in which I have selected and treated the extant figures, which

[33]The population of the USA is estimated at 246,113,000 on 30 June 1988 (see HMSO 1990, p. 49). The estimated early modern population stands in relation to this figure at a ratio of 1:60·25. The figures for executions by hanging and by the *peine*, and those for prison deaths have therefore been multiplied by a factor of 60·25 to yield the figures given.

[34]I am no more a statistical demographer than I am an anthropologist. These modern equivalent figures are in no sense meant to represent a scientifically accurate extrapolation based on a serious comparative analysis of demographic and social structure from the early modern population of England and Wales to the present-day populations. They are meant as an indicator of the scale rather than the number of the deaths. If the scaling up of the Home Circuit, Middlesex and London figures to aggregates for England and Wales in the sixteenth and seventeenth centuries is already speculative (given that where statistics survive from the period there are no reliable ones, and that there were in any case no national totals recorded in the period, whether trustworthy or otherwise), still less can mere multiplication provide a reliable value for the equivalent modern number of executions to those carried out in Elizabethan and Stuart England and Wales. Strictly speaking the results are no more than what they appear to be: the values achieved when the calculated period aggregates are multiplied in the same ratio as that which relates the modern population(s) to the population then. But *as an indicator*, as a suggestion of how many of the modern population would have to be killed in order to correspond to the equivalent proportion of the period population who *were* being killed each year, they are chilling, radical underestimates as they are.

Perhaps more appropriate figures would be produced not by a comparative analysis of population, but by one of crime and punishment. I leave it to the reader to estimate how many people would have to be killed in modern Britain (or in the USA, which has an annual murder rate of over 25,000) if we sought to execute everyone convicted of crimes more serious than the theft of goods worth the equivalent of 12 pence.

suggest that the real values were significantly greater than those recorded. Secondly, consideration of the county assizes and the Middlesex sessions (with their equivalents in the city of London) by no means exhausts the judicial, para-judicial, summary and other means by which the state could and did dispose of its subjects. And thirdly, if one wishes to assess not only the figures but the violence they articulate, it is important to remember that the documents only record – with whatever degree of accuracy or error – those whom the state was *successful* in killing, as distinct from those it failed to apprehend, try, convict and execute, or otherwise destroy.

Regarding the first of these matters, two kinds of consideration are important – the nature and quality of the original records, and their condition when analysed by modern scholars. The documents from which the figures for the county assizes are drawn are largely the bills of indictment rather than full records of the outcome of trials, and these bills were not consistently annotated with that information.[35] The most reliable accounts of actual executions are not the records of indictment but the so-called 'hanging books'. These, however, have only survived (or perhaps were only originally kept) haphazardly. As far as the Home Circuit is concerned, there are no hanging books from before 1650, well after our period, and for Middlesex the hanging books are of variable reliability, as we have seen. The cause or gaol books, which also recorded the actual disposition of cases in a more systematic way than the bills of indictment did or were designed to, are also fragmentary or missing. Thus even if the available assize records were to have been perfectly kept and perfectly preserved they were not necessarily designed to yield the sort of information I am requiring of them. The lack, particularly in the early part of the period, of a clear jurisdictional division between the assize judges and the Justices of the Peace, who continued dealing with felonies although these were strictly issues for the judges, also results in the assize records being a necessarily incomplete account of capital offences and their punishment within the overall jurisdiction of these courts (cf. above, where I have had to estimate a quotient for executions ordered by the justices, based on the exceptional Devon records). Or again, the fact

[35]In fact the Home Circuit documents are what Cockburn calls 'composite files' (1985, p.12) in as much as they contain other documents besides indictments; the general point I am making here – that they are nonetheless not the direct and full record of sentences and executions as such – holds good.

that the indictments of those allowed benefit of clergy were returned to the Court of King's Bench at Westminster and that the assize documents bear scant or no information about what became of these prisoners and of others who were referred from the provincial to the superior courts, would be a further example of the way in which the records of the assizes, even where they have survived in perfect condition, are of necessity incomplete records even of the number of indictments for felonies on the circuits, let alone the number of convictions and subsequent executions.[36] But of course the records were not kept perfectly. The value of the figures which Jeaffreson draws from the Middlesex hanging book in James's reign depends, for example, precisely on the contrast between the apparent assiduity of the clerk who kept it during the ten years cited and the very inadequate record-keeping of his immediate predecessor and successor. There is other evidence of similarly inefficient and incoherent initial compilation and maintenance of the Home Circuit files.

And if the records were not originally kept well, neither have they survived intact. The assizes being essentially itinerant courts meant that records were often not stored consistently in one place, and were subjected to all sorts of accidental loss and damage. Even where the relatively full records of the Home Circuit are concerned, Cockburn reports that 'There are no records for Hertfordshire before 1573; but from 1605 the run for that county is complete. Conversely, records for Kent and Sussex, which are substantially complete for much of Elizabeth's reign, are fragmentary in the 17th century' (1985, pp. 11–12). And even where there are good sequences of records there are nonetheless missing indictments. The fullest series are for Essex and Surrey, but even these have lost – 'the records of over thirty assizes are totally missing' (Cockburn 1985, p. 12) – or damaged files. And so on. For a host of reasons to do with the nature of the original documents and the vicissitudes of their subsequent treatment, there is every ground for believing them to be a very incomplete record of what must actually have taken place, and one yielding figures which are much below the real values.

The same general pattern holds true for the Middlesex records.

[36]To a certain extent Cockburn has been able to supply this kind of deficiency by resort to the records of King's Bench (see Cockburn 1985, p. 12), but the degree to which this procedure remedies the gaps in the assize records remains incalculable in as much as the Westminster records are also both imperfect and incomplete.

Not only do they seem to have been kept with variable accuracy in the first place, but they too suffer from what Cockburn refers to in the Home Circuit records as 'concealed deficiences': in other words, they do not always even attempt to record what they purport to, and nor were they necessarily designed to record the information which I am now seeking to derive from them. And by the same token, they too have been subject to varying degrees of material damage – in some instances quite extensive – both in the period and subsequently.

But if the documents themselves are less than a full record, I have nonetheless treated them as if they were perfect. That is to say that I have not – except in the specific controlled instance noted above[37] – sought by selection, speculation or calculation to build into my fig-ures any amount designed to compensate for their incompleteness. This in turn is part of a more general methodological principle by which I have been careful at every stage in my choice of data and subsequent arithmetical or statistical treatment of the figures to underestimate rather than risk exaggerating the numerical values involved. Precisely because it is part of my wider argument to show how great the extent of coercive violence was, I have thought it appropriate at every point to be as conservative as possible in my empirical procedures and in my methods of inference both from the data and from the palpable inadequacy of the data. In selecting values where variant figures are available, I have chosen the lower or lowest quanta; when calculating arithmetically, or projecting statistically, from the empirical calculations, I have rounded results down rather than up, and chosen methods of calculation which tend to err in the direction of low rather than high sums. Both where mathematical procedures, and methodological operation based on the nature and quality of the records are concerned, I have been careful throughout to give 'the Age of Shakespeare', that high point of English 'culture', the maximum benefit of the doubt.

The second set of reasons for regarding the overall numbers of executions presented here as dramatically fewer than the actual figure, relates to the choice of assize records as the basis for these aggre-gates. It is a choice which although it has its reasons, as I shall show below, nonetheless leads of itself to a very restricted account of penal executions. Although the assizes were the principal instruments of

[37]I.e. the use of the evidence of the Middlesex Gaol Delivery Register rather than that of the general sessional rolls (see above p. 172).

judicial intervention in the counties of England and Wales outside London and Middlesex, it is by no means the case that the royal justices sitting on assize benches yet retained in this period a monopoly on ordering the use of the rope. I have mentioned above, and included in my estimated figures an allowance for, the overlapping jurisdiction over felons of the quarter sessions which continued to be exercised despite the policy of restricting felony trials to the assizes. But beyond this there are a number of other kinds of jurisdictions which either competed with or duplicated that of the assize circuits. Overlapping with the Oxford circuit was the jurisdiction of the Council in the Marches, to which commissions of oyer and terminer and gaol delivery were also issued. Similarly, the jurisdiction of organs of conciliar goverment overlaid that of the assizes on the Northern Circuit, where a very complex judicial hierarchy under the Council of the North makes it difficult now to disentangle the precise role of the assize judges, particularly after the union of the English and Scottish crowns in 1603. There were also a number of other important judicial franchises which continued to retain some independence from the assize system even when they may have duplicated it. The Bishop of Ely, for example, maintained a franchise – and a gaol – on the Isle of Ely, appointing his own Chief Justice, and issuing his own commissions; and in a similar way the county palatine of Chester had been a 'jurisdictional enclave' (Cockburn 1975, p. 38) throughout the Middle Ages, also with its own Chief Justice, who was nonetheless a royal nominee. In addition to these major franchises and others like them, there was also a host of other ecclesiastical, municipal and other local jurisdictions – especially for gaol delivery – which even if they tended over the period to be brought, in reality or in name, within the assize system, nonetheless represent a further power to punish, which was doubtless exercised, beyond that which has been included in the present calculations.[38]

But even beyond the purview of the assizes, that of the competing jurisdictions in the provincial counties, and that of the equivalent courts in London and Middlesex, there were a number of other forms of judicial and quasi-judicial jurisdiction which were also busily hanging people throughout the period, but of which I have also taken

[38]For the information given here and further details of the multiplicity of jurisdictions beyond that of the assizes, and the complexity of the relations among them, see Cockburn 1975, pp. 23-48 and *passim*.

no notice in this essay. No account has been taken of the myriad special commissions of oyer and terminer which were empowered, outside the regular sessions, to deal with particular outbreaks of so-called disorder, and which put to death anyone from participants in gatherings deemed to be unlawful protests or riots, through to the likes of participants in Essex's rebellion. Nor have I taken any account of the frequent occasions on which martial law was declared with the consequent – undeniably summary – execution of yet further numbers of the population.[39] I have given no place in these calculations to the criminal trials in the higher courts at Westminster such as King's Bench (except to the small extent that these records supplement those of the Home Circuit; see above n. 36). And, finally, I have in particular excluded from consideration the religious and political trials, mainly conducted at the centre, whether the big state trials of notorious rebels and traitors, or the more routine but nonetheless political trials of less prominent opponents or alleged opponents of the regime, which were conducted in the Westminster courts and elsewhere.[40]

Taking into account, then, the variety of other jurisdictions beyond that of the assize courts – not to mention the summary disposal of opponents of the regime by para- or extra-judicial means – it is clear that the data yielded by the records of the assizes and their equivalents in London and Middlesex represent only a proportion of the number of those who were hanged in the period concerned, even if

[39]For a discussion of martial law in the Tudor period see Bellamy 1979, pp. 228-35.

[40]In contrasting the 'routine' character of the hangings ordered by assize courts with the more spectacular trials and executions at the centre, it is important nonetheless to avoid two erroneous implications. It is no part of my argument to suggest that these deaths were less central: on the contrary. Nor is it to allow that the 'administration of justice' is somehow neutral, where a show trial or a martial law execution is clearly 'political': again, on the contrary. The claim that the ordinary work of the judicial apparatus is not political is a mystification which has served successive regimes well. At a very fundamental level, routine administration of justice daily promulgates and reinforces dominant ideologies, protects the existing social structure (its property relations especially), and either subordinates or eliminates those who fail or refuse to serve or satisfy its values and norms of behaviour. And as for the Elizabethan and Stuart assize courts in particular, there is no doubt that they were an integral part not only of the transmission and enforcement in the provincial counties of state policy (and not only in judicial matters but across the board of governmental policy) but that they were also sites – I say this at the risk of appearing to concede something of the argument I am opposing – of the spectacular display and practice of the power of the state, and in particular the monarch, whose agents the judges were and whose supremacy they represented. The assize judges gathered in Star Chamber before they left for the circuits and were 'charged' with the task not only of carrying out their judicial

we were to suppose that they were perfect figures in themselves, which, as I have already shown, they were not.[41] In the light, then, both of the imperfections of the records and the extent to which the assize jurisdiction is itself limited in these various ways, it is clear that the figures given above – those derived directly from the surviving documents, as well as the aggregates and projections generated from them – must fall very far short of the likely actual totals of people hanged or otherwise put to death by the authorities. In other words, in working exclusively on the assize records one is in fact looking at an imperfect record of what was, when compared with the probable if finally unquantifiable whole, an in any case restricted means by which the killing was done.

But there is a third dimension to what is in fact the relative modesty of the figures I have adduced from the assize records and those of the equivalent metropolitan courts, a third class of reasons for thinking that even if it were possible to obtain perfect information about the actual incidence of all executions, such a total would itself markedly underestimate the scale and intensity of what would be involved in trying to assess the general violence of the 'culture'. My subject is, after all, violence and not merely punishment. In any case, there is evidence which suggests that even the figures we have seen so far represent but a fraction of the whole when compared with what the scale of the killing would have been had what we might call – borrowing or altering a phrase from Foucault – 'the will to punish' operated absolutely unimpeded. Ranging from examples of leniency in effecting prosecutions and determining sentences, through corruption and inefficiency in the processes of arrest and incarceration, to overt or subtle resistance, a number of factors indicate willed or accidental limitations on the effectivity of a power which would have been even more devastating in its effects if these limitations had not affected it.

---

commissions but also of conveying and reinforcing current policy at large. On arrival in the counties they convened – with, indeed, some display of authority – the great and the good of the locality and in turn charged them with the responsibility of the government of the place according to how the state was currently defining this task. And then set about hanging the less great and the less good. For an account of the political and governmental function of the assize judges see Cockburn 1972, pp. 1-11; and for another account, particularly of the coercive spectacle of the convocation of a session of assize, see Fletcher and Stevenson 1985, p. 21.

In the light of what we have already seen in the figures, it sounds startling, on the first of these counts, to say that there seems to have been a certain leniency in the operation of the courts, especially when assize proceedings seem to have fallen very far short of the standards of probity and fairness which, it is often held, characterise modern-day courts: hearings were conducted at great speed,[42] the accused had no defence counsel,[43] and the entire conduct of the trial was dominated by judges who often made no pretence of impartiality or detachment, as a matter of common practice hectoring, brow-beating and intimidating witnesses and jurors alike, and frequently unambiguously instructing both in what they, the judges, wanted to hear and having no truck with alternative testimony or verdicts (see Cockburn 1972, p. 122 and *passim*; 1985, pp. 70, 112 and *passim*). But nonetheless circuit judges were often criticised in the counties for their leniency, especially, it seems, by local magistrates who 'failed to comprehend the sterility of a system which in practice allowed no meaningful punishment short of death'.[44] Even if the evidential value of such views needs to be treated with a certain scepticism (then as now the local lay benches were composed of people not themselves noted for their liberal views, people predisposed to find any level of judicial ferocity wanting), it is nonetheless possible for the modern commentator to remark with some conviction that 'Judicial conduct in routine trials on circuit ... was ... often distinguished by an independence and humanity noticeably absent in political trials at Westminster' (Cockburn 1972, p. 125).

One area in particular in which the judges of assize were noted,

[41] What relation the assize data bears to the likely whole is difficult to estimate without conducting the equivalent research – in so far as records exist – for the other formal and informal jurisdictions, research which, for the reasons given, I have excluded from this study. My *impression* is that this built-in underestimation would be considerable.

[42] Cockburn notes that courts on the Home Circuit 'dealt with an average of between ten and twenty cases a day...and as many as forty cases a day during some periods' and that 'routine trials probably averaged between fifteen and twenty minutes each' (1985, p. 110). There was also 'little, if any, time for jury deliberations', not least because the practice of multiple arraignment and verdict meant that as many as fifteen prisoners were considered together *(ibid.)*.

[43] ' ... the accused commonly had no counsel, no notice of the evidence against him, and no opportunity to frame his defence' (Cockburn 1972, p. 122).

[44] Cockburn 1972, p. 132; see also here and *passim* on the leniency of trial judges. He also gives the tariff: 'In cases of capital felony the penalty prescribed by law was hanging. Men sentenced for petty treason were drawn upon a hurdle to the place of

both at the time and subsequently, for leniency was that of the granting of benefit of clergy.[45] Originally the *privelegium clericale* had exempted clerks in holy orders from criminal trial before secular judges, but eventually it was extended to all male felons who could establish their clerical status by showing themselves able to read the 'neck verse', traditionally the first or fourteenth verse of Psalm 51. Felons so allowed their clergy were branded on the thumb as a sign that it had been granted. There is evidence that 'judges usually interpreted the literacy test leniently, helped the prisoner, condoned prompting or allowed the plea on compassionate grounds' (Cockburn 1985, p. 119). And if 'official criticism' of judicial latitude in granting benefit of clergy seems to have resulted in judges 'temporarily abandoning their liberal attitude', particularly to granting clergy a second time, after about 1589 (p. 120), the general point holds good: judges exercised large measures of discretion in granting the benefit, if only, as Cockburn puts it, 'in order to establish control over the application of the death penalty' (p. 121).[46] Women were not allowed benefit of clergy fully until 1693, although a partial form of the privilege was allowed from 1623. They could, however, claim 'benefit of belly' (see Cockburn 1985, pp. 121–3). A woman claiming that she was pregnant was examined by a panel of twelve matrons and if she was found to be 'quick' with child, the death sentence was automatically stayed. In theory the felon should have been hanged after giving birth, but in practice she was often imprisoned at the judge's discretion, or simply released. There is evidence that the rules governing benefit of

---

execution and then hanged; male high-traitors were in addition disembowelled, beheaded and quartered. Women convicted of either high or petty treason were burned'. He continues, 'Judges had no power to vary the form of those punishments, but the executive ... could order additional or aggravated penalties where the offence was considered to be particularly heinous' (1985, p. 124).

[45]See Cockburn 1985, pp. 117-21; Jeaffreson 1972, pp. xxxiii-xxxviii.

[46]It should be pointed out that the grant of benefit of clergy did not mean getting off, apart from the branding, scot-free. For a brief period in the reign of Edward VI felons who successfully pleaded their clergy were *enslaved*, either for one year or for five depending on the precise form allowed (Jeaffreson 1972, p. xxxvi). And as benefit of clergy strictly speaking exempted clerks only from secular judgement, felons so allowed were handed over – in the early part of our period, until 1576 – to the jurisdiction of the bishop with, in the case of those granted benefit 'without power of making purgation', the expectation of 'no brighter prospect than that of remaining in prison to the end of [their] days'. Jeaffreson continues dryly, 'there is no reason for thinking the discipline of a bishop's prison milder than the discipline of a secular gaol' (*ibid.*).

pregnancy were sometimes manipulated to defend the women from execution. There seem to have been some remarkably extended preganciees, for example, and often women claiming pregnancy were remanded to the next assizes for examination, with the clear implication that if they were not already pregnant, they should take steps to see that they were by then.

If 'leniency' played a limiting part,[47] so too did inefficiency and corruption, the as it were 'accidental' failure of the system to do its worst. It is impossible to know with any certainty how many 'offenders' were either not apprehended or not brought to trial, but at least one magistrate, Edward Hext, a Justice of the Peace in Somerset 'thought in 1596 that eighty per cent of all offenders evaded trial', a figure which Cockburn, on the basis of modern statistics, finds 'not implausible' (1985, p. 89), and there was considerable contemporary comment on the ineffectiveness and even the complicity of local constables (pp. 89–90). Prisons were notoriously insecure – 150 escapes are recorded in the files of the Home Circuit alone (p. 37), and the real figure must have been, as usual, considerably higher – and gaolers were not always noted for high levels of dedication to their calling (pp. 37–42).

Leniency and inefficiency might be regarded from within certain sociological and anthropological perspectives as disfunctions inherent to the power system itself. But resisting arrest and gaol-breaking surely represent active efforts on the part of the system's victims to contest or at least to resist the power of the judicial and 'police' machinery. And these should not be allowed, because more dramatic, to obscure in turn more subtle but probably more widespread resist-

[47]Not only does it go against the grain of my prejudices (although the analysis demands it at this point) to seek out instances of leniency on the part of the judges of assize (as distinct from members of the local community), but the concept itself may be a very loose one. Benefit of clergy and of pregancy were, after all, statutory rights (reflecting or resulting from whatever earlier social and political struggles) and not in themselves acts of mercy; mitigation by reason of insanity (concerning which I have at present no information from the period) was also not in itself discretionary, even if its actual application may have involved some such. In general judges had wide powers to reprieve but not to pardon. It seems that judge-granted reprieves were issued very largely in instances where a royal pardon was in any case already likely. Not all reprieved or pardoned felons were released; some were conscripted into the army, others were condemned to service in the galleys (see Cockburn 1985, pp. 126–7). Analysis suggests that the granting of benefits and other reprieves may not have stemmed from the humanity of the judges so much as from a desire to assert their control over sentencing policy, less a mitigation of the will to punish than a component part of it.

ance which was indirect and recalcitrant in form. There are strong indications of local behaviour designed to impede or mitigate the process. Evidence of a 'general unwillingness to prosecute crime' (Cockburn 1985, p. 90), and in particular reluctance 'to hazard a suspect's life by accusing him of a felony' (p. 91), can be laid alongside unwillingness to convict: juries would name imaginary killers in order to protect real people who might otherwise have been indicted or convicted (Cockburn 1985, p. 113); they would value stolen goods which were manifestly more costly at less than the statutory value of 12 pence in order to convert grand larceny, which was a capital offence, into petty larceny which was not;[48] they would return partial verdicts (Cockburn 1985, p. 115); or they would simply ignore the judge – and often, doubtless, the facts of the case – and return reduced verdicts or acquittals, sometimes at the risk of themselves being committed to Star Chamber in London by the thwarted judge of assize whose instruction they had flouted and whose authority they had defied (see p. 71). In general it is possible to speak of 'the independent line habitually taken by trial jurors attempting to save felons from the gallows' (Cockburn 1972, p. 113).

In considering this third class of reasons for distrusting the figures given above as an accurate account of the actual levels of violence offered, it is, of course, impossible to gauge what the effects would have been of a 'will to punish' which had not been mitigated in these and in similar ways. But we can be certain that without these limitations many more people than we can even begin to know about on evidential grounds would have died on the gallows in early modern England and Wales. The data we do have, whatever the level of their intrinsic accuracy or imperfection, record, badly or well, not the pure operation of power but result from the dialectical relation between the coercive violence of the authorities on the one hand, and the various forces which attempt to oppose, block or mitigate that violence on the other. The general problem with empirical computation of the kind ventured above, is always, of course, that it tends to reveal nothing of the social forces whose contestation results in the effects such enumeration describes. Behind the arithmetic is a dialectic of

[48]See Cockburn 1985, p. 116, according to whom there is evidence of confusion in the minds of both jurors and trial judges about the level of value at which petty larceny became capital; Jeaffreson (1972, p. xxxi) is more categorical. In any case, the substantive point that stolen goods were deliberately undervalued in order to protect defendants from the rope holds good.

conflict: the figures given are the result not of a *unitary* historical process, but of what can only be imperfectly labelled a 'will to punish' as it has been modified by coming up against, not just its 'own' disfunctions but also, and most importantly, whatever and whoever resisted the ideological authority and the physical capacity of the state to do violence to its subjects.

V

The tradition of the oppressed teaches us that the 'state of emergency' in which we live is not the exception but the rule. We must attain to a conception of history that is in keeping with this insight.

Walter Benjamin, 'Theses on the Philosophy of History'

In defence of property and the established social order the Elizabethan and Jacobean crown killed huge numbers of the people of England. Their names not wholly unknown, the circumstances of their demise often recorded, the sheer number of them estimable, men, women and children in 'Shakespeare's England' were strung up on permanent or makeshift gallows by a hempen noose. Sometimes the spinal chord was snapped at once; or they hung by their necks until they suffocated or drowned; until their brains died of hypoxeia, or until the shock killed them. Pissing and shitting themselves. Bleeding from their eyes. Thinking.

Or they were crushed under slabs of stone and iron. Or they 'took their own lives', as the exculpatory phrase has it. Or they became just 'prison deaths'.

But nothing of this is dramatised in *Titus Andronicus*. The relationship between the text and the 'quiet', steady slaughter of the people by hanging is not one of ostentation but occlusion. The play does make violence, extravagant violence, the centre of its, and our, attention, but the graphic violence of the drama serves to direct attention away from, rather than towards, the elimination of huge numbers of the population. For the barbarisms so spectacularly performed by the play are nothing like the common violence of the times. I make no comment on the real incidence of cannibalism in early modern England, only on the diversionary effect of such a practice being foregrounded in *Titus Andronicus* at the expense of the representation of a systematic violence which is recoverable but which is thus occluded. Indeed, one might be forgiven for thinking that *Titus Andronicus* is organised around this very occlusion. So extravagant and so insistent is the violence of the play, for which of course it has been dismissed by criticism, that even without attempting to bring to light the material it occludes, an analysis based on the idea that it 'has something to hide' would seem almost to suggest itself.

It is the anthropology of *Titus Andronicus* that plays the main part in organising this occlusion: the 'othering' structure of its categorial and topographical anthropology of civility and barbarism locates significant violence in another time, in another place, among other people. I noted above the way in which the Shakespearean anthropology simplified the structuration of otherness (n. 4). It is now important to see how the oversimplification serves the occlusion I am discussing: the clear and simple expulsion of the savage beyond the limits of the civil seeks to locate safely 'out there' the violence which it codes as barbarism but which may in fact belong dangerously 'in here'. But in making violence into the spectacle of the exotic, it serves in a curious way also to domesticate that violence, or at least to render violence – in a manner which New Historicism will later 'remember' – *merely* theatrical. No one alive in early modern England could fully have *believed* that the location of violence was elsewhere, but we know that ideology – perhaps especially when deployed in the form of 'cultural performance' – works in mysterious but effective ways.

The occlusion at work in *Titus Andronicus* – to return to the strange episode of the Clown which precipitated these reflections on occluded violence in the first place – is, however, both subtle and complex. For example, I myself was led to investigate systematic execution by an uncanny moment in the play itself, by the odd flatness of the incident's intrusion into its otherwise extravagant decorum. It is an incident which lies at the unnoticed margins of the cultural text: the play has its guilty secret, *which it keeps*. Certainly it keeps very quiet compared with what an analysis which prioritises spectacular display would expect. But the incident is, of course, nonetheless 'there'. And just as no repression disappears 'without trace', so the occlusion of the violence marks the text from which it is excluded. The episode is a marginalised 'representation' which but barely represents, an articulation which disarticulates, leaving everything unsaid when viewed in the light of what I have demonstrated above as the actual incidence, both in extent and intensity, of death by hanging among the ludic rustics and non-elite clowns of early modern England and Wales – the real dead. It suggests in this way that the achievement of occlusion depends, thus, on an inherently complex form of representation which does not entail a simple suppression of the occluded material. It could be argued, for example, that Shakespeare does not so much obscure as frequently acknowledge – in examples like the hanging of Cordelia in *Lear* – the killing of the people.[49] But this only seems to me to be clear from a certain, rather specific, class perspective. The death, by hanging, of aristocrats like Cordelia – sentimentalised as 'my poor fool' – is represented as tragic, and with appropriate affect. The deaths of some plebeian figures are poignant on condition that they form part of the aristocratic story: the hanging of Bardolph, at which the king nods, is part of Henry's 'tragedy' and only barely part of Bardolph's – 'comic' – narrative. But the lack of affect associated with the demise of the Clown in *Titus Andronicus* makes it casual, more like the reference to the 'gallows-maker' whose 'frame outlives a thousand tenants' in the gravedigger's scene in *Hamlet* (V.i.43–4), part of the routine, 'natural' landscape and lifescape of the poor. And we have noticed how the discrepancy among the class idioms involved contributes to the sense in which *Titus Andronicus* has comedic effects, and is not, in that guise, as 'flattened' as all that. But if hanging is 'addressed', as in the episode of the execution of the Clown in a sense it is, it is nonetheless impossible to claim that because this play glancingly dispatches a minor character in this way – uncanny as the episode itself is – it therefore does not occlude the massive social, historical and political phenomenon of the execution by hanging of huge numbers of the common people, even although the play is otherwise so massively 'centred' in the extravagant, 'exotic' violences that it actually does foreground. And still less does the 'culture' in which this play, and 'Shakespeare' as a whole, has been subsequently embedded, address this and similar material. On the contrary, this glancing attention – which is in turn quite distinct from theatrical display – is the very form of the occlusion. To be sure occlusion does not entail a complete erasure of death by hanging; rather it puts death by hanging 'under erasure'. Not exactly hidden, it is more naturalised and exscribed at the

---

[49] I am particularly indebted to Jonathan White for his interrogation of this point.

same time.

This sense of the intricacy of occlusion is particularly important if we consider that there are ways, for example, in which what I have called above the 'structural anthropology' of *Titus Andronicus* is in the practice of the drama unable to function. Indeed, in a fuller reading of the play – if that were an objective – it would be important to take seriously the complexity of the way in which the categorial structure of barbarism and civility, as well as the boundaries established by their symbolic and topographical distribution, are unable always to be sustained. Consider these three examples. It is Rome – not the barbarian, Gothic exterior – which Titus describes, in a language redolent of the play's anthropology, as 'a wilderness of tigers' (III. i. 54). Or when the purging resolution comes, or at least when something like order is restored at the end, it comes only partly out of the Roman tradition, but more mainly from a source and a place which, according to the structure of anthropology, is entirely inappropriate: from Gothic barbarity. Lucius, Titus's son, flees the city, allies himself with the enemy and enters Rome triumphant but at the head of a *Gothic* army.[50] Or, in the central act of the eating of human flesh, what is to be made of the fact that Titus cooks Tamora's sons but does not eat; while Tamora eats but does not *know* what she eats? Who, in such circumstances, is the cannibal, and where, in such circumstances, is the line between civilisation and barbarism? In each case – and there are many others – there seems to be a transgression of the line which demarcates the boundary between the civil and the savage. It is often a line which can, throughout the play, be drawn, but not, it seems, held.

But also it is worth remembering the insistence of Mary Douglas – whose work provides so much of our sense of the importance of anthropological limits – that boundaries have to be symbolically crossed *in order* to act effectively as cultural demarcations. Indeed, according to Douglas, order, and even the limits of culture 'as such', may be not only confirmed by their being transgressed, as a fashionable word has it, but may even be *produced* in the passage. Dirt is necessary to a clean place, and to the idea of cleanliness. Thus, if the civil and the savage in *Titus Andronicus* seem to be at times in the wrong places, and the line between those places is confused, the sense of the wrongness involved in the confusion is not always itself confused. This is so even if these

[50] I am grateful to Maurizio Calbi, my colleague in the Essex Early Modern Research Group, for alerting me to this aspect of the text.

signs of the limits of the civilised and the human are all transgressed or negated, as, in fact, they are. The prohibition on eating human flesh is contravened, and in general – apart perhaps from the transgression of the incest taboo – there seems little that is prohibited which does not in fact occur at the other, barbarous, extreme.[51] But this is, again, how the occlusion works: the exoticisation of significant violence depends upon the affirmation, in however remarkably complex forms, of the difference between the indigent and the strange, which occurs both when the line is firmly drawn, and when it is crossed or blurred, and even if sometimes it is unsettled altogether.

I am suggesting that even when violence is shown it is occluded, and that occlusion is more than a mere lack of ostentation. This raises questions about the politics of representation in the given play *Titus Andronicus*, in Shakespeare's *oeuvre* more widely, and in the Elizabethan and Jacobean theatre as a whole, questions in particular of the extent to which the theatre either underwrites the signifying practices of the dominant culture (and by way of that the political and social power of the dominant, as well as its cultural authority), or alternatively unsettles such structures and institutions by transgressing,

---

[51]Hulme comments in these terms on the marginal character of the eating of human flesh: 'Human beings who eat other human beings have always been placed on the very borders of humanity. They are not regarded as *in*human because if they were animals their behaviour would be natural and could not cause the outrage and fear that "cannibalism" has always provoked' (1986, p. 14).

On the matter of incest compare Levi-Strauss's claim that the prohibition on incest is the one universal taboo: in *Titus Andronicus* there is certainly no overtly incestuous sexuality in the form of a sexual act committed, although Elizabethan and Jacobean tragedy was quite capable of addressing the issue. But there may be an element of displacement in the fact that Tamora eats her sons.

[52]I have already discussed the complexity of the relationship between what I see as the master-discourse of the Shakespearean tragic text and the failure or the inability, in what I call the 'event' of the drama, of that project to be sustained in its full form: see above, *Signs of Invasion*.

Connected with this, I am grateful to Peter Hulme in discussion for raising the question of whether the intrusion, in the language of the representation of the Clown, of Englishness, isn't also the intrusion of 'England' in the sense that by virtue of that episode *Titus Andronicus* could be read not so much as an occlusion but a critique, albeit one which is inevitably coded and displaced. I have to say that I doubt it. The question of *Shakespeare's* historicism and his sense of cultural otherness is very difficult of course, but in *Titus Andronicus* there does seem to be an attempt to imagine another society, suggested not least by the explicit and somewhat self-conscious classical borrowing, especially of Ovid, which could be seen as functioning very much

erasing, confusing, contesting or making 'disfunctional' the categories and representations they support and which in turn support them.[52] And if the relationship between *Titus Andronicus* and the reality of hanging is as I suggest, then important questions are also raised about the political orientation and purposes of an interpretative approach which in the New Historicism has depended upon the view that the encratic effectivity of the Shakespearean text lies in its explicit display of power. In fact, if the main interpretative assumptions of the New Historicism are brought to bear both on the anthropology of *Titus Andronicus*, and on the evidence of hanging in early modern England which I have presented, a major discrepancy in its vaunted ability to interpret ought to become apparent. Power is not made visible by *Titus Andronicus*; it is hidden, as we have seen, by other visualities. At best it leaves complex, oblique, easily unnoticeable traces as the signs of its occlusion. To be sure, there is theatrical display, and it is largely violence that is theatrically displayed; and indeed, many have commented, from the earliest moment of Shakespearean criticism, on the way in which the play seems to be composed of almost nothing but such extravagant theatricality. But it is not, as I have suggested, the common violence of the times which is made thus so spectacular.

But as we have seen, a sense of groundlessness has been prepared in advance for the New Historicism. I have traced out above some links between Clifford Geertz's cultural anthropology (and by extension the other anthropological perspectives engaged) and the New Historicist figurations of power and the political. Compared with the scientistic, objectifying gaze of much preceding anthropology,

---

like tribal lore in ethnographic description, or the cultural level of some more 'developed' imagined other society; and above all by way of the structuration of otherness I have discussed above. This is not to say, of course, that some very fully imagined representation of another society – and *Titus Andronicus* is certainly not that, no more than it is simply an allegory for England – could not be inflected or disrupted by pressures from within the home society. But in any case, I have looked without success for historically particular instances of death by hanging – some especially noted intensification of the norm, or an exceptional atrocity – which would explain contextually this suggestion of 'intrusion'. By the same token I am sceptical about the 'radical tragedy' reading, most famously and persuasively represented in the book of that name by Jonathan Dollimore (1984), which may risk a recuperation of 'Shakespeare', this time as a great, if coded, critic of his society.

It is at least interesting to note that the very same question – whether the political foreshortening is the result of occlusion, or is a kind of coded and displaced critique – can be asked of the New Historicism.

Geertz's interpretative culturalism, with its reflexivity and its liberal politics, has been perhaps welcome and progressive in the field of anthropology itself.[53] But the appropriation of these perspectives and their application in the field of Renaissance studies by New Historicism has legitimated altogether more ambiguous, if not disturbing, interpretative consequences, connected both with the theoretical localism of its culturalism – attractive as 'self-validating interpretation' may be – and with its tendency to de-realise power.[54]

Despite the avowed and apparent refusal of general theory, there are in fact three distinct phases of New Historicist thinking about – cultural – power which *are* 'generally' – if inadequately – theorised; at least they appear systemic even as they refuse to be systematic. The early emphasis on a 'cultural poetics' in *Renaissance Self-Fashioning*, which I have discussed already, gives way, in a strange meeting of phenomenology with functionalism, to a second phase, characterised by the prominence of the notorious 'subversion and containment'

[53]This cannot be the place to carry out a full critique of anthropology (although that task is ongoing and necessary), or even of Geertz's place in it. It should be said that recently anthropology in some of its forms, by questioning what Renato Rosaldo, who is a significant figure here, calls the 'classic norms' of anthropology (1989, pp. 25-45), has sought to free itself from its historical connections with imperialism and its epistemological consonance with objectifying, colonising perspectives, and its tendency to depoliticise, via functionalism and in other ways, the culture of the object-society; see e.g. Clifford and Marcus (1986) and Marcus and Fischer (1986). My task here has been more to focus and criticise some of the effects of anthropological perspectives and methods on the theoretical and cultural politics of recent interpretations of the literature and indeed the 'culture' of the early modern period.

[54]As a matter of fact I have considerable reservations about Geertz's work, not least in respect of what I see as a central contradiction in it, or at the very least a slippage, between differently empowered perspectives. Even as Geertz opts for a weakened scientificity in his theory and method, there is some surprise in the way in which he chooses not for the defamiliarisation of the native culture, but for making it familiar. His whole emphasis on anthropology as 'another country heard from' (1973, p. 23) and especially on its status as 'conversation' (p. 13), depends upon an assumption that this conversation is possible in the first place, and also agreeable and useful – *to the anthropologist*. There is no hint in the essay that 'native' agreement with these assumptions is sought or offered. In addition, this 'conversational' model of anthropology sits in some contradiction with the fact that it remains true that it is native behaviour which is being *described, by the anthropologist*. Geertz recognises that the anthropologist's interpretations are second and third order, whereas only native interpretations can be first order ones (p. 15), but nonetheless description remains within the ambit of an anthropological 'gaze' which records for consumption elsewhere (and for purposes defined elsewhere) the native country, which is thus not in any meaningful sense in 'conversation' with the anthropologist's culture. There is something disingenuous in the conflation of conversation and description, however the latter is hedged about with weakened scientificity, reflexiveness, and other genial disclaimers.

model of the key essay 'Invisible Bullets', in which the theatricalisation of power reaches its apogee: 'Within this theatrical setting', Greenblatt writes, with some ambiguity as to whether the theatrical setting in question is the power of the theatre, or the theatricality of power apart from the theatre, 'there is a remarkable insistence upon the paradoxes, ambiguities, and tensions of authority, but this apparent production of subversion is ... the very condition of power' (Greenblatt 1985, pp. 44–5).[55] Confounding authority and power in a way which is characteristic of New Historicism, and seeming to invoke the dark and fatalistic reading of the middle to late Foucault, who thought liberation impossible because he held resistance and power to be constitutive of each other, Greenblatt here again rehearses a model which depends on cultural groundlessness, in as much as it resolves apparently contradictory or antagonistic forces into a functional unity with each other.[56]

The conceptual lexicon of New Historicism is then transformed, in a third phase represented by *Shakespearean Negotiations*, into the language of the circulation and exchange of social 'energy' (see Greenblatt 1988, pp. 1–20). This is a quintessentially anthropological language, of course, and one which purchases much of its rhetorical effect by borrowing the caché of political economy for a position

[55]It is open to question as to whether a profounder influence on the New Historicism than the cultural anthropology of the sixties and seventies hasn't been that of the functionalist sociology of the US fifties and sixties. Seeming to desire what might be thought of as the functionalism of an open system, the model of subversion and containment, when linked with the circularity and groundlessness I have remarked, is inseparable from the way in which functionalisms of closed systems have characterised 'disfunction' as operational for the larger stability of the social structure.

[56]It has become almost axiomatic in the light of the New Historicism (not least in a climate of the effects of the work of the late Michel Foucault, which influenced it in complex ways) to foreground the notion of power, whether this be the abstract, somewhat hypostatised 'Power' of some of Foucault's theoretical formulations, where the possibility of resistance seems to be fatalistically subsumed under the operation of power 'itself' in ways which fully resemble the ambivalences of the New Historicist model of the production and containment of subversion; or the sense (which is in my view more productive) of an historical *dispositif*, a practical deployment – constitutive as well as repressive – of force and domination in given historical circumstances, which can also be derived from Foucault's work. This is not the place for a full account of the influence of Foucault's power, or the effects of the climates of those accounts, on the New Historicism: that would demand another paper in itself. But compare the pessimism of the last phrase of *The History of Sexuality* (1979a) (together with the somewhat elusive formulations of pp. 92-102 where power and resistance are made disablingly productive of each other), with the more clearly historically articulated themes and methods of *Discipline and Punish* (1977).

H

which is actually culturalist, and where again the groundlessness of interpretation matches and is matched by the flow of the circulation of cultural patterns in the society itself.[57]

It may be argued, in defence of the failure of these perspectives to

[57] This language begins to emerge in Greenblatt's 'Towards a Poetics of Culture' (1987), at the time something of a long-awaited theoretical statement, in which Greenblatt undertakes 'if not to define the new historicism, at least to situate it as a practice' (p. 3). The argument invokes two different accounts of capitalism, derived from the writing of Fredric Jameson and Jean-François Lyotard respectively:

> If capitalism is invoked not as a unitary demonic principle, but as a complex historical movement in a world without paradisal origins or chiliastic expectations, then an inquiry into the relation between art and society in capitalist cultures must address both the formation of the working distinction upon which Jameson remarks and the totalising impulse on which Lyotard remarks. For capitalism has characteristically generated neither regimes in which all discourses seem coordinated, nor regimes in which they seem radically isolated or discontinuous, but regimes in which the drive towards differentiation and the drive towards monological organisation operate simultaneously, or at least oscillate so rapidly as to create the impression of simultaneity. (Greenblatt 1987, p. 7).

Greenblatt then proceeds to oscillate between them. He gives three examples, which function as theoretical anecdotes: Ronald Reagan's observation of 'no distinction between simulation and reality' (1987, p. 8) in his disconcerting habit of quoting his own films; the 'interpenetration of artifice and nature that makes the distinction possible' (p. 11), communed with during a walk on the Nevada Falls Trail in the Yosemite National Park; and the complex, folded, intricacies of Norman Mailer's 'true life novel' about Gary Gilmore and a series of related texts and real events which also simultaneously cross and confirm the distinction between reality and fiction. Each example instantiates the 'complex dialectic of differentiation and identity' (p. 9) on which the essay insists as it tries to inhabit *both* of what it identifies as the two main theoretical positions available today. It is not a Reaganite document, but it is less than critically a document of Reagan's America:

> My use of the term *circulation* here is influenced by the work of Derrida, but sensitivity to the practical strategies of negotiation and exchange depends less on post-structuralist theory than upon the circulatory rhythms of American politics. (1987, p. 9)

Certainly the language and the metaphors it uses (words which become the 'theoretical' idiom of *Shakespearean Negotiations*) when specifying its account of the relationship between culture and society belong very fully to the meretriciousness of capitalism in the 1980s:

> In order to achieve the negotiation, artists need to create a currency that is valid for a meaningful, mutually profitable exchange. It is important to emphasise that the process involves not simply appropriation but exchange, since the existence of art always implies a return, a return normally measured in pleasure and interest. I should add that the society's dominant currencies, money and prestige, are invariably involved, but here I am using the term 'currency' metaphorically to designate the systematic adjustments, symbolisations and lines of credit necessary to enable an exchange to take place. The terms 'currency' and 'negotiation' are the signs of our manipulation and adjustment of the relative systems. (1987, p. 13)

engage with those modes of effective power which are not wholly representational, that they deliberately address the 'cultural', as their proper object. But this, surely, is exactly the point. The New Historicism seems unwilling or unable to specify the meta-critical theory of the social whole that informs both its practical interpretations and also the particular instances of theoretical articulation which mark, but do not seem consistently to govern, the critical texts.[58] The theoretical formulations hover low over their material, seeming systemi-

[58]This is not to say that the New Historicism is not theoretically informed, or indeed that it is not certainly a major – perhaps the most important – literary critical movement to have taken account of what is often called, simply, Theory (cf. Culler 1983, p. 9). Nor is it to say that its 'localism' never implies more general cases at the theoretical or historical levels. On the contrary, its local formulations, as many have remarked, frequently contain hints of allegory, suggestions of a wider application or more general privilege than is actually articulated in them, and invariably do so with not a little ambivalence towards a possibility which is thus both offered and withdrawn at the same time. Consider, for example, a well-known passage in *Renaissance Self-Fashioning* when Greenblatt addresses his choice of the handful of – utterly canonical – aristocratic and middle-class men whose lives and texts provide the book's subject-matter:

> In attempting to glimpse the formation of identity in the English Renaissance, we cannot rest content with statistical tables, nor are we patient enough to tell over a thousand stories, each with its slight variants. The problem is not only a lack of patience but a sense of hopelessness: after a thousand, there would be another thousand, then another, and it is not at all clear that we would be closer to the understanding we seek. So from the thousands, we seize upon a handful of arresting figures who seem to contain within themselves much of what we need, who both reward intense, individual attention and promise access to larger cultural patterns. (Greenblatt 1980, p. 6)

The effect of Greenblatt's 'hopelessness' in the face of the evidence (nonetheless 'stories') conforms quite exactly to one of Geertz's *caveats* concerning the localist method, that there may be no sufficiently articulated reason for believing its findings, and several rather obvious ones for not doing so:

> You either grasp an interpretation or you do not, see the point of it or you do not, accept it or you do not. Imprisoned in the immediacy of its own detail, it is presented as self-validating, or, worse, as validated by the supposedly developed sensitivities of the person who presents it. ... (Geertz 1973, p. 24)

Greenblatt believes, without any real explanation of how this might be so, that his 'arresting figures' who 'reward intense, individual attention' do in fact 'promise access to wider cultural patterns'. The mode of that access, if, that is, it evades Geertz's warnings about the dangers built into his own method, remains opaque, and the critical discourse remains ambivalent in respect of its theorisation of the relationship between the local interpretation and the wider pattern. The demonisation of systemic thinking entailed in offering to substitute the anecdote for statistics alibies both an impressionistic *belles-lettrisme* and the traditional canon by implying that the *summa* of social analysis consists in nothing more than the quantitative. This is, by the way, an antithesis between the poetics of culture and the possibility of comprehensive cultural thought which is almost purely internal to the philistinism of *bourgeois* culture.

cally to theorise culture as social power, but if scrutinised as system-atic theory, they simultaneously retreat into the specialised address to culture. Culture is at once totalised and regional.[59]

It would doubtless be extravagant to suggest that Greenblatt is an adherent of the nostalgia for a vanished organic society which has peren-nially organised the interpretative strategies of Renaissance studies. It is, however, striking that his sense of the theatricality of power, and the dramatic containment of subversion – despite what is often thought of as its projection of a dark totalitarianism – approximates to the view that if there was social control in early modern England, it was achieved by essentially benign social – that is, 'cultural' – means. But within the parameters of culturalism it is probably inevitable that the – undeniably important – emphasis on the interpretative power of metaphor – the view that 'particular cultures and the observers of these cultures are inevitably drawn to a metaphorical grasp of reality' (Greenblatt 1980, p. 4) – grows over into the notion that power is itself a metaphor, and, in effect, *no more than a metaphor*: a wholly appropriate attention to the power of representation can, it seems, easily topple over into figuring power as *merely* invested in the representational. But if the turning of society into discourse and power into theatre are not instances of the aestheticisation of politics that Walter Benjamin warned against, it would be important to know how the New Historicism's view of culture as representation and its theatricalisation of power are actually to be theorised. For, returning to the culturalist reading of the interpenetration of all social forms and the lack of epistemological or ontological differentiation among them – Tennenhouse's 'transgeneric logic' of the theatre with other social practices – it is important to ask for some further clarity over the *precise* sense in which the strategies of the theatre, or indeed those of court performances, can be said to *resemble* those of the scaffold, as Tennenhouse claims in the passage I have quoted above. Was it that they were all – merely – *spectacles* perhaps? And how is it that they *both* 'testified to' *and* 'sustained' the monarch's power? And what, quite, might be at stake in the degree to which, under the general impetus towards the theatricalisation of

[59]There is a similar tension in Geertz who does, after all, make general claims about what culture is and how it may be interpreted, although in the light of his theoretical and methodological localism it is difficult to know how the generalisation, or indeed the generation, of the – apparently unitary – concept of culture across distinct particular cultures is possible. In other words, it is hard to see how the very theoretical formulations advanced could survive being taken seriously.

power, the scaffold of punishment becomes, or risks becoming, indeed *aestheticised* by identification with the scaffold of playing?[60] At its most fantastic, New Historicist culturalism figures society, or power in society, as no more structured a formation than a variously patterned reciprocation and replication of the forms of spectacle and display, in regard to which an interpretative poetics of power is most the trenchant form of imaginable critique.

In response to these deficiencies in the culturalism of the New Historicism, I have not myself commented 'interpretatively' on the occluded material itself. Mainly for polemical, but partly for epistemological reasons, I have presented instead blank 'facts', very thinly described, or not described at all. But despite a perspective which believes that power *'is constituted in theatrical celebrations of royal glory and theatrical violence visited upon the enemies of that glory'*, the record of death by hanging suggests there was an extensive, ruthless and effective coercive apparatus that was putting to death vast numbers of the people, overwhelmingly the low-born and the poor.[61] A standing army, a highly developed bureaucracy, an extensive police force, and so on, may have been lacking (although these assertions in themselves need scrutiny), but means to deal with recalcitrant or transgressive, rebellious or merely delinquent members of the 'society' clearly were

[60]The 'connection' between the two scaffolds was made frequently in the early modern period and has played an emphatic role in the recent theory on which Tennenhouse draws (Foucault 1977). I have written about it myself (Barker 1984). But the difference between the aestheticisation of politics and the politicisation of aesthetics remains crucial.

[61]Curt Breight (1990, p. 5) accuses Peter Hulme and myself of de-politicising Caliban's conspiracy against Prospero in our work on *The Tempest* (Barker and Hulme 1985 and Hulme 1986). I find this suggestion incomprehensible in substance and slightly hurtful in tone. I am in very substantial agreement, however, with the general line of Breight's article, and his closing remarks about the dangers involved in conceiving power in terms of 'cultural production' are wholly apposite to the present argument: 'Late Elizabethan and early Jacobean government featured no hegemony based on "consensus". It can be described only as "domination" based on 'coercion'. (Breight 1990, p. 28). And see *passim*.

[62]In particular I have not seriously attempted to develop or invoke a theory of the state. This is a notoriously difficult problem in the pre-revolutionary period when, it can be cogently argued, there was not yet such a thing as a 'state' in the modern sense (cf. Barker 1984 and forthcoming 1994, *passim*). My current view is that 'state apparatuses' certainly existed and should be called by that name, but the theoretical and historical justification of this would need another paper.

not. Means were available not so much to impress them with theatrical celebrations as to kill them.[62]

Nor have I commented interpretatively on the precise nature of the general relationship between the occluded material as such and the text of *Titus Andronicus*, apart of course from positing both the occlusion itself and the complexity of the way in which it works, seeking what the culturalist reading and the cultural performance hide as well as what they disclose, and excavating in the particular case what has been occluded but which ought, according to the interpretative predispositions I have been discussing, to be very fully 'on display'. And in particular I have not attempted to specify precisely the ratio of significance between coercive violence and cultural legitimation. This is a matter which would need considerable further theoretical elaboration, for surely there was a 'moral economy' organised around the assizes, surely hangings were in this way 'cultural' events and of course there is meaning in what cannot otherwise be thought of as acts of purely physical violence. At least it is not impossible to presume, on the basis of the evidence I have offered above, that if there was such widespread state violence there was also an estimable dissemination of fear. The process of arrest, imprisonment, trial and execution cannot be taken in isolation from some sense of the effects that the awareness of this process must have had on those members of the population who were not presently caught up by or involved in it, not least, presumably, because the minatory effect of the process was effective in keeping them 'within the law'. But howsoever those further analyses may be developed, it is in any case clear that a very different account will be needed of the relationship between the

[63]In using the term 'moral economy', and in my deployment of archival material on the assize courts, I might be seen to be privileging a certain kind of social history. Indeed at 'wisemens threasure' I thought it important to point out that the balance between symbolic authority and coercive violence in the exercise of Elizabethan and Stuart power had been debated by – British – social historians *years* before New Historicism had truncated the importance of the latter in favour of its near celebration of the former. In this connection (and I am particularly grateful to Margaret Ferguson for pressing this point) I was taken to task in the discussion which followed my lecture for allegedly valorising the Real ... It is difficult to be believed when I point out that despite the national academic stereotypes I no more accept the unconditional reality of the empirical than I give credence to the hypostatisation of the symbolic. At the risk, to be sure, of raising some – doubtless unwelcome – epistemological problems (and there *are* problems with associating too closely the empirical with the real, of course) I would insist that even at the theoretical level the evidence of mass execution I have reported on above stands opposed to culturalism, even if no allowance is made for the extent to which I have deliberately flattened it into the numerical.

theatre and power, between culture and violence, than that which is currently so available.[63]

In trying to uncover, to de-occlude, by the citation of brute and brutal evidence, a considerable coercive apparatus which rather than abutting, or being in some way continuous with, theatrical performance, is in fact effectively occluded by it – as it is by the subsequent tradition of 'culture' – I have tried to suggest that Elizabethan power certainly did not operate by theatrical spectacle, cultural display or circulation and exchange alone.[64] Failing to perceive either that power can be hidden by cultural performance, or – worse – that power may not consist simply in cultural performance, the New Historicism would seem to be in some deep complicity with the occlusive strategy of *Titus Andronicus*, and the Shakespearean text more widely. I truly hope that there will be no end to meaning and interpretation, and that there are senses in which human culture will prove inexhaustible. But I cannot rest content with an analysis that finds itself unable or unwilling to specify any cultural relations more poignant, limiting or coercive than those of inference at the level of social ontology, or, at the level of interpretation, interpretation. Indeed, the culturalism supposedly engendered by 'the desire to speak with the dead' (Greenblatt 1988, p. 1) seems grotesquely disorientated. It looks for the dead in the

[64] It was suggested at the Symposium that the key phrases from 'Invisible Bullets' – that power is 'constituted in theatrical celebrations of royal glory and theatrical violence visited upon the enemies of that glory', and that 'Elizabethan power ... depends upon its privileged visibility' (Greenblatt 1985, p. 44), and the similar passages in the New Historicism read more widely – may not actually mean what they appear to mean, as if inadvertantly some qualifying conditionals had been omitted from them. This somewhat unlikely attempt to save appearances suggests that I would be content with the insertion of a single qualifying adverb in, for example, the passage quoted from 'Invisible Bullets' above; to the effect that Elizabethan power is *partly* constituted in celebratory or minatory spectacles. Perhaps. The addition would make the particular sentences truer, but the wider position more wholly false. At least it would entail a whole recentring of the work which has resulted. Such a recentring could do worse than be organised along the lines promised by striking passages in Greenblatt's own 'Murdering Peasants' (1983) where he writes, in terms, I discover, similar to those of the present essay, of the English literary representations which 'rarely depict the actual method most often used to punish those whom the magistrates deemed serious threats: the thousands of hangings carried out locally throughout Tudor and Stuart England'. The view that in the literature of the period we get 'tales of mass rebellion and knightly victories' instead of 'the assizes and a hempen rope' (1983, p.15), would seem to beckon a theory of occlusion. These have not been the directions in which New Historicist work has subsequently developed.

wrong places, and at best it ignores and at worst it hides what was done to them. Perhaps, under the state of emergency in which they died, 'a metaphorical grasp of reality' was to the fore. Perhaps, the 'proper goal, however difficult to realise', was 'a *poetics of culture*'. But I doubt very much whether for the people whose killing is recorded in the archives I have cited above it was 'turtles all the way down'. For them there was a point where interpretation very definitely stopped.

VI

... if one asks with whom the adherents of historicism actually empathize [t]he answer is inevitable: with the victor. And all rulers are the heirs of those who conquered before them. Hence, empathy with the victor invariably benefits the rulers. Historical materialists know what that means. Whoever has emerged victorious participates to this day in the triumphal procession in which the present rulers step over those who are lying prostrate. According to traditional practice, the spoils are carried along in the procession. They are called cultural treasures, and a historical materialist views them with cautious detachment. For without exception the cultural treasures he surveys have an origin which he cannot contemplate without horror. They owe their existence not only to the efforts of the great minds and talents who have created them, but also to the anonymous toil of their contemporaries. There is no document of civilization which is not at the same time a document of barbarism. ... A historical materialist therefore dissociates himself from it as far as possible. He regards it as his task to brush history against the grain.'

Walter Benjamin, 'Theses on the Philosophy of History'.

There is nothing that I or anyone else can do for the dead of early modern England, other than to remember in the practical, active, historically redemptive sense that Benjamin recommended. That part of the past which has passed is truly gone.

But that part of the present which we call the past, that part which flashes up at a moment of danger, is another matter ...

I began with cultural treasures borne along in the triumphal procession of ruling tradition and I shall end with them. From the begining of the formation of Western modernity in the moment of first contact with 'America', anthropological thought, in the constitution of which Shakespeare participates, has shadowed the idea of culture. But the anthropology of *Titus Andronicus*, and of the Shakespearean text at large, in effect legitimates an entire historical culture of violence which it domesticates, in its own society and for us, by the strategies of occlusion and exoticisation I have addressed. Cultural criticism becomes complicit with this violence if it does not free itself from the same strategies, remaining equally content to remember in order to forget.[65] To a terrifying extent, what now counts as culture *is* the occlusion of that historical violence, then and now. Thus Benjamin's *dictum* that 'there is no document of civilization which is not at the same time a document of barbarism' is resonant.

Clearly the Shakespearean text, and its culturalist readings actual and potential, belong among the documents of our civilisation; indeed there are ways in which for the literary culture of the English-speaking world Shakespeare has come to serve as the very epitome of civilisation. But Benjamin's thesis holds good even when the document in question is not so apparently 'about' the antithetical couple civilisation and barbarism as *Titus Andronicus*. Texts which are by their own definition the most civilised, must most occult the barbarism of which he speaks. It is thus that they are documents of violence, as they occlude the violence which is culture. Or, in the case of *Titus*, it is as if the process works first, by means of an inversion, the other way round. This dreadful play, so often estimated as itself a kind of barbarism, and thereby not authentically Shakespearean, serves to confirm by exception the normally civilised protocols of what we can recuperate as Shakespeare's art, as our tradition, as a secure past and a cultured present.[66] Even the barbaric text under-

---

[65]For more on the idea of remembering in order to forget, rather than *simple* forgetting, see below, 'Tragedy and the Ends of History'.

[66]*Titus Andronicus* is a play I have come not to regard, in the course of working in detail on it, as all that inferior either by the – in fact somewhat ramshackle – structural standards of Shakespeare's dramaturgy, or by the claims made for the cogency of his skills of characterisation and versification. In II.iii.10-29, for example, it has some of Shakespeare's best early verse. But the play has been scorned or ignored from a very early moment in a way which suggests to me that more is at stake than bad artistic work. There is something insistent in the warding off of *Titus*, as if the rejection of material which is unacceptable for other reasons has been disguised as aesthetic criticism. Edward Ravenscroft, one of its earliest recorded commentators, remarked in 1678 that it was 'rather a heap of rubbish than a structure' (quoted in Waith 1984, p. 1); a recent critic, Gustav Cross, begins his Introduction to the play thus: *"Titus*

206 | violence and interpretation

writes the civilisation, which is itself in turn barbaric. It is a barbarism which is concealed not least in the occlusion of violence achieved in the very spectacles of the text's own strange savagery. In the evidence of mass execution I have adduced I have tried to show that that tradition of 'civilisation' has been abstracted from the history of early modern England and Wales, an occlusion of the violence – by its own terms, 'barbarism' – which is its inner structure.

I, for one, will not be party to that violence, nor to its occlusion. Nor to its 'anthropology'.

Andronicus is a ridiculous play' (Shakespeare 1969, p. 11). Its Shakespearean authenticity has been from the beginning repeatedly questioned, and generally the work has been dismissed as early, immature, crude, sensationalist. The common view is, under the circumstances, a happy one: that *Titus Andronicus* is a 'primitive' play, in the sense that it is what the language of literary taste used to call a 'barbarism' ....

Part Three

TRACES

1

TRAGEDY AND THE ENDS OF HISTORY*

'... it is possible to trace the path which leads from the haunted work to that which haunts it'.

Pierre Macherey, A *Theory of Literary Production*

I

Despite pretensions to contrariety, and for all its refusal of epistemology, postmodernist theory, especially when it treats of knowledge, continues to tend to take either the rationalist form of a discourse of the knowing subject, or the empiricist one of a discourse about the existing object. Failing thus to escape a founding Cartesianism, it is either 'theoretical' in the sense of being a more or less rigorous discourse about discourse; or it purports to describe – or even to participate in the existence of – a 'condition'.[1] On the one hand it proposes that, because the erstwhile guarantees which it takes once to have secured knowledge are now without foundation, we cannot know what we know (and never could), but only and merely 'know' (in the sense that knowledges simply take their epistemologically indifferent places among all other, equally non-privileged discourses). Or, on the other hand – the 'problem of knowledge' notwithstanding (and not, apparently, applying to the theory of postmodernism itself) – postmodernism can confidently

*An initial draft of this essay was presented to the first of the Essex Symposia on Literature, Politics and Theory, 'Marxism, postmodernism and the Renaissance: the uses of history', which was held at the University of Essex in March, 1989. A developed version of that draft was published as 'Which Dead? *Hamlet* and the Ends of History', in the volume based on the Symposium (see Barker *et al.* (eds.) 1991, pp. 47–75). Readers interested in pursuing the issues addressed here in relation to the theme of historical memory in the particular instance of *Hamlet*, but in the context, still, of a critique of contemporary culturalism and historicism, are referred to that earlier version. It has been reshaped and revised for publication in this volume.

The thematics of memory in *Hamlet*, has already played a part here, of course; see above, *Signs of Invasion*, esp. pp. 32–51.

[1] I am taking Lyotard's work as the instance which is by now classical; partly because of its substance, and partly because of the widespread influence of the name of his text, not least in as much as it claims to name a 'condition'. See Lyotard 1984 *passim*.

adduce not just the loss of the privilege of knowledge, but a whole new state of affairs (which includes, but is not exhausted by, new forms of non-guaranteed knowledge). This is a state of affairs which it purports to describe well, even truthfully, while other discourses rest on illusion because they have failed to notice the changes and have not understood that where once they were secure they cannot now, under a changed 'condition', remain so.

But if, in each case, 'incredulity towards meta-narratives' is involved, all this begins to become serious when one of the simultaneous localisations and globalisations of its account of knowledge in particular, and of the present moment more generally, occurs when the post-industrial theme of the end of ideology has grown over into senses of the end of history.[2] And where again these two forms insist. Either, it has become near orthodox to hold, we must abandon, epistemo-theoretically, historical discourse as now understood to be overweaningly objectivist or, worse, totalising; or, history in an objective sense has come to an end, supplanted by the famous new condition which is not, in its own self-estimation or in any received sense, historical.

[2]For Lyotard's famous 'definition' of the postmodern as 'incredulity towards metanarratives' – among which 'history' is prominent – see Lyotard 1984, p. xxiv. But the ground has been in preparation for some time: the cognate 'end of ideology' is properly associated with the name of Daniel Bell, whose *The End of Ideology* (1960) and more recent *The Coming of Post-Industrial Society* (1973) and *The Cultural Contradictions of Capitalism* (1976) are notorious landmarks.

And the company kept ... If Lyotard will have us be incredulous before certain kinds of – historical – discourse, others will more bluntly announce the ending of historical process itself, with the politics of this gesture very close to the surface. Published in the US conservative journal *The National Interest* in the summer of 1989, Francis Fukuyama's essay 'The End of History' was first influential in Washington and then widely disseminated in many countries, even to the extent of being deemed sufficiently topical for the British newspapers to reprint it (Fukuyama 1989). (The second part of the article appeared, transparently enough, under the title 'Marxism's Failure'.) Fukuyama's claims have subsequently been published at book length (1992).

The *best* that can be said for Fukuyama's celebration of the global triumph of capitalism, and the 'end' of any alternative to economic and political liberalism, is that it is tinged with regret: 'The end of history will be a sad time ... In the post-historical period there will be neither art nor philosophy, just the perpetual caretaking of the museum of human history. I can feel in myself – and see in others around me – a powerful nostalgia for the time when history existed. Such nostalgia, in fact, will continue to fuel competition and conflict, even in the post-historical world, for some time to come.'

The 'post-political' is part of this powerful fantasy; cf. below, n. 32.

In both cases surely, some grave problems would be entailed for those who study historical literature, let alone for those who still use historical discourse for the wider purposes of the explanation of the present and the formation of strategies for a future?

Of course, historicism and its culturalist avatars and recensions have ever been symbiotes, if not simply mediated synonyms, and there is no surprise therefore in the mutual emergence recently of empowered forms of de-historicisation and a concurrent 'new' historicism – keen co-celebrants at the wishful reburial of dialectic. The postmodernists denounce the historical as of the past; newly re-empowered historicism is pronounced in terms which cannot be differentiated on every occasion, as we have seen, from this indifference. 'New' can seem to mean 'old'; and 'old', 'new'. Ending, totalisation and anthropology rehearse their familiar roles.

But if these 'ends' (and the word may disclose more than it knows) are radical, are they not also signs of crisis and able to be read as such? If they do indeed present *grave* problems – the death of history, the end of the possibility of the intelligibility of its writing in the form of its cultural interpretation – are they new problems? It seems unlikely when so many other contexts, and earlier conjunctures, with – by definition – less novelty, have also developed languages not just of the end of history but of incredulity and death.[3] Of tragedy and farce; of gay and melancholy anti-historicism.

[3]There is no particular surprise, as I have said above, in the simultaneous emergence – 'back to back' – of a recent urgency in the promotion of the theme of the end of history, and a new historicism. They are no less than two commensurable, and arguably complicit, facets of the broader postmodernism. To the extent that this volume has been concerned with the New Historicism in Renaissance studies, and with its wider implications for the political analysis of culture, it is worth noting here again the figural trajectory of the New Historicism – however narrow in itself the instance is – from a morbid anecdote between Baltimore and Boston, to the opening sentence of *Shakespearean Negotiations*: 'I began with the desire to speak with the dead'. This trip from death to death, this 'speaking' of the past as the dead, of history as death, of death-history, requires at least some clarification. (See above, 'A Wilderness of Tigers,' pp. 144–9, 152–3, 169–90, 203–4).

II

GHOST. Adieu, adieu, adieu. Remember me.

Hamlet (I.v.91)

Early modern tragedy dramatises the ends of history: inherently in its formation, and as a near explicit thematic.[4] Even if saying so meant being, in the name of something 'fundamental',[5] incredulous about incredulity, the crisis of memory turned out to be a crisis in the governing sovereignty of the tragic texts and their discursive regime.[6] Indeed, we have little choice but to witness in tragedy a compelling sense of the ways in which the problematics of forgetfulness and paranoid recall invest the figuration of power, and those in which remembrance and amnesia traverse the forms of resistance.

[4]See above, *Signs of Invasion* esp. pp. 32–51, 91–2, but also *passim*.

[5]Fundamental? One of the characteristics of characteristically 'postmodernist' analysis is, of course, to deny, in its own theory and methodology, and in the objects of analysis, any hierarchisation of significance: this is paradoxical in discourses which claim to attend to representation. But even if we agreed to remain at the level of mere 'representation', surely the history of human societies is littered with – and even, arguably, constituted by – the claims of their discursive regimes to locate and to valorise in various patterns of dominance, subordination and dependency: value ranking, logical derivation, material or ideal causality, formations of phenomena and epiphenomena, and so on? These structures cannot be wished out of existence by remarking that it's all representation; nor understood without seeing that it is power which assembles them, and that it's not merely a case of earlier forms of thought which can now be triumphantly pronounced as being, or having been, in error. Postmodernist theory (which I am taking to be different from postmodern theory) routinely makes these idealist assumptions, which are, in the circumstances, rather touchingly traditional.

[6]Although at the level of the master-discourse, not always, to be sure, a crisis necessarily disclosed 'as such': for as texts and historical structures, these 'dramas' are constrained to resort so wholly to displacement and compromise in order to live (or to die) with the radical historical difficulty of the present, and at least to 'save the appearances' of the high cultural text as one of the mastery even of its own depredation. Then as now, for the sovereign text, the pronunciation 'crisis', and its subsequent manipulation, themselves form and legitimate strategies of management or control. And – by definition of the function of 'ruling class' or 'dominant culture' texts – the representation of crisis, even when historical and profound, will seek to be 'managed' rather than disclosed or acknowledged (to the extent that the ruling culture remains capable of such manipulation in the circumstances of its historical crisis and in view of the current strength of the forces which dissent from or oppose it).

In connection with these slippages between the pressure of historicity and the ruling representations of history, John Joughin asks a trenchant question in the very title of his 'Whose Crisis?' (1991).

Tragedy, with its celebration of sovereign presence in the form of lost plenitude, its doubled, hollowed formation caught up between project and event, is constituted in the incoherence – with its attendant declination in cultural authority – between the powerfully nostalgic drive toward restitution, and the deployments of actuality where recovery is impossible. Indeed, as we have seen, the crisis of the master discourse – graphically instantiated by networks of dying voices and failing audiences, by the dramatic and thematic concatenation of lost places and deracinated identities, of unknowing and reduction – represents tragedy longingly to us as an erstwhile sovereign presence nonetheless having become subject to a radically dehistoricising violence, a violence apparently against time, presence and place, and, as dominantly defined, one seemingly against sense itself. And this doubleness – or duplicity – leads, as we have seen, to the strangulated catastrophe of the compromised ending, the strategies of displacement and substitution whereby the diminishment of affect and charge – as the place of the sovereign gives way to the rule of the military – wins the battle for monarchical nostalgia, for defining history as the question of the lost body of the king, but loses the war for the continuity of that discourse and that power. The closure, and 'settlement', are achieved only and explicitly – and with however inadvertent an effect of demystification – by armed forced.[7] Sovereign history, not able to be recognised in the cultural text as ended but unable further to be proclaimed, is suspended, and reserved in compromise, at the same time.[8]

But end of history is structural and narrational to tragedy, rather than merely episodic, punctual or empirically final. And this prompts

[7]'Demystification' in this context means 'no longer being able, or desiring, historically and culturally – representationally – to claim the automatic authority of the sacred'. Compared with the classically Marxist usage which refers a cultural form structurally to its decoded grounding elsewhere in the social formation, the sense here is that quasi-'anthropological' (but better historical) idiom which probably began with Machiavelli – and which Marx, to be sure, understood and adopted – that practically rather than diagnostically, abandons the transcendentally charged – while continuing to manipulate the latter as a mode of ideological coercion – in favour of force and rationality. See also Franco Moretti's account of this dramatic, ideological and historical trajectory (Moretti 1988).

[8]This is certainly less grand (although perhaps more historically poignant) than other 'theories' of tragedy. But so be it. Not figuring universal and absolute (the word is instructive) loss of value, but – transitional – inability to render value into either dramatic or political practice, at least it doesn't function, compared with some other accounts of the idea of tragedy, as an alibi for its own depoliticisation.

again that at least double reading which must also trace the underside of the structure of the project and the event, where, for all the investment of the cultural text in the pathos of the power of the voice of the sovereign having become reduced to a ghostly trace, that double of need and loss is always implicitly articulated against the ground of an historicity which cannot be present in the event. And which is figured, moreover, as something more radical and vertiginous, and more complex, than a simply temporal or linear discontinuity. For the signs of crisis must be apprehended as the symptoms, the symptomisations, the very symptomatology, of crisis itself. We can wonder what more catastrophic rending of the things that are there could be than this depicted and enacted cutting off, this discontinuation, this inability to perpetuate or renew; and indeed, if we seek, historically, the end of history, it would be hard, surely, to ignore this articulation of the demise of the empowered sequence which the master discourse – the project – of a culture counted, affirmed and produced as the historical itself, as the very sovereignty of the real. But yet, even behind this depredation, there is that always-already forgotten denial of form, life, validity and place – barely even registered in the vicissitudes of the master-discourse and the sovereign text – to those who are dispossessed before even possessing, delegitimated before ever identified, and unaccommodated in every significant register of this word. Even beneath the hollowed configuration of sovereign history and its depredation, there is to be apprehended, as I have already argued, the historical non-realm, the limitless delimitation, where are – under seemingly permanent erasure, their voices hardly able to be heard – the unsovereign dead whose remembering and forgetting is barely even predicated by the sovereign cultural text; at most so, only in the inadvertent and symptomatic interstices of its own critical depredation.

If the formation of tragedy is itself in this way doubled, and if it is legible as such today, no less temporally complex – and politically insistent – may be the necessary effects of reading the crisis as, in parallax, not only on the threshold – historically – of modernity, but *at* the threshold – theoretically – for the critical re-reading of that modernity and its postmodernity. In short, nothing should prevent *a priori* the thinking of 'ends of history' as being anything other than fully historical. In the very effort, under the form and pressure of its crisis, to displace, substitute and compromise, the tragic formation signals the historicity it both is and at the same time structurally and thematically denies, and which informs and determines both the impossibility and the insistent return of what it counts as history. In fact, for all its manoeuvres, and failed symbologies, the only thing it doesn't escape is historicity. The more it seeks to evade *that*, the more it signals the need against the grain of which it is formed.

And the more inescapable, against the grain of the manoeuvres, the insistence that the substance and structure of the historical inheres thus in domination.

III

Hegel remarks somewhere that all facts and personages of great importance in world history occur, as it were, twice. He forgot to add: the first time as tragedy, the second as farce.

Karl Marx, *The Eighteenth Brumaire*

Remembering and forgetting. Unsurprisingly really, Shakespearean tragedy, and postmodern ends of history, are not the only contexts for imbrications of the representation of history and the figure of death. Other texts, other historical conjunctures, as we have seen already, have figured the past as 'the dead'. I invoked above the diacritical sense of historicity at work in the texts of Marx and Benjamin: here it is important to recall that temporal complexity.

The insistence of the memory of the dead is there, certainly, but it is not easy to make precise – and certainly not precisely historicist – interpretations of those first pages of Marx's text, with their famous invocation and supplementation of Hegel. But if it does without the costumes of previous epochs, and leaves the dead behind, the key imperative of the revolution Marx both addresses and imagines could be said to be 'forget'.[9] And then generations later, Walter Benjamin struggled with the positive memory of Marx's text, and on the face of

[9] In this it seems to approximate to the fashionably pleasing, if reductive, reading of that other relevant text, Friedrich Nietzsche's 'The Uses and Abuses of History for Life', whose drift is also commonly taken to entail not historical forgetting but the forgetting of history. Even Fredric Jameson, in his Foreword to *The Postmodern Condi-*

it there is a contradiction or even an antagonism between their positions.[10] If, for Marx, 'the tradition of all the dead generations weighs
like a nightmare on the brains of the living' (1970, p. 96), the new
revolutionary task, by contrast, will have to figure itself as radically
distinct from that figuration of the past, and 'let the dead bury their
dead' (p. 98). But Benjamin will say the opposite: his motto might be
said to be 'remember'. Rather than leaving the dead to their burying,
he will say that if the enemy wins not even the dead will be safe.
Should the figure of the dead merely serve in such a formulation to
name (and it is much more than this) a reference point for –
unnegotiable – value in the form of providing a measure of how great
the threat of the enemy is, they are not, in Benjamin's theses, and
must and cannot be, as easily forgotten as Marx's words suggest.
Benjamin even ventures, against the progressivist logic of post-Enlightenment liberalism, the valorisation of enslaved ancestors over
liberated grandchildren.[11]

Political and historical contextualisation may focus the apparency
of the antagonism between these temporal and metaphysical
orientations. Marx, it could be argued, writes in a heroically futuristic
moment, prospective of the proletarian revolution (and not
unaffected by the heroic progressivism of his own characterisations
of the bourgeoisie),[12] while Benjamin wrote in the dark night of
Nazism. For Marx, in this reading, the dead can be safely dead (even
if they mock – or make a mock of – the present, by providing the

---

tion, speaks of 'the great and still influential essay of Nietzsche on the debilitating
influence of historiography and of the fidelity to the past and the dead that an obses-
sion with history seems to encourage'. See Lyotard 1984, p. xii. This has a certain
currency, to be sure, but it remains a misreading and one whose simple consonance
with Marx's text, as well as being politically implausible, is only constructable on the
basis of the latter also being reduced to an essential proposal of amnesia. Cf. above pp.
105 ff; Nietzsche 1983, p. 63: 'This, precisely, is the proposition the reader is invited to
meditate upon: *the unhistorical and the historical are necessary in equal measure for the
health of an individual, of a people and of a culture*' (emphasis original).

[10]See Benjamin, *Theses on the Philosophy of History* (1973), from which the quotations here are taken.

[11]It is especially understandable today, without countenancing postmodern cri-
tiques of the legacy of the Enlightenment, why this reversal of the expectations of
progressivist ethico-genealogical chronology made sense to Benjamin and should
make now a similar sense to the *critique* of postmodernist *doxa*: the complexity of
Benjamin's sense of historical time, and the time of history, resists the conventional
postmodern flattening.

[12]For an apposite reading of the positivity of the Marxist text in respect of nineteenth-century capitalism, see Berman 1983, esp. pp. 87–129.

guises and the disguises of the past in which the revolutionaries costume themselves). For Benjamin the dead are the only ones who are *not* 'safely' dead, both in the sense that they are not beyond the reach of the enemy, but also, more importantly, in the sense that they do continue to haunt the present (if not in the way that Marx imagines).

But a fully critical account of the proximity and divergence of the Marxist and Benjaminian vocabularies would prompt an interrogation of what Marx means by 'tradition', and be compelled to ask whether his use of the word is not one already critical and interrogative, and whether that interrogation isn't further conducted – and 'completed' – by Benjamin's even more explicitly diacritical sense of history. Marx urges the revolution of the nineteenth century, to abandon the dead in favour of the poetry of the future. For Benjamin the angel of history has its back to the future even as the wind from Paradise compels it forward. If the present generation is 'endowed with a *weak* Messianic power' (p. 256) – whatever that shall prove to be – it is also the power of the present as a radical discontinuity and not a traditional succession. 'History is the subject of a structure whose site is not homogenous, empty time', but time filled by the *jetztzeit*, the 'presence of the now' (p. 263), it is also 'shot through' with charged fragments, with chips of Messianic time' (p. 265); it is apprehended as that 'memory' which 'flashes up at a moment of danger' (p. 257), it is 'the continuum of history' blasted apart (p. 264). In other words, Benjaminian time is complex dialectical and diacritical time. If abandoning tradition is what Marx is arguing for, then Benjamin agreed. Tradition, when not articulated historically, constitutes the time of historicism, and continually threatens to become the tool of the ruling classes, unless wrested away from conformism by historians – or, presumably, revolutionaries – who have 'the gift of fanning the spark of hope in the past' (p. 257).

The essential questions are: which forgetting and which remembering? what relation of the past to the present and the future? Which dead? There is no contradiction between 'forgetting' the costumes of previous epochs and 'remembering' the tradition of the oppressed.

The diacritical question needs to be put to the postmodern end of history, which in knowing more than it knows, knows thus a lot less.

Its erasure of the history of its own vocabulary of forgetting, or ends of history, has, in turn, a history. The end of history is historical, whether we are discussing postmodernism as theory or condition (and its own theoretical bad faith needs to be put to it in this way). Postmodernism's end of history is not a new thing but a farcical – ignorant – 'recall' of earlier tragedy. Farcical in its breathless novelty because it does not remember – or systematically forgets – that the end of history has always been the theme and condition of any radical, historical (and radically historical), practical, thought. The radical break with the past, in these other contexts which postmodernism knowingly (unknowingly) elides, is not the end of history, but history. If the slogan of the revolution of the nineteenth century and, (or it may be 'or'), the proletarian revolution, is 'forget the dead', elsewhere Marx will figure the break with the past as the *beginning* of history. If 'we communists are dead men on leave', no less is the proletarian revolution thought as the end of pre-history, and communism as the start of human history. History is the move into the radically unknowable future (although not in indeterminate circumstances).[13] It is that dialectical tiger's leap of which Benjamin spoke (p. 263). For Marx history and tradition are not the same thing. And again, Benjamin agreed. One makes possible the future; it remembers. The other weighs like a nightmare; it forgets.[14] And in neither case is the figuration of history flattened into the singular, filled and complete time of historicism.

---

[13]Postmodernism routinely conflates unknowability with indeterminacy, and either or both with 'undecideability' ...

[14]Benjamin's 'flashes of memory' apparently bespeak radical discontinuity. But as we have seen already (cf. 'A Wilderness of Tigers,' above), it is important to distinguish nonetheless between his sense of the tradition of the ruling class, the procession of the victors and their cultural spoils, and the altogether different 'tradition of the oppressed' which has to be wrested from 'history' and from historicism, and which inspires – or indeed, *is* – that historical action. See Benjamin 1973, pp. 258–9 and *passim*. (I am grateful to Paula Hutchings for insisting on this clarification in particular).

[15]Lyotard's periodisation is precise: the second substantive sentence of his text has the transition to the postmodern age 'under way since at least the end of the 1950s' (1984, p. 1). This very precision, in respect especially of history conceived as chronological sequence, should be an embarrassment in as much as it discloses, against its alternative novelty, the continued attachment of the discourse to the (Cartesian) epistemology inaugurated at the beginning of the modern period.

IV

> Human anatomy contains a key to the anatomy of the ape. The intimations of higher development ... however, can be understood only after the higher development is already known.
>
> Karl Marx, Grundrisse

Postmodernist *history*, if it is not to rest at the description of a *condition*, would be hard to write. Such a 'history' would have to be done in one of at least two ways: either as the eternal recurrence of certain themes, or as the articulation of a dimension of successive, essentially identical, historical conjunctures – successive 'presents'.

In the first sense it would stretch, paradoxically, not from about 1960, but from, say, Shakespeare, or – especially if the model of the subject and the object persists in it – from Descartes.[15] It would extend from the Descartes who, at the beginnings of capitalism as a potential world system, left the West the, in one sense, radically demystified, artificial man which amounts of liberal humanism have subsequently strained to animate and recuperate, to, say, *Blade Runner*, where the artificial men and women (figured by the film as intimately and intrinsically products of corporation capitalism) search, in a postmodern Los Angeles, for an identity and a past. Their human, all too human, questions: 'Where do I come from? Where am I going? How long have I got?'; the search for the past as the memory of the future.[16] And at least there would be a certain symmetry (although this is hardly a postmodern form) in a history that would have the theme of time, if not 'History', begin in the 'Renaissance' – it would cite Cartesianism or even early modern

---

[16] *Blade Runner* is frequently cited as exemplary of postmodernism. It plays in Los Angeles in November, 2019. It rains continuously. Coca Cola and TDK adverts hang overhead. Passing aerial vehicles pronounce strangulated, disembodied messages. Gothic-metallic technology and glamourised immiseration; decay. Genetic engineering is available in *sushi* bars. There are blue light effects. And there is Deckard's hardboiled cop voice-over (now removed from the re-issued 'director's cut') with the usual sentimental half-tones, and Gaff's menacing and ultimately sardonically forgiving *origami*. But the most poignant of the narrative and generic strands of the movie is the quest of the replicants for their own past. As artificial beings they have no authentic history; their search is dominated by the fact that all Nexus 6 replicants have built-in termination dates. Memory.

See *Blade Runner* (1982); cf. Francis Barker, *Breathing Simulacra: The Dream of the Artificial Man* (forthcoming).

tragedy as the evidence – and have it end 'now' in the postmodern moment itself.

Or, in the second sense, it would have to be argued that since it has been possible to think a notion of the present as 'modern' at all (i.e. since the Renaissance), successive conjunctures have had their modern, if not modernist, and postmodern, if not postmodernist, moments.[17] This would come a little closer, in my view, to a more acceptable history of several 'crises of representation', exemplified for present purposes by the readings here of early modern tragedy, and of Marx and Benjamin, and by the famous simulacra of postmodernism 'itself'.[18]

But not just crises of *representation*, surely? If the moments of the early modern, of full blown modernity, and of postmodernity, are thought as crises historically, and structurally *as crisis*, then we come to the present not as condition but as crisis, to history as crisis, the crisis of the present, and to the present as history. And if that may seem itself to resemble the articulation of a perpetual 'condition', it is only so in as much as it coheres with Benjamin's sense of the violence of the continuum: 'the tradition of the oppressed teaches us that the 'state of emergency' in which we live is not the exception but the rule' (1973, p. 259).

And that is very far from a 'merely' aesthetic, or representational sense of crisis, especially if we remember the revolutionary character of the conjunctures in question.

But of course there cannot be a history of postmodernism, at least not from within the terms of its own characteristic discourse, whether we think of its high theory or the flattened, lapidary reticence of its fiction. Despite its avowal of change, if not unknowability, postmodernism in practice figures what we might better refer to as the stasis – or perhaps better, the hypostasis – of change. Transformation reified, as difference. The present is figured not as crisis but as, indeed, condition. And if we think of the celebratory dimensions of cultural postmodernism in particular, even condition becomes too 'situated' a word for its taste. Easy to recognise but hard

---

[17]Although see also Habermas 1985, pp. 3–4 and *passim*, for a discussion of the historical possibility of the conception of the modern and therefore also of the postmodern.

[18]For the 'crisis of representation', connected to a discussion of postmodernity as also a crisis of legitimation, see again, in an appropriate context, Jameson in his Foreword to Lyotard 1984, p. viii and *passim*.

to define, it is difficult to resist the thought that postmodernism amounts to little more here than the unnoticed affirmation of a certain consumerism, glossed, relativised, hardened, and turned into something like a rootless aesthetic of the momentary, which then claims in turn the pseudo-historical authority of the description of a condition. Descriptively, phenomenally, this may catch something, to be sure. But postmodernism purchases its own theoretical indeterminacy – which should properly be seen at least as imprecision – by just such an evocation of an ethos, an atmosphere, a style; while abandoning as meta-discursive any account of the determinate production of this condition or aesthetic, or of its historical situation or situatedness.[19]

If the capitalism of this postmodernity is a condition instead of a history, postmodernism cannot but be certain transactions of the aesthetic. At least, although not exhaustively these four: non-representational representation of representations, and often connected with, in particular, 'representation' of 'the' 'other'; representational technology and the representation of technology; and, the figuration of the space rather than the time of technology in particular, and of that of the condition and the aesthetic in general:

● Postmodernism has its capital cities. New York, or 'New York', is often cited. Or the Los Angeles of *Blade Runner*. Simulacral cities, of course, where the signs are on the streets, and where substance generally has been replaced by sign, in a double sense: it is not just that we see a representation of a real city, but that the 'reality' represented is itself representational in its fabric; not just that *Blade Runner* is a film, representational in the ordinary sense, and its Los Angeles a fiction, but that the 'real' experience of being in New York is often read as fictional in this way.

● And, when not 'pure' simulacra, Baudrillard's 'America' say, the *topoi* of postmodernism are, in geopolitical and representational terms, hybrid. The postmodern is produced out of the mixing of

[19]Situatedness? It is an ugly word which I began to use because it seemed to help with articulating what cannot be articulated: a sense at once of contingency and determination, of the density of an event without resorting to the banality of regarding the context merely as 'background'. It was subsequently elaborated as a – dialectical – concept by the Essex Early Modern Research Group.

the metropolitan modern with what has been called 'the modern-ism of underdevelopment'.[20] The 'charm' of this insists in the glossing of signs of immiseration, usually in significantly 'Third World' forms. If New York can be credibly spoken of as a Third World city, (it has been), equally the Los Angeles of *Blade Runner* gets its quasi-exotic postmodernity from signs of the 'other' among the ruins of the ideal modern city. The other is not 'there' but 'here'; modernity is and has been now everywhere; the postmodern is the synthetic-aesthetic overdetermination of the numinous presence of the absence of both, or the presence in one of the absence of the other and *vice versa*. The aesthetic of the postmodern is thus produced as a representational complex of 'over-development' and 'underdevelopment'.

At an academic meeting not many years ago, only too aware that it was taking place in a British colony, I asked the speaker about the political geography of postmodernism: I was invited to walk out of the conference building into the streets of Hong Kong if I wanted to 'see' the 'postmodern'...[21] Multi-national capital, presumably, and the signs of 'China'. Banks and ghosts.[22]

---

[20]For Marshall Berman's discussion of the modernism of underdevelopment see Berman 1983, pp. 173–286.

[21]The invitation was issued by an American – that is, US – academic who is committed to postmodern*ism*. Doubtless, it would be wrong to overinterpret, but perhaps the current 'theoretical' audibility of the anecdote will license the following speculation. My question was about empire, and about whether the espoused postmodernism wasn't part of at least a *representational* complex which includes senses of the provincial and the local as the identical other side of globalisation – I had in mind, contrastively, the Roman figure of the empire compared with which the US imperium apparently lacks both a capital, a Rome, and, relatively speaking, territorial possession in the empirical sense. The answer didn't convince me that in one major respect postmodernism is not simply 'America' – whether Baudrillard's simulacra or Fukuyama's sad paradise. An undertow in the discussion is inescapably the way in which some American representations of the present as the end of history (and some European representations – Lyotard? Baudrillard? – which are essentially American, or, rather, 'American') may participate, knowingly or not, in a (politically *ex post facto*, to be sure) repetition of an originary sense of US historicism, founded as it was on two kinds of break from history: revolutionary severance from Europe, and the erasure of an indigenous history up to and including genocide. The signs of invasion are often of other histories, but recently of history 'itself'.

[22]Capitalism is presumably mitigated. Until recently a hazard for motorists in Hong Kong was the fine timing with which elderly Chinese would cross the road. A speeding vehicle, even one driven by a foreign ghost apparently, was an effective way of dispersing the bad spirits which follow at the heels. On Cheung Chau island each year pyramids of bread are made for the ghosts of a band of robbers, and other Departed

It would be tempting to dialecticise, recuperate, and detect in this geopolitically narcissistic complex a progressive moment in its apparent undermining of the substance of the metropolitan. But it would be an uneven dialectic, dominated by the reactionary moment of the complacence of the erasure of the relations which secure this aesthetic by abstraction from, and immunise it against political analysis of, the processes of its production as simulacrum and style.

● Because it *is* an aesthetic, and the aestheticisation of politics, as Benjamin remembered, has its vicissitudes.[23] In, for example, the consumerisation of a certain politically depoliticised representation, of, say, the 'Sudan' or 'Ethiopia' or 'Somalia', where in part the 'reality' of the aesthetic of the postmodern is constructed. Those finally comforting television images of 'the starving' – representationally fetishised, however compassionately – which have provided, via the iconography of the ethnic, so much when mixed with first world-forms, of the visual 'feel' (if not the controlling aesthetic) of filmic postmodernism in particular. 'The other' as the end of history before it has begun, subject to the double bind of history as Western history, in form *and* substance. There are glosses and glosses. Relatively painless forms of the 'condition'. The complex re-exported, videoed, beamed back again.

● But if 'we' do indeed live in a world of 'staccato signals of constant information', is it not also one of 'lasers in the jungle somewhere'?[24] If the 'magical is optical' then isn't it so also on a seemingly 'automatic earth' in which military technology – ranged

---

Spirits, who live there. At the culmination of the festival a priest, who alone can see them, observes the ghosts through a jade monocle. When they have eaten their fill he gives a sign and anyone else may take the bread; even the intellectual tourists.

It is a peculiar but telling assumption that the postmodern can be *seen* (i.e. that it belongs *in this form* to the sphere of the aesthetic). In this respect, even though properly speaking signs cannot be sensuous-empirical, the signs of 'China' are particularly numinous. But they have a history, in the aestheticised *chinoiserie* of Western artists and collectors, of course, but perhaps as well in the trade and warfare which also stretches back at least to the *European* seventeenth century?

[23]See 'The Work of Art in the Age of Mechanical Reproduction' in Benjamin's *Illuminations*, (1973), esp. p. 244.

[24]From Paul Simon's lyric 'The Boy in the Bubble' on the arguably postmodern album *Graceland* (1986).

I am grateful to Thele Moema for clarifying just how politically ambiguous Paul Simon's 'hybrid' encounter with South African music was. But for its following hard on 'Music for Peace', and its lack of negotiation with the African National Congress

against a mass democratic movement – is the cutting edge of the postmodern: although *that* doesn't figure so prominently in the celebrations of the joyful challenges of post-historical indeterminacy? The celebration of machine intelligence and machine aesthetics might be subjected – at least momentarily – to the criticism of machine use. Even to that of the imagination of a world run, roughly, by 'a loose affiliation of millionaires and billionaires'? Why not? Why should such a 'totalisation' be *a priori* fantastic? After all, 'These are the days of miracle and wonder, this is the long distance call'.

— And if space rather than time, why not the space of – military – 'technology'? In the cartographies of the 'postmodern' another *locus* is Michael Herr's *Dispatches* (1978). In his 'Vietnam' of high speed airmobility, Herr writes, attending the multiple ironies of his title, the postmodern war, interpretable, it is said, as space – 'as we moved about the war' – rather than time (or history). There is 'the war' and there is 'back in the world'. Spatialisation.[25] Beyond the modernist theme of the futility of war (not that distant in fact from wider cultural pessimisms of modernism), the postmodern form: the war is post-futile futility: the 'loss of affect'.[26] It is not wholly innocent for that, although Herr – in another register of the consequences of the erasure of the historical – went to Vietnam for himself, listened to the language, stuck with the hermeneutic of rock and roll, and didn't presume to speak for anyone else, evading

---

and the mass democratic movement of the cultural boycott of South Africa, it might have been otherwise. The Graceland concert in Zimbabwe with, among others, Miriam Makeba and Hugh Masekela, belatedly mitigated the ambiguity somewhat.

[25]A major theme of Fredric Jameson's seminal article, 'Postmodernism, or The Cultural Logic of Late Capitalism' (Jameson 1984) is that of postmodern emphases on space: 'the conception of space that has been developed here suggests that a model of political culture appropriate to our own situation will necessarily have to raise spatial issues *as its fundamental organizing concern*' (p. 89, emphasis added). He too is struck by Herr's writing of the Vietnam War, and associates that representation, along with its imbrication in military technology, with postmodern spatialisation, figured, often, over against time. It is easy to see why: 'Airmobility, dig it, you weren't going anywhere. It made you feel safe, it made you feel Omni, but it was only a stunt, technology. Mobility was just mobility, it saved lives or took them all the time ... ' (Herr 1978, p. 19). But Jameson's reading of postmodernity may concede too much to postmodernism and its 'ends of history', both in general, and in his use of *Dispatches* in particular: key terms for Herr, after all, are *time* and information; see below, n. 27.

[26]See Jameson 1984, p. 61ff., for the 'waning of affect' which he, among others, sees as another of the principal features of postmodernity.

that other sense of representation as not an analytic problem but an imperial weapon.[27] As we have seen, there are representational discourses which produce the other as the dead, the ghosts, in which, for Herr, not even the criticism of a technology of major applied death, 'forgetting' on a massive scale, licenses participation.

And since Vietnam, not only has the technology of 'information' and 'representation' moved on, together, of course, with the military technology itself – both raised to another power of simulacral facticity and military lethality – but so have those of its apologists who are disguised as cultural 'critics'. If the smart bomb and the cruise missile have come into being, if the militarisation of the language of death has let into the world the obscene comfort of such phrases as 'the surgical strike', 'collateral damage', 'target acquisition' and 'friendly fire', with no less assiduous attention to the sanitisation of the violence of what I have called the event, has a Baudrillard given currency to the 'theory' of the 'hyperreality' which allowed him in January 1991 the hateful mystification of declaring that the war in the Persian Gulf first would not, and then had not taken place.[28] Dispatches ...

[27]'Talk about impersonating an identity, about locking into a role, about irony: I went to cover the war and the war covered me; an old story, unless of course you've never heard it. I went there behind the crude but serious belief that you had to be able to look at anything, serious because I acted on it and went, crude because I didn't know, it took the war to teach it, that you were as responsible for everything you saw as you were for everything you did. The problem was that you didn't always know what you were seeing until later, maybe years later, that a lot of it never made it in at all, it just stayed stored there in your eyes. Time and information, rock and roll, life itself, the information isn't frozen, you are' (Herr 1978, p. 22).

[28]According to Christopher Norris's *Uncritical Theory* (1992) – a sustained, timely and powerful critique of this, and other instances of what he rightly refers to as 'ludicrous theses' (p. 17) and 'sheer nonsense' (p. 15) – 'the whole campaign'. for Baudrillard, was 'a media benefit, an extension of video war games technology by other means, a hyperreal scenario (Baudrillard's phrase) where truth is defined solely in performative or rhetorical terms' (p. 13). Professor Norris is perhaps too kind when he remarks that Baudrillard, 'a cult figure on the current "postmodernist" scene', is 'the purveyor of some of the silliest ideas yet to gain a hearing' (p. 11); 'sublimely offensive' later (p. 195), is nearer the mark. We do not know how many hundreds of thousands of people were, or have yet to be, killed and maimed in this 'war that never took place' and its aftermath. Thanks to Norris we do know a great deal about the complicity between such 'postmodernism' and the ideological conditions of the possibility of the slaughter.

V

Under the general demand for slackening and for appeasement, we can hear the mutterings of the desire for a return of terror, for the realization of the fantasy to seize reality. The answer is: Let us wage a war on totality; let us be witnesses to the unpresentable; let us activate the differences and save the honor of the name.

Jean-François Lyotard, *The Postmodern Condition*

The difference, or differance, assiduously promoted by some forms of theory today, is pallid when compared either descriptively or agonistically with the difference that a Marx or a Benjamin were trying to make.[29] It pales into distracting insignificance when taken as an historical diagnosis rather than a critical tool, and when it is brought thereby into what amounts to a symbiotic contact with these relentless, postmodernist underwritings of the aestheticisation of the current effects of transnational capitalism which it is so frequently used, wittingly or not, to celebrate. This seems to me a shame, because something fundamental *is* disclosed in this elaboration of the way in which we have to think today the continual departure of meaning from itself. Shameful, and sad, that it could have been lent to an unrelieved sameness in the aestheticised celebrations of an increasing, and increasingly global (and *thus* undifferentiated), violence. As 'insubstantial' as, but less efficacious than, the staccato bursts of constant information and the lasers in the jungle somewhere which otherwise define the frontline 'experience' of today.

[29]Perhaps it would assist some critics if it were pointed out that (although cognate, of course) Derridean *différance* and currently easily fashionable *difference* are not the same thing. To take the now famous *dictum* as a case in point, in one sense of course there *is* 'nothing outside the text'. But this may be a platitude. To be sure, there is no uncultural nature which can act as the guarantee of the truth of the analysis of history. But on the other hand, if – to take one limit case – history becomes 'second nature', the problem remains. Weak (in the analytico-philosophical sense) versions of 'the text' implicitly address not the textual (cultural and historical) character of Nature, but retain the traditional (and, more importantly, traditionalist) understanding of text as – empirically – books, writing, etc., and the traditional distinction between words and things. Substituting one for the other, the world is made susceptible of *literary* criticism ... Short of some more articulate refutation of this idealism, one might as well suppose that this was not what Derrida 'had in mind'. But then to equate these 'philosophical' problems in the theory of écriture with a positive ethics or aesthetics – it's hardly a 'politics' – of *unqualified* difference, is, as I argue, dangerously if not disingenuously mistaken.

When 'poverty' becomes televisual, and otherness provides the style of the lure of consumption, difference ought, surely, to have come up against the test of the nightmare of its own neo-liberalism, or worse. The promotion of difference, and conceptual undermining, are not – and certainly not *necessarily* – the same as radical political initiatives. In the hectic *fashion* for intellectual and cultural postmodernism, far too little thought has been given to ascertaining these distinctions and thinking through their strategic implications. Or rather, it is not so much a matter of deficient or insufficient thought, but of the determined, even intended, politics of these positions and representations. And after all, only the crassest – and today, perhaps, few and decreasingly viable – tyrannies prevent difference. Oppressive societies thrive on difference, even when they are officially democratic, even radically so. Unacceptable, undemocratic regimes persistently secure entrenched, if dynamic, difference(s) – between, for example, the rich and the poor, the fed and the hungry, between those who have power of various kinds and those who have none – and these 'differences' are real and social as well as formal and aesthetic. Whatever their official ideology, most such political formations rather 'prefer', in this practical sense, a certain legitimating 'play'. And are at least untouched by the intellectuals, of the otherwise apparently ubiquitous West, granting themselves that coy privilege.[30]

It is clear that difference in and of itself will not do. Which differences? Which criteria of evaluation of differences? Which projects for the construction of difference in the future? The questions have to be asked. And answered. If there is a 'postmodern *condition*', for whom is it a condition? Who is conditioned by it, whose existence and practice – if 'humans' are still in the information stream – is conditional upon it, whose existence and practice is *it* conditional upon? *These* questions are no doubt cast in a mode which would appear to postmodernists as all too philosophically realist, and, prefaced as they are by a personal pronoun (albeit relative and interrogative) decidedly humanist in derivation. That will be, or at least appear, as it may: is it still necessary, even today, to explain *theoretical* anti-humanism? But the line of questioning remains: is there not too easily available in such discussion a willingness 'merely' to abandon the 'nineteenth-century' questions of history and totality in favour of the fragmentary,

[30] If disorientation seems to organise the postmodern, might not this loss of the East be a complicity with the globalisation of the West? So much for difference.

delirious or even ecstatic *jouissance* of the postmodern conceived as an emblem of what is culturally *avant-garde*, without paying any attention to the real power of the political manipulation (and the politics of the means of the manipulation) of representation? Will not the vertiginous move beyond the cultural authority of the modern prove only too commodious and supportive of the projects of late capital, provided that that rejection is of its metaphysics alone? And behind the back of the declaration of the advent of the ungrounded time of hybridity and difference, will not the engines of oppression continue inexorably to turn?

But nor should to oppose undifferentiated difference be to allow the charge of having accepted a position of support for sameness, for totalisation read quickly as totalitarianism. Nothing in the cultural diagnosis at work in these pages hinges on the alleged failure, or on a consignment to the political problematic of the nineteenth century, or on the assertion of the impossibility of the imagination – amid the operations of power today – of the project of social transformation. There *are*, unsurprisingly enough, implications for the forms and methods of political struggle, and in particular for the critique of various kinds of totalisation, whether the perennial debility of a social democracy that still seeks for electoral respectability a metaphysic of 'consensus' or common sense, and hands over the radical project of changing 'sense' to the political right; or the 'revolutionary' centralisations of the Leninism which will encode authoritarian teleology in the very organisational forms of the struggle or the revolution. And it is, of course, hard to think rationally the dispersal of struggle and, at the the the same time, the idea of generalised transformation. But only so, of course, because of the legacy of thinking revolution from within a totalistic conceptual framework which *always was* idealist and hubristic in respect of the complexity of social reality (which included, naturally, that metaphysic itself). Another practice altogether must be imagined in the project of the historical relinquishment of historicism in the name of the history of the new. For the postmodernists, the proper abandoning of historicism entails, when it does not mask, the jettisoning of historicity or history as such. But any such shallow and voluntaristic negligence of history will be futile as an overcoming of historicism, so long as it is conceived – as it normally is in postmodernism – merely intellectually and culturally, and merely negatively. The negative and celebratory objective of the lifting of repression or the removal of constraint remains trapped within the problematic of the historicisms of the modern. What has to be thought through is the positive and productive, and newly revolutionary, task of constructing strategies of freedom.

Postmodern cancellations of the historical frequently take the form of reinstating the subject – in the substitution of ethics for politics.[31] The *Hamlet* syndrome. I have some sympathy with the idea of a renewed ethical discourse, especially if more epistemology is the alternative. But it might be worth offsetting against that substitution a *political* ethics. The sense, like Benjamin's, that the forces of the enemy are currently formidable and strong, should be read as current, historical – and by no means minor, it should not be underestimated – difficulty. But this melancholy historicisation is decisively not an historicism. Instead it recognises the struggle for what it is, a struggle, not a teleology, a destiny or a mission (terms which are each currently talismanic in various contexts). There is no right to a chiliastic outcome, given in advance by the gods, or even determined by historical process. Certainly neither history nor historicity can be appealed to in this way. But because of this, the stance imagined by the politics of the end of historicism entails an optimistic openness to the future, and in many respects. But in one dimension in particular this perspective is inescapably urgent: that of the refusal, in the face of countervailing material force – ideological as well as physical – and even the appearance of defeat, to comply with the enemy by giving up the original project, conceived under that historicity which is marked by the diacritic of struggle, of generalised and redemptive social transformation.

[31]Whether or not it is quite accurate to group him with the postmodernists, a version of this move by the Michel Foucault of the later volumes of *The History of Sexuality* (if indeed they are volumes of the project which was begun under that name) has taken up an influential place among the figurations of postmodernity.

But ethics may not be *necessarily* subjective in the sense of subject-based, although postmodernism – paradoxically, given its other positions on the fragmented self – does not always free itself from the positivity of this assumption. Or, given that postmodern experience is actually the opposite of experience in that it tends to disorientate the subject born into the modern humanist assumptions and practices which are still the cultural and ideological dominant of the West, and to undermine in concept any notion of the stability or unity of a subject able to have experience in the first place, postmodernism tends to resist the ethical as having no foundation. This too misses at least half of the point.

Postmodernism, by contrast, *is thus* an historicism.

Gramsci's 'pessimism of the intellect, optimism of the will' is sometimes invoked. There are, of course, difficulties with the concept of 'the will', a term which may belong more to the political vocabulary of what Gramsci opposed than what he sought to see overcome; perhaps Gramsci's acute sense of the problematical and historically embedded character of language – not to mention the political centrality of the question of language – would put the silent inverted commas of irony around the word? Certainly, if the dark night of difficult language is there for Benjamin, no less was it so for Gramsci, localised only too palpably in his case by Fascism's prisons. But, the real 'pessimism', it seems to me, is not the metaphysical reflex of looking into the face of the defeat which Benjamin and Gramsci each resisted, but that of theorising the post-historical, or even (as fashionable but defeatist postmodernist 'theoretical' formulations have it), the post-political.[32]

Fashionable surrender.

VI

I can't stop myself from thinking that if the end of history is to be figured (and the dangers of culturalism are ever-present), that the complex transactions of tragedy are more acute to the present than the knowing velleities of postmodern ends of history. At least they form a richer symptomatology. Tragedy is the text that signals a reactionary continuity – the memory of the dead coded as the loss of the sovereign – but then falls into a practice of impossibility. It is a text which displaces that conservative historical substance, but the displacements then fail, as signs of the absence of the historical for which they were substituted. A secular declination caught in a network of failing voices, useless audiences, impossible hearing and necessary but inefficient narration, undercuts both the form and the substance of the nostalgic continuity the tragic formation can neither dramatise nor be. History is at once signalled and 'ends'.

But it is a peculiar 'end', of course, that takes the form of the

---

[32]At the same meeting in Hong Kong – the context remains significant – Ihab Hassan, who is credited with using the term postmodernism as early as any (although Olson, with doubtless a quite different valency, also has a claim), announced the onset of the post-political period ... He is not alone; cf. above, n. 2.

impossibility of history. Because the end in question is not that of history 'as such', but of a certain sovereign discourse still then powerful enough dominantly to code what might count as the historical, but already residual enough to need to offer to drag into its end the end of everything; or dominant *and* residual enough to figure 'survival' only in the diminished compromise of the tragic endings. And yet persisting, hardly content with that. Isn't, then, the announcement of the end of history intrinsically bound up with the question of history? In other words, is it not the sign, despite itself and unknown to the sovereign discourse, at a moment of crisis, indeed of historicity? Ineluctably so; and irremediable.

The same hermeneutic – of the perdurance of historicity in the figure of the end of history – subtends more recent and contemporary ends.

In the text of tragedy, and in this 'postmodern condition', there are analogous systems of denial. Summarily, the erasure may be described thus: the denial of historicity is the effacing of the signs of domination. They are the same. History, in the critical sense, must be consituted as *difference from domination*: at the descriptive level, as the underside of what 'is' and what we have been told, whether the official lies or, more fundamentally, the naturalised facticity of 'things as they are'; and at the political level, as the dialectical ground of the possibility of the practice of the overcoming of the fact of the present. In this sense, even the Nietzschean 'forget' is a call for historicity in that it rejects the way in which the burden of the past has been made to substitute for properly diacritical history, and has thus effectuated the latter term, in its grand forms and its historicist recensions,[33] not as the sign of change but one, as I have argued, of stasis.

In any case, a fundamental critical question always to be asked concerning the emergence of a discourse, is of what and whom does the emergence, and the emergency, serve? If early modern tragedy signals history when it dramatises the breakdown of the controllingly historicist discourses of its epoch, postmodernism signals historicity not by 'innocent' failure but by knowing rejection. 'Innocent', only in the sense, to be sure, that the overarching project in the tragic text is knowingly committed, as I have argued, to the retention of the dominant and the sovereign, and that its encounter with the resistance of the event is unbargained for and not to be laid at 'its' door; even as a

[33]Heritage; the anecdote; for examples.

textual form, the tragic formation is itself thus an uncontrolled event
rather than a governed intention. 'Knowing', to the extent that most
forms of postmodernist discourse implicitly or explicitly claim, with a
somewhat less than tragic ignorance, to have dealt with the question
of history, one way or another: it is often the form of their sophistication. But both offer or impose, ultimately, an impossible and coercive
'choice' between historical tragedy figured merely as a complex of
signs of nostalgia, and a historicity so flattened figurally,
epistemologically and politically as to cancel the question of tragedy,
and much besides. And yet I no more read the Shakespearean text
and mourn the passing of either feudal or absolutist forms of presence and domination, than I read Lyotard – or Fukuyama – and
lament as unsustainable the project of a full sociality and a full
liberation, which the one resists weakly because decrepit and the
other resists strongly because it fancies that the time of its own banal
historicism has come. To be sure, in one sense the end of history *is* a
banally familiar theme. But it is important to risk imagining the
difference between an 'end of history' which produces the stasis of
change, the one-dimensionality of postmodernism, and those figured
ends of history which have both their past and future versions, turn-
ings and orientations, imbricated in an historical diacritic of the
historicity of the present. For in another sense end-of-history has still
yet to be brought into historically actual contact with the ways in
which a Marx or a Benjamin could think the end of a certain history
as the beginning of another. Or perhaps, better, the ending of some
history as the beginning of others.[34] The agonistic – in both available
senses – of the hollowing of any present, may be hard to think, but
perhaps not so difficult to feel. But counter either to *any* historicism,
or to *any* confident – and in any case equally historicist – announce-
ments of the advent of the postmodern (they are often apocalyptic,
but not in Benjamin's way that messianic), there are, as we have seen,
both artistic and theoretical texts which inhabit in this way the register of the complexity of historical time, however violent the entail-
ment of this historicity.

---

[34]Renaissance studies today, with which this volume might seem to have begun to
be engaged, lacks much sense of what in this way might actually be, and be *actually*, at
stake. For it is finally important to get the historicisation right. It is the critical value of
alterity on the – revolutionary but then amnesiac – threshold of 'our own' determining
history which alone can legitimate the critical value of the study, and its implications

VII

If we must, then, in a special sense, remember (and forget) history, the question of which – or even what – history, remains at this stage open. As a diagnosis of the historicity of the present, is it the diacritic of that which makes a society a society and not merely a machine for domination? Or a life a life, and not just a subjection? Is it perhaps the history promised in those whose lives have largely been written out? As a turning to the future, it is indeed the tiger's leap. In contrast to the fetishised memorialisation of a dead past, it will certainly have to be a history of the present, shot through with the knowledge and the poetry of that critical part of the present which is the dangerous past. In other words the memory of the future, the history that remains always to be made.

And notwithstanding those who confuse memory with nostalgia – they are committed to the charm of the bad new days – it will have to be a historical practice, deploying – in practice – the sense which is not anecdotal but structural to both history and the possibility of thought, the sense that things have not always been like this nor need remain so. Where 'this' and 'so' are not as much particles of grammar as the diacritical sites of historical signs. The sense, in other words, that if historicity is lost, so too is the capacity to formulate (not just to desire and embrace, but also to know and shape) change.

VIII

The situation in which we who inhabit a seemingly common earth do not all do so with space, validity and pleasure, may properly be described as tragic. But not declined as an inescapable and irremediable given, an unrelievable historicism, or a mysterious condition.

---

for practice. And not just alterity of empirical substance, but also of an interpretative strategy which might have its beginnings – not origins – in a counter-reading of the founding moment of modernity. It is worth repeating the remark of Foucault's which served as an epigraph to an essay above: 'I believe that it is not to the great model of signs and language [*la langue*] that reference should be made, but to war and battle. The history which bears and determines us is war-like, not language-like. Relations of power, not relations of sense. History has no "sense", which is not to say that it is absurd or incoherent. On the contrary, it is intelligible and should be able to be analysed down to the slightest detail: but according to the intelligibility of struggles, of strategies and tactics.' (Foucault 1979, p. 33).

These are all the same howsoever the apologists of culture and criticism seek to legitimate or question them.

But what is the question? Is it this? How long will we tolerate *this*?

Bibliography

Adelman, J. (1987), '"Born of woman": fantasies of maternal power in *Macbeth*' in Marjorie Garber (ed.) *Cannibals, Witches and Divorce: Estranging the Renaissance*, selected papers from the English Institute 1985, New Series, 11, Johns Hopkins University Press, Baltimore and London, pp. 90–121.

Adorno, T. W. (1990), *Negative Dialectics*, trans. E. B. Ashton, Routledge, London.

Althusser, L. (1970), 'Marxism is not an historicism' in *Reading Capital* [1968], trans. Ben Brewster, repr. 1975, New Left Books, London, pp. 119–44.

—— (1971), 'Ideology and ideological state apparatuses' in *Lenin and Philosophy and Other Essays*, trans. Ben Brewster, New Left Books, London, pp. 121–73.

Altman, J. B. (1991), '"Vile participation": the amplification of violence in the theatre of *Henry V*', *Shakespeare Quarterly*, 42(1) (Spring), pp. 1–32.

Anderson, P. S. (1986), 'The fragile world of *Lear*' in Clifford Davidson *et al.* (eds.) *Drama in the Renaissance: Comparative and Critical Essays*, AMS Press, New York, pp. 178–91.

Andrews, M. C. (1978), '*Hamlet*: revenge and the critical mirror', *English Literary Renaissance*, 8(1) (Winter), pp. 9–23.

Arens, W. (1979), *The Man-Eating Myth: Anthropology and Anthropophagy*, Oxford University Press, Oxford.

Armstrong, N. and L. Tennenhouse (1989), *The Violence of Representation: Literature and the History of Violence*, Routledge, London.

Asp, C. (1981), '"Be bloody, strong and resolute": tragic action and sexual stereotyping in *Macbeth*', *Studies in Philology*, 78, pp. 153–69.

Axton, M. (1977), *The Queen's Two Bodies: Drama and the Elizabethan Succession*, Royal Historical Society, London.

Axton, M. and R. Williams (eds.) (1977), *English Drama: Forms and Development. Essays in Honour of Muriel Clara Bradbrook*, Cambridge University Press, Cambridge.

Barber, C. L. (1972), *Shakespeare's Festive Comedy: A Study in Dramatic Form and its Relation to Social Custom* [1959], Princeton University Press, Princeton, NJ.

Barker, F. (1984), *The Tremulous Private Body: Essays on Subjection*, Methuen, London and New York.

—— (1987), 'In the wars of Truth', *Southern Review*, 20(2) (July), pp. 111–25.

—— (1990), 'In the wars of Truth: violence, true knowledge and power in Milton and Hobbes', in Thomas Healy and Jonathan Sawday (eds.), *Literature and the English Civil War*, pp. 91–109.

—— (1991), 'Which dead? *Hamlet* and the ends of history' in Barker *et al.* (eds.), *Uses of History*, pp. 47–75.

—— (forthcoming 1994), *The Tremulous Private Body: Essays on Subjection*, 2nd. rev. edn., University of Michigan Press, Ann Arbor.

—— (forthcoming), *Breathing Simulacra: The Dream of the Artificial Man*, University of Michigan Press, Ann Arbor.

—— (forthcoming) 'Treasures of culture: *Titus Andronicus* and death by hanging' in Miller, O'Dair and Weber (eds.), *The Production of English Renaissance Culture*.

—— and Peter Hulme (1985), '"Nymphs and reapers heavily vanish": the discursive contexts of *The Tempest*' in John Drakakis (ed.), *Alternative Shakespeares*, pp. 191–205.

—— *et al.* (eds.) (1981), *1642: Literature and Power in the Seventeenth Century*, University of Essex, Colchester.

—— *et al.* (eds.) (1991), *Uses of History: Marxism, Postmodernism and the Renaissance*, Manchester University Press, Manchester and New York.

—— *et al.* (eds.) (1992), *Postmodernism and the Re-Reading of Modernity*, Manchester University Press, Manchester and New York.

Barroll, L. J. (1988), 'A new history for Shakespeare and his time', *Shakespeare Quarterly*, 39(4) (Winter), pp. 441–64.

Baudrillard, J. (1985), 'The ecstasy of communication' in H. Foster (ed.), *Postmodern Culture*, Pluto Press, London, pp. 126–34.

—— (1988), *America*, trans. Chris Turner, repr. 1989, Verso, London and New York.

Bell, D. (1960), *The End of Ideology: On the Exhaustion of Political Ideas in the Fifties*, Free Press, Glencoe, Ill.

—— (1973), *The Coming of Post-Industrial Society: A Venture in Social Forecasting*, Basic Books, New York.

—— (1976), *The Cultural Contradictions of Capitalism*, Basic Books, New York.

Bellamy, J. (1979), *The Tudor Law of Treason: An Introduction*, Routledge and Kegan Paul, London; University of Toronto Press, Toronto and Buffalo.

Belsey, C. (1979), 'The case of Hamlet's conscience', *Studies in Philology*, 79, pp. 127–48.

—— (1981), 'Tragedy, justice and the subject' in F. Barker *et al.* (eds.), *1642: Literature and Power in the Seventeenth Century*, University of Essex, Colchester, pp. 166–86.

—— (1985), *The Subject of Tragedy: Identity and Difference in Renaissance Drama*, Methuen, London and New York.

Benjamin, E. B. (1958), 'Fame, poetry and the order of history in the literature of the English Renaissance', *Studies in the Renaissance*, 6, pp. 64–84.

Benjamin, W. (1973), 'Theses on the philosophy of history' [1940], in *Illuminations*, trans. Harry Zohn, ed. and introd. Hannah Arendt, Fontana/Collins, London, pp. 255–66.

Bennet, J. Walters (1962), 'The storm within: the madness of Lear', *Shakespeare Quarterly*, 13 (2), pp. 137–56.

Bennet, R. B, (1987), 'Four stages of time: the shape of history in Shakespeare's second tetralogy', *Shakespeare Studies*, 19, pp. 61–85.

Berger, Jr., H. (1980), 'The early scenes of *Macbeth*: preface to a new interpretation', *English Literary History*, 47(1) (Spring), pp. 1–31.

—— (1982), 'Text against performance in Shakespeare: the example of *Macbeth*', *Genre*, 15, pp. 49–79.

—— (1989), 'What did the King know and when did he know it? Shakespearean discourses and psychoanalysis', *South Atlantic Quarterly*, 88(4) (Autumn), pp. 811–62.

Berman, M. (1983), *All that is Solid Melts into Air: The Experience of Modernity* [1982], Verso, London.

Biggins, D. (1975), 'Sexuality, witchcraft and violence in Macbeth', *Shakespeare Studies*, 8, pp. 255–77.

Blade Runner (1982), Dir. Ridley Scott. Prod. Michael Deeley. With Harrison Ford, Rutger Hauer and Sean Young. The Ladd Company/Warner Communications.

Blanpied, J. W. (1975), '"Unfathered heirs and loathly births of nature": bringing history to crisis in *2 Henry IV*', *English Literary Renaissance*, 5 (2) (Spring), pp. 212–31.

Bloom, A. and H. V. Jaffa (1964), *Shakespeare's Politics*, Basic Books, New York and London.

Booth, S. (1983), *King Lear, Macbeth, Indefinition and Tragedy*, Yale University Press, New Haven.

Boris, E. Zwick (1978), *Shakespeare's English Kings: The People and the Law*, Associated University Presses, New Jersey.

Bradley, A. C. (1986), *Shakespearean Tragedy: Lectures on Hamlet, Othello, King Lear, Macbeth* [1904], Macmillan, London.

Braunmuller, A. R. (1988), '*King John* and historiography', *English Literary History*, 55(2) (Summer), pp. 309–32.

Breight, C. (1990), '"Treason doth never prosper": *The Tempest* and the Discourse of Treason', *Shakespeare Quarterly*, 41(1), pp. 1–28.

Breuer, H. (1976), 'Disintegration of time in Macbeth's soliloquy "Tomorrow, tomorrow, tomorrow … "', *Modern Language Review*, 71, pp. 256–71.

Briggs, J. (1983), *This Stage-Play World: English Literature and its Background 1580–1625*, Oxford University Press, Oxford and New York.

Brown, P. (1985), '"This thing of darkness I acknowledge mine": *The Tempest* and the discourse of colonialism' in Dollimore and Sinfield (eds.) *Political Shakespeare*, pp. 48–71.

Brucher, R. T. (1981), 'Fantasies of violence: *Hamlet* and *The Revenger's Tragedy*', *Studies in English Literature*, 21, pp. 257–70.

Burckhardt, S. (1966), '*King John*: the ordering of the present time', *English Literary History*, 33(2) (Summer), pp. 133–53.

Calderwood, J. L. (1983), *To Be and Not to Be: Negation and Metadrama in Hamlet*, Columbia University Press, New York.

—— (1985), '*Macbeth*: counter-*Hamlet*', *Shakespeare Studies*, 17, pp. 103–21.

—— (1986), *If It Were Done: 'Macbeth' and Tragic Action*, University of Massachusetts Press, Amherst, MA.

—— (1986), 'Creative uncreation in *King Lear*', *Shakespeare Quarterly*, 37(1) (Spring), pp. 5-19.

Callaghan, D. (1989), *Woman and Gender in Renaissance Tragedy: A Study of King Lear, Othello, The Duchess of Malfi and The White Devil*, Harvester Wheatsheaf, Hemel Hempstead.

Camden, C. (1964), 'On Ophelia's madness', *Shakespeare Quarterly*, 15(2), pp. 247–55.

Campbell, L. B. (1951), 'Political ideas in *Macbeth* IV iii', *Shakespeare Quarterly*, 2(4) (Autumn), pp. 281–6.

Carr, S. L. and P. A. Knapp (1981), 'Seeing through *Macbeth*', *P.M.L.A.*, 96, pp. 837–47.

Carroll, W. C. (1987), '"The base shall top th'legitimate": the Bedlam beggar and the role of Edgar in *King Lear*', *Shakespeare Quarterly*, 38(4) (Winter), pp. 426–41.

Cartelli, T. (1986), 'Ideology and subversion in the Shakespearean set speech', *English Literary History*, 53(1) (Spring), pp. 1–25.

Cavell, S. (1976), 'The avoidance of love: a reading of *King Lear*' in *Must We Mean What We Say?*, Cambridge University Press, Cambridge.

Cespedes, F. V. (1980), '"We are one in fortunes": the sense of history in *Henry VIII*', *English Literary Renaissance*, 10(3) (Autumn), pp. 413–38.

Charney, M. (1969), 'The persuasiveness of violence in Elizabethan plays', *Renaissance Drama*, New Series, 2, pp. 59–70.

Clifford, J. and G. E. Marcus (eds.) (1986), *Writing Culture: The Poetics and Politics of Ethnography*, University of California Press, Berkeley and London.

Cockburn, J. S. (1972), *A History of English Assizes 1558–1714*, Cambridge University Press, Cambridge.

—— (1985), *Calendar of Assize Records: Home Circuit Indictments, Elizabeth I and James I: Introduction*, HMSO, London.

Coddon, K. S. (1989), '"Unreal mockery": unreason and the problem of spectacle in *Macbeth*', *English Literary History*, 56(3) (Autumn), pp. 485–501.

Cohen, W. (1982), '*The Merchant of Venice* and the possibilities of historical criticism', *English Literary History*, 49(4) (Winter), pp. 765–89.

—— (1987), 'Political criticism of Shakespeare' in Howard and O'Connor (eds.) *Shakespeare Reproduced*, pp. 18–46.

Coleman, D. C. (1977), *The Economy of England: 1450–1750*, Oxford University Press, Oxford and New York.

Coursen, H. R. (1982), *The Leasing Out of England: Shakespeare's Second Henriad*, University Press of America, Washington, DC.

Cox, J. D. (1989), *Shakespeare and the Dramaturgy of Power*, Princeton University Press, Princeton, NJ.

Culler, J. (1983), *On Deconstruction: Theory and Criticism after Structuralism*, Routledge and Kegan Paul, London.

Danby, J. F. (1961), *Shakespeare's Doctrine of Nature: A Study of King Lear* [1948], Faber and Faber, London.

Davidson, C. (1975), 'Death in his court: iconography in Shakespeare's tragedies', *Studies in Iconography*, 1, pp. 74–86.

Dean, L. F. (1952), '*Richard II*: the state and the image of the theatre', *P.M.L.A.*, 67, pp. 211–18.

Delany, P. (1977), '*King Lear* and the decline of feudalism', *P.M.L.A.*, 92, pp. 429–40.

DeNeef, A. Leigh (1987), 'Of dialogues and historicisms', *South Atlantic Quarterly*, 86(4) (Autumn), pp. 497–517.

Derrida, J. (1976), *Of Grammatology*, trans. and introd. Gayatri Chakravorty Spivak, Johns Hopkins University Press, Baltimore and London.

—— (1978), *Writing and Difference*, trans. and introd. Alan Bass, Routledge and Kegan Paul, London and Henley.

Dollimore, J. (1984), *Radical Tragedy: Religion, Ideology and Power in the Drama of Shakespeare and His Contemporaries*, Harvester, Brighton; University of Chicago Press, Chicago.

—— (1985), 'Introduction: Shakespeare, cultural materialism and the new historicism' in J. Dollimore and A. Sinfield (eds.), *Political Shakespeare*, pp. 2–17.

—— and A. Sinfield (1985), 'History and ideology: the instance of *Henry V*' in J. Drakakis (ed.), *Alternative Shakespeares*, pp. 206–27.

—— and A. Sinfield (1990), 'Culture and textuality: debating cultural materialism', *Textual Practice*, 4(1) (Spring), pp. 91–100.

—— and Alan Sinfield (eds.) (1985), *Political Shakespeare: New Essays in Cultural Materialism*, Manchester University Press, Manchester; Cornell University Press, Ithaca, NY.

Douglas, M. (1984), *Purity and Danger: An Analysis of the Concepts of Pollution and Taboo* [1966], ARK, London and New York.

Drakakis, J. (ed.) (1985), *Alternative Shakespeares*, Methuen, London and New York.

Eagleton, T. (1970), *Shakespeare and Society: Critical Studies in Shakespearean Drama*, Chatto and Windus, London.

—— (1986), *William Shakespeare*, Basil Blackwell, Oxford and New York.

Easlea, B. (1983), *Fathering the Unthinkable: Masculinity, Scientists and the Nuclear Arms Race*, Pluto Press, London.

Elliot, J. R. (1968), 'History and tragedy in *Richard II*', *Studies in English Literature*, 8, pp. 253–71.

Ellis, J. (1972), 'The gulling of Gloucester: credibility in the subplot of *King Lear*', *Studies in English Literature*, 12, pp. 275–89.

Emmison, F. G. (1970), *Elizabethan Life: Disorder, Mainly from the Essex Sessions and Assize Records*, Essex County Council, Chelmsford.

Erickson, P. (1985), *Patriarchal Structures in Shakespeare's Drama*, University of California Press, Berkeley, CA.

Evans, M. (1986), *Signifying Nothing: Truth's True Contents in Shakespeare's Text*, Harvester, Brighton; University of Georgia Press, Athens, GA.

Everett, B. (1977), '*Hamlet*: a time to die', *Shakespeare Survey*, 30, pp. 117–23.

Felperin, H. (1987), 'Making it "neo": the New Historicism and Renaissance literature', *Textual Practice*, 1(3) (Winter), pp. 262–77.

Ferguson, M. W. (1985), '*Hamlet*: letters and spirits' in P. Parker and G. Hartman (eds.) *Shakespeare and the Question of Theory*, pp. 292–309.

Fleissner, R. F. (1962), 'The "nothing" element in *King Lear*', *Shakespeare Quarterly*, 13(1), pp. 67–70.

Fletcher, A. and J. Stevenson (eds.) (1985), *Order and Disorder in Early Modern England*, Cambridge University Press, Cambridge.

Foakes, R. A. (1987), '*King Lear* and the displacement of *Hamlet*', *Huntingdon Library Quarterly*, 50, (3) (Summer), pp. 263–78.

Forker, C. R. (1963), 'Shakespeare's theatrical symbolism and its function in *Hamlet*', *Shakespeare Quarterly*, 14(2), pp. 215–29.

Foster, D. W. (1986), 'Macbeth's war on time', *English Literary Renaissance*, 16(2) (Spring), pp. 319–42.

Foucault, M. (1972), *The Archaeology of Knowledge* [1969], trans. A. M. Sheridan Smith, Tavistock, London.

—— (1974), *The Order of Things: An Archaeology of the Human Sciences,* Tavistock, London.

—— (1977), *Discipline and Punish: The Birth of the Prison,* trans. A. Sheridan, Allen Lane, London.

—— (1978), 'Politics and the study of discourse' [1968], *Ideology and Consciousness,* 3, 1978, pp. 7–26.

—— (1979), 'Truth and power', in M. Morris and P. Patton (eds.) *Michel Foucault: Power, Truth, Strategy,* Feral Publications, Sydney, pp. 29–48.

—— (1979a), The History of Sexuality Volume 1: An *Introduction,* trans. R. Hurley, Allen Lane, London.

Fukuyama, F. (1989), 'The end of history', *The Independent,* London, 20 and 21 September.

—— (1992), *The End of History and the Last Man,* Hamish Hamilton, London; Free Press, New York.

Garber, M. (1981), '"Remember me": memento mori figures in Shakespeare's plays', *Renaissance Drama,* New Series, 12, pp. 3–25.

—— (1987), *Shakespeare's Ghost Writers: Literature as Uncanny Causality,* Methuen, New York and London.

Geertz, C. (1973), *The Interpretation of Cultures: Selected Essays,* Basic Books, New York.

Giddings, R. (1988), 'A king and no king: monarchy and royalty as discourse in Elizabethan and Jacobean drama' in C. Bloom (ed.) *Jacobean Poetry and Prose: Rhetoric, representation and the popular imagination,* Macmillan, London, pp. 164–93.

Gilman, E. B. (1976), '*Richard II* and the perspectives of history', *Renaissance Drama,* New Series, 7, pp. 85–116.

Girard, R. (1986), 'Hamlet's dull revenge', in P. Parker and D. Quint (eds.), *Literary Theory/Renaissance Texts,* Johns Hopkins University Press, Baltimore, MD, pp. 280–302.

Goldberg, J. (1983), *James I and the Politics of Literature: Jonson, Shakespeare, Donne and Their Contemporaries,* Johns Hopkins University Press, Baltimore, MD and London.

—— (1985), 'Shakespearean inscriptions: the voicing of power' in P. Parker and G. Hartman (eds.), *Shakespeare and the Question of Theory,* Methuen, London and New York, pp. 116–137.

—— (1987), 'Speculations: *Macbeth* and source', in Jean E. Howard and M. F. O'Connor (eds.), *Shakespeare Reproduced,* pp. 242–64.

Gottschalk, P. (1974), 'Hamlet and the scanning of revenge', *Shakespeare Quarterly,* 25(2) (Summer), pp. 155–70.

Greenblatt, S. (1980), *Renaissance Self-Fashioning: From More to Shakespeare,* University of Chicago Press, Chicago and London.

—— (1982), '*King Lear* and Harsnett's "Devil Fiction"', *Genre,* 15, pp. 239–42.

—— (1983), 'Murdering peasants: status, genre and the representation of rebellion', *Representations,* 1(1), pp. 1–29.

—— (1985), 'Invisible bullets: Renaissance authority and its subversion, *Henry IV* and *Henry V*' in Dollimore and Sinfield (eds.), *Political Shakespeares,* pp. 18–47.

—— (1985a), 'Shakespeare and the exorcists' in P. Parker and G. Hartman (eds.), *Shakespeare and the Question of Theory,* pp. 163–87.

—— (1987), 'Towards a poetics of culture', *Southern Review*, 20(1) (March), pp. 3–15.

—— (1988), *Shakespearean Negotiations: The Circulation of Social Energy in Renaissance England*, University of California Press, Berkeley; Clarendon Press, Oxford.

Greenfield, T. Nelson (1954), 'The clothing motif in *King Lear*', *Shakespeare Quarterly*, 5 (3), pp. 281–96.

Greg, W. W. (1966), 'Time, place and politics in *King Lear*' in J.C. Maxwell (ed.) *Collected Papers of W. W. Greg*, Oxford University Press, Oxford.

Guj, L. (1986), '*Macbeth* and the seeds of time', *Shakespeare Studies*, 18, pp. 175–88.

Gurr, A. (1987), *Playgoing in Shakespeare's London*, Cambridge University Press, Cambridge.

Habermas, J. (1985), 'Modernity – an incomplete project' in H. Foster (ed.), *Postmodern Culture*, Pluto Press, London and Sydney.

Hall, . and A. Abbas (eds.) (1986), *Literature and Anthropology*, Hong Kong University Press, Hong Kong.

Hammersmith, J. P. (1978), '*Hamlet* and the myth of memory', *English Literary History*, 45, pp. 597–605.

Hardison, Jr., O. B. (1975), 'Myth and history in *King Lear*', *Shakespeare Quarterly*, 26 (3) (Summer), pp. 227–42.

Hawkes, T. (1985), 'Telmah' in P. Parker and G. Hartman (eds.), *Shakespeare and the Question of Theory*, pp. 310–32.

—— (1986), *That Shakespeherian Rag: Essays on a Critical Process*, Methuen, London and New York.

Healy, T. and J. Sawday (eds.) (1990), *Literature and the English Civil War*, Cambridge University Press, Cambridge.

Helgerson, R. (1977), 'What Hamlet remembers', Shakespeare Studies, 10, pp. 67–97.

Herr, M. (1978), *Dispatches* [1968–77], Picador/Pan, London.

HMSO (1990), *Population Trends: Journal of the Office of Censuses and Surveys*, 61 (Autumn), London.

Hobbes, T. (1981), *Leviathan*, ed. C.B. Macpherson, Penguin Books, Harmondsworth.

Holderness, G. (1981), 'Shakespeare's history: *Richard II*', *Literature and History*, 7, pp. 2–23.

—— (1985), *Shakespeare's History*, Gill & Macmillan, Dublin; St. Martin's Press, New York.

—— N. Potter and J. Turner (1988), *Shakespeare: The Play of History*, Macmillan, Basingstoke.

—— (ed.). (1988), *The Shakespeare Myth*, Manchester University Press, Manchester.

Hodges, D. Leigh (1981), 'Cut adrift and "cut to the brains": the anatomized world of *King Lear*', *English Literary Renaissance*, 11 (2) (Spring), pp. 194–212.

Holleran, J. V. (1989), 'Maimed funeral rites in *Hamlet*', *English Literary Renaissance*, 19 (1) (Winter), pp. 65–93.

Holstun, J. (1989), 'Ranting at the New Historicism', *English Literary Renaissance*, 19 (2) (Spring), pp.189–225.

Horwich, R. (1978), 'Integrity in *Macbeth*: the search for the "single state of man",' *Shakespeare Quarterly*, 29 (3) (Summer), pp. 365–73.

Horwitz, H. (1988), '"I can't remember": scepticism, synthetic histories, critical action', *South Atlantic Quarterly*, 87 (4) (Autumn), pp. 787–820.

Howard, J. E. (1986), 'The new historicism in Renaissance studies', *English Literary Renaissance*, 16 (1), pp. 13–43.

—— and M. F. O'Connor (eds.) (1987), *Shakespeare Reproduced: The Text in History and Ideology*, Methuen, London and New York 1987.

Hulme, P. (1986), *Colonial Encounters: Europe and the Native Caribbean 1492–1797*, Methuen, London and New York.

Ide, R. S. (1975), 'The theatre of the mind: an essay on *Macbeth*', *English Literary History*, 42, pp. 338–61.

Isenberg, A. (1951), 'Cordelia absent', *Shakespeare Quarterly*, 2 (3), pp. 185–94.

Ives, E. W. (1985), 'Shakespeare and history: divergences and agreements', *Shakespeare Survey*, 38, pp. 19–35.

Jackson, E. M. (1966), '*King Lear*: the grammar of tragedy', *Shakespeare Quarterly*, 17 (1) (Winter), pp. 25–40.

Jagendorf, Z. (1976), 'The life of memory: the experience of the past in Shakespeare's History plays', *Hebrew University Studies in Literature*, 4, pp. 138–53.

Jameson, F. (1979), 'Marxism and historicism', *New Literary History*, 11(1) (Autumn), pp. 41–73.

—— (1984), 'Postmodernism, or the cultural logic of late capitalism', *New Left Review*, 146, pp. 53–92.

Jardine, L. (1983), *Still Harping on Daughters: Women and Drama in the Age of Shakespeare*, Harvester, Brighton.

Jeaffreson, J. C. (ed.) (1972), *Middlesex County Records I: Indictments, Coroners' Inquests-Post-Mortem and Recognizances from 3 Edward VI to the End of the Reign of Queen Elizabeth*, The Greater London Council, London.

—— (ed.) (1974), *Middlesex County Records, II: Indictments, Recognizances, Coroners' Inquests-Post-Mortem, Orders and Memoranda, temp. James I [With summaries from 1549]*, The Greater London Council, London.

Johnson, J. (1967), 'The concept of the "king's two bodies" in *Hamlet*', *Shakespeare Quarterly*, 18(4) (Winter), pp. 430–4.

Joughin, J. (1991), 'Whose crisis? AIDS/plague and the subject of history' in Barker *et al.* (eds) *Uses of History*, pp. 140–52.

Kahn, C. (1986), 'The absent mother in *King Lear*' in M. W. Ferguson, M. Quilligan and N. J. Vickers (eds.), *Rewriting the Renaissance: The Discourses of Sexual Difference in Early Modern Europe*, University of Chicago Press, Chicago and London, pp. 33–49.

Kastan, D. S. (1982), *Shakespeare and the Shapes of Time*, Macmillan, London; University Press of New England, Hanover, NH.

—— (1986), 'Proud majesty made a subject: Shakespeare and the spectacle of rule', *Shakespeare Quarterly*, 37(4) (Winter), pp. 459–75.

—— (1987), '"His semblance is his mirror": *Hamlet* and the imitation of revenge', *Shakespeare Studies*, 19, pp. 111–24.

Kirsch, A. (1984), 'Macbeth's suicide', *English Literary History*, 51 (2) (Summer), pp. 269–96.

Kocher, P. H. (1954), 'Lady Macbeth and the doctor', *Shakespeare Quarterly*, 59 (4), pp. 341–50.

Lacan, J. (1982), 'Desire and the interpretation of desire in *Hamlet*' in S. Felman (ed.), *Literature and Psychoanalysis: The Question of Reading: Otherwise*, Johns Hopkins University Press, Baltimore, MD.

Legatt, A. (1988), *Shakespeare's Political Drama: The History Plays and the Roman Plays*, Routledge, London and New York.

Lever, J. W. (1971), *The Tragedy of State: A Study of Jacobean Drama*, repr. 1987, Methuen, London and New York.

Leverenz, D. (1980), 'The woman in *Hamlet*: an interpersonal view' in Murray M. Schwartz and C. Kahn (eds.), *Representing Shakespeare: New Psychoanalytic Essays*, Johns Hopkins University Press, Baltimore and London, pp. 110–28.

Linville, S. E. (1990), '"Truth is the daughter of time": formalism and realism in *Lear's* last scene', *Shakespeare Quarterly*, 41 (3) (Autumn), pp. 309–18.

Long, M. (1976), *The Unnatural Scene: A Study in Shakespearean Tragedy*, Methuen, London.

Lui, A. (1989), 'The power of formalism: the New Historicism', *English Literary History*, 56 (4) (Winter), pp. 721–72.

Lyons, B. (1977), 'The iconography of Ophelia', *English Literary History*, 44, pp. 60–74.

Lyotard, J. F. (1984), *The Postmodern Condition: A Report on Knowledge* [1979], trans. G. Bennington and B. Massumi, repr. 1986, Manchester University Press, Manchester.

Macdonald, D. J. (1978), '*Hamlet* and the mimesis of absence: a post-structuralist analysis', *Educational Theatre Journal*, 30, pp. 36–53.

Macdonald, R. R. (1984), 'Uneasy lies: language and history in Shakespeare's Lancastrian tetralogy', *Shakespeare Quarterly*, 35(1) (Spring), pp. 22–39.

Macherey, P. (1978), *A Theory of Literary Production*, trans. G. W. Routledge and Kegan Paul, London, Henley and Boston.

McLauchlan, J. (1974), 'The Prince of Denmark and Claudius's court', *Shakespeare Survey*, 27, pp. 43–57.

McLaughlin, A. L. (1972), 'The journeys in *King Lear*', *American Imago*, 29, pp. 384–99.

Maclean, H. (1960), 'Disguise in *King Lear*: Kent and Edgar', *Shakespeare Quarterly*, 11 (1), pp. 49–54.

Mack, M. (1973), *Killing the King: Three studies in Shakespeare's tragic structure*, Yale University Press, New Haven, Conn.

Manheim, M. (1969), 'The weak king history play of the early 1590s', *Renaissance Drama*, New Series, 2, pp. 71–80.

—— (1973), *The Weak King Dilemma in the Shakespearean History Play*, Syracuse University Press, Syracuse, NY.

Marcus, G. E. and M. M. J. Fischer (1986), *Anthropology as Cultural Critique: An Experimental Moment in the Human Sciences*, University of Chicago Press, Chicago and London.

Marcus, L. S. (1989), *Puzzling Shakespeare: Local Reading and Its Discontents*, University of California Press, Berkeley, CA.

Marx, K. (1970), *The Eighteenth Brumaire of Louis Bonaparte* [1851–2], in Marx, K. and F. Engels (1970), *Selected Works*, Progress Publishers, Moscow; Lawrence and Wishart, London; International Publishers, New York.

——(1973), *Grundrisse* [1857–8], trans. M. Nicolaus, Penguin/New Left Books, London.

Mazzaro, J. (1985), 'Madness and memory: Shakespeare's *Hamlet* and *King Lear*', *Comparative Drama*, 19(2) (Summer), pp. 97–116.

Meszaros, P. K. (1976), '"There is a world elsewhere": tragedy and history in *Coriolanus*', *Studies in English Literature*, 16, pp. 273–85.

Miller, A. (1985–6), '*Hamlet*, II.ii – III.iv: mirrors of revenge', *Sydney Studies in English*, 11, pp. 3–22.

Miller, D. L., S. O'Dair and H. Weber (eds.) (forthcoming), *The Production of English Renaissance Culture*, Cornell University Press, Ithaca, NY.

Milton, J. (1958), *Areopagitica*, in *Milton's Prose Writings*, introd. K.M. Burton, Dent, London, pp. 145–85.

Montrose, L. A. (1980), 'The purpose of playing: reflections on a Shakespearean anthropology', *Helios*, 7, pp. 51–74.

—— (1986), 'Renaissance literary studies and the subject of history', *English Literary Renaissance*, 16(1), pp. 5–12.

Moretti, F. (1988), 'The great eclipse: tragic form as the deconsecration of sovereignty' in *Signs Taken for Wonders: Essays in the Sociology of Literature*, trans. S. Fischer, D. Forgacs and D. Miller, rev. edn., Verso, London and New York, pp. 42–82.

Murphy, J. L. (1984), *Darkness and Devils: Exorcism and 'King Lear'*, Ohio University Press, Athens, OH.

Neill, M. (1975), 'Shakespeare's Halle of Mirrors: play, politics and psychology in *Richard III*', *Shakespeare Studies*, 8, pp. 99–129.

Newton, J. (1987), 'History as usual?: feminism and the "new historicism"', *Cultural Critique*, 9, pp. 87–121.

Nietzsche, F. (1967), *The Birth of Tragedy, or Hellenism and Pessimism* [1872], Vintage Books, New York.

—— (1983), 'On the uses and disadvantages of history for life' [1874], in *Untimely Meditations*, trans. R. J. Hollingdale, Cambridge University Press, Cambridge.

Norbrook, D. (1987), '*Macbeth* and the politics of historiography' in K. Sharpe and S. N. Zwicker (eds.) *Politics of Discourse: The Literature and History of Seventeenth-Century England*, University of California Press, Berkeley and London, pp. 78–116.

Norford, D. P. (1979), '"Very like a whale": the problem of knowledge in *Hamlet*', *English Literary History*, 46, pp. 559–76.

Norris, C. (1985), 'Post-structuralist Shakespeare: text and ideology' in J. Drakakis (ed.) *Alternative Shakespeares*, pp. 47–66.

—— (1992), *Uncritical Theory: Postmodernism, Intellectuals and the Gulf War*, Lawrence and Wishart, London.

Novy, M. (1979), 'Patriarchy, mutuality and forgiveness in *King Lear*', *Southern Humanities Review*, 13, pp. 281–92.

Ornstein, R. (1972), *A Kingdom for a Stage: The Achievement of Shakespeare's History Plays*, Harvard University Press, Cambridge, Mass.

Osborne, P. (1992), 'Modernity is a qualitative, not a chronological category: notes on the dialectics of differential historical time' in F. Barker *et al.* (eds.), *Postmodernism and the Re-Reading of Modernity*, Manchester University Press, Manchester and New York, pp. 23–45.

Parker, P. and G. Hartman (eds.) (1985), *Shakespeare and the Question of Theory*, Methuen, London and New York.

Patterson, A. (1989), '"The very age and body of the time his form and pressure": rehistoricizing Shakespeare's theatre', *New Literary History*, 20(1) (Autumn), pp. 83–104.

—— (1989), *Shakespeare and the Popular Voice*, Blackwell, Oxford.

Pechter, E. (1987), 'The New Historicism and its discontents – politicising Renaissance drama', *P.M.L.A.*, 102, pp. 292–303.

Pirie, D. (1980), 'Lear as King', *Critical Quarterly*, 22(2) (Summer), pp. 5–26.

Porter, C. (1988), 'Are we being historical yet?', *South Atlantic Quarterly*, 87 (4) (Autumn), pp. 743–86.

Prior, M. E. (1973), *The Drama of Power*, Northwestern University, Evanston, Il.

Pye, C. (1984), 'The sovereign, the theatre and the kingdome of darknesse: Hobbes and the spectacle of power', *Representations*, 8 (Fall), pp. 85–106.

—— (1988), 'The betrayal of the gaze: theatricality and power in Shakespeare's *Richard II*', *English Literary History*, 55(3) (Autumn), pp. 575–98.

—— (1990), *The Regal Phantasm: Shakespeare and the politics of spectacle*, Routledge, London and New York.

Ranald, M. L. (1977), 'The degredation of Richard II: an enquiry into the ritual backgrounds', *English Literary Renaissance*, 7 (2) (Spring), pp. 170–96.

Reese, M. M. (1961), *The Cease of Majesty: a study of Shakespeare's history plays*, Edward Arnold, London.

Ribner, I. (1953), 'Political doctrine in *Macbeth*', *Shakespeare Quarterly*, 4 (2) (Spring), pp. 202–05.

—— (1956), 'Shakespeare and legendary history: *Lear* and *Cymbeline*', *Shakespeare Quarterly*, 7 (1), pp. 47–52.

—— (1965), *The English History PLay in the Age of Shakespeare*, Methuen, London.

Richmond, H. M. (1978), *Shakespeare's Political Plays*, Random House, New York.

Rosaldo, R. (1989), *Culture and Truth: The Remaking of Social Analysis*, Beacon Press, Boston.

Rose, J. (1985), 'Sexuality in the reading of Shakespeare: *Hamlet* and *Measure for Measure*' in J. Drakakis (ed.) *Alternative Shakespeares*, Methuen, London and New York, pp. 95–118.

Rosenberg, M. (1978), *The Masks of Macbeth*, University of California Press, Berkeley, CA.

Rothwell, K. S. (1988), 'Hamlet's "glass of fashion": power, self and the Reformation' in L. H. Martin, H. Gutman and P. H. Hutton (eds.), *Technologies of the Self. A seminar with Michel Foucault*, Tavistock Publications, London, pp. 80–98.

Rozett, M.T. (1984), *The Doctrine of Election and the Emergence of Elizabethan Tragedy*, Princeton University Press, Princeton, NJ.

Ryan, K. (1989), *Shakespeare*, Harvester Wheatsheaf, Hemel Hempstead and New York.

Saccio, P. (1977), *Shakespeare's English Kings: History, chronicle, and drama*, Oxford University Press, Oxford.

Sacks, D. Harris (1988), 'Searching for "culture" in the English Renaissance', *Shakespeare Quarterly*, 39(4) (Winter), pp. 465–88.

Sahel, P. (1986), 'History in Shakespeare's tragedies, tragedy in Shakespeare's histories' in T. R. Sharma (ed.), *Essays on Shakespeare in Honour of A. A. Ansari*, Shalabh Book House, Meerut, India, pp. 58–69.

Schoenbaum, S. (1975), 'Richard II and the realities of power', *Shakespeare Survey*, 28, pp. 1–13.

Schoff, F. G. (1962), 'King Lear: moral example or tragic protagonist?', *Shakespeare Quarterly*, 13(2) (Spring), pp. 157–72.

Scott, W. O. (1986), 'Macbeth's – and our – self-equivocations', *Shakespeare Quarterly*, 37(2) (Summer), pp. 160–74.

Selden, R. (1987), '*King Lear* and true need', *Shakespeare Studies*, 19, pp. 143–69.

Shakespeare, W. (1962), *Macbeth*, ed. K. Muir, Methuen, The Arden Shakespeare, London.

—— (1968), *Titus Andronicus*, ed. J.C. Maxwell, Methuen, The Arden Shakespeare, London.

—— (1969), *The Tragedies*, ed. A. Harbage, Penguin, Complete Pelican Shakespeare, Harmondsworth.

—— (1972), *King Lear*, ed. K. Muir, Methuen, The Arden Shakespeare, London.

—— (1982), *Hamlet*, ed. H. Jenkins, Methuen, The Arden Shakespeare, London and New York.

—— (1984), *Titus Andronicus*, ed. E. M. Waith, Clarendon Press, The Oxford Shakespeare, Oxford.

Showalter, E. (1985), 'Representing Ophelia: women, madness, and the responsibilities of feminist criticism' in P. Parker and G. Hartman (eds.) *Shakespeare and the Question of Theory*, pp. 77–94.

Sibony, D. (1977), '*Hamlet*: a writing effect', *Yale French Studies*, 55–6, pp. 53–93.

Siegel, P. N. (1957), *Shakespearean Tragedy and the Elizabethan Compromise*, New York University Press, New York.

—— (1986), *Shakespeare's English and Roman History Plays: A Marxist Approach*, Fairleigh Dickinson University Press, Rutherford, NJ,; Associated University Presses, London.

Simon, P. (1986), *Graceland*. With Ladysmith Black Mombazo *et al.* Warner Bros., 925 447–4 WX52C.

Sinfield, A. (1986), '*Macbeth*: history, ideology and intellectuals', *Critical Quarterly*, 28(2) (Summer), pp. 63–77.

Skulsky, H. (1966), '*King Lear* and the meaning of chaos', *Shakespeare Quarterly*, 17 (1) (Winter), pp. 3–18.

Slights, W. W. E. (1979), 'The sacrificial crisis in *Titus Andronicus*', *University of Toronto Quarterly*, 49(1) (Autumn), pp. 18–32.

Smith, R. (1980), 'A heart cleft in twain: the dilemma of Shakespeare's Gertrude' in C. R. Swift Lenz, G. Greene and C. Thomas Neely (eds.), *The Woman's Part: Feminist*

Criticism of Shakespeare, University of Illinois Press, pp. 194–210.

Stallybrass, P. (1982), 'Macbeth and witchcraft' in J. Russell Brown (ed.), *Focus on Macbeth*, Routledge and Kegan Paul, London, pp. 189–209.

Stern, J. (1990), '*King Lear*: the transference of the Kingdom', *Shakespeare Quarterly*, 41 (3) (Autumn), pp. 299–308.

Tayler, E. W. (1990), '*King Lear* and negation', *English Literary Renaissance*, 20 (1) (Winter), pp. 17–39.

Taylor, G. (1980), 'The war in *King Lear*', *Shakespeare Studies*, 33, pp. 27–34.

Tennenhouse, L. (1986), *Power on Display: The Politics of Shakespeare's Genres*, Methuen, London and New York.

Tillyard, E. M. W. (1972), *The Elizabethan World Picture*, Penguin/Chatto and Windus, London.

Veeser, H. Aram (ed.) (1989), *The New Historicism*, Routledge, New York and London.

Waith, E. M. (1984), 'Introduction' in W. Shakespeare *Titus Andronicus*, pp. 1–69.

Wayne, D. E. (1987), 'Power, politics, and the Shakespearean text: recent criticism in England and the United States' in Howard and O'Connor (eds.) *Shakespeare Reproduced*, pp. 47–67.

Weidhorn, M. (1969), 'The relation of title and name to identity in Shakespearean tragedy', *Studies in English Literature*, 9, pp. 303–19.

Weimann, R. (1985), 'Mimesis in *Hamlet*' in P. Parker and G. Hartman (eds.), *Shakespeare and the Question of Theory*, pp. 275–91.

—— (1986), 'History and the issue of authority in representation: the Elizabethan theatre and the Reformation', *New Literary History*, 17(3) (Spring), pp. 449–76.

—— (1987), 'Towards a literary theory of ideology: mimesis, representation, authority' in J. E. Howard and M., F. O'Connor (eds) *Shakespeare Reproduced: The Text in History and Ideology*, pp. 265–72.

—— (1988), 'Shakespeare (De)canonized: conflicting uses of "authority" and "representation"', *New Literary History*, 20 (1) (Autumn), pp. 65–81.

—— (1988), 'Bifold authority in Shakespeare's theatre', *Shakespeare Quarterly*, 39 (4) (Winter), pp. 401–17.

Weisinger, H. (1955), 'The study of Shakespearean tragedy since Bradley', *Shakespeare Quarterly*, 6 (4), pp. 387–96.

Wells, R. Headlam (1985), 'The fortunes of Tillyard: twentieth-century critical debate on Shakespeare's history plays', *English Studies*, 66 (5), pp. 391–403.

—— (1986), *Shakespeare, Politics and the State*, Macmillan, London.

White, R. S. (1988), 'Lear and philosophical anarchism', *English*, 37 (159) (Autumn), pp. 181–200.

Willbern, D. (1986), 'Phantasmagoric *Macbeth*', *English Literary Renaissance*, 16(3) (Autumn), pp. 520–49.

Yates, F. (1969), *Theatre of the World*, Routledge and Kegan Paul, London.

Index

absolute, the, 83, 135, 138, 213 n.7
absolutism, 30, 65, 71, 232
actuality, 72, 76, 82, 110, 158
aesthetic, the, 23, 30, 51, 97, 98,
    100–1, 128, 163–4, 166, 168,
    200, 201 n.60, 205 n.66,
    220–3, 226–7
aestheticisation of politics, 200,
    201 n.60, 223; *see also*
    Benjamin, Walter
affect, loss of, 31, 51, 84, 101, 224
African National Congress, 223
    n.24
against the grain, 49, 65, 78, 80,
    90, 111, 204, 215
airmobility, 154, 224
Althusser, Louis, 109, 132
America, 135, 205, 221, 222 n.21
amnesia, 49–50, 80, 88, 105–6,
    212, 216 n.9, 232 n.34
ancestors, 113, 145–6, 216
anecdote, 108, 123, 152, 160–1, 198
    n.57, 211 n.3, 222 n.21, 231
    n.33
anthropic principle, 102
anthropology, 60, 85, 144, 146–52,
    152–65, 169, 179 n.34, 188,
    191, 193, 195–7, 205, 206,
    211, 213 n.7; *see also* cultural
    anthropology
anti-humanism, 127, 227; *see also*
    humanism
artificial man, 219
Assize circuits, 169–71, 175–7,
    180–4, 186 n.42, 188

Assize courts, 169–71, 173, 180–6,
    188, 202, 203 n.64
Australia and New Zealand Asso-
    ciation for Medieval and
    Renaissance Studies, 121–
    2n.
autonomy, 16, 78–9, 94, 100, 153

banishment, 8, 149
barbarism, 73, 146, 148, 150–1,
    165, 168, 190–1, 193–4,
    204–6
Barber, C. L., 152 n.6
Baudelaire, Charles, 97
Baudrillard, Jean, 221, 222 n.21,
    225
Bell, Daniel, 210 n.2
benefit of belly, 187–8
benefit of clergy, 172 n.22, 181, 187,
    188 n.47
Benjamin, Walter, 105–6, 108,
    110–13, 114, 200, 204–5,
    215–18, 220, 226, 229–30,
    232
Berman, Marshall, 222 n.20
bestiality, 19, 54, 148
Blade Runner, 219, 221–22
body, the, 7, 22, 23, 25–6, 38, 58–9,
    62, 71, 76–7, 81, 98, 101, 130,
    134, 139–40, 213; *see also*
    corporeality; incorporeality
Boon, James, 152
boundary, 60, 147–51, 161, 193
Breight, Curt, 201 n.61
Brotherston, Gordon, 116

Brotton, Jerry, x
brutality, 93, 165, 203
burial rites, 145–7, 149

Calbi, Maurizio, x, 193 n.50
cannibalism, 143, 190, 193, 194
    n.51
capitalism, 97, 99, 198 n.57, 210
    n.2, 216 n.12, 219, 221–2,
    226, 228
Cartesianism, see Descartes, René
cautious detachment, 204
censorship, 126–7, 132, 138
ceremony, 144
China, 222, 223 n.22
circulation, 124–5, 133, 141, 197,
    198 n.57, 203
city, the, 124, 148–9, 222
civility/civilisation, 148–51, 191,
    193–4, 204–6
Civil War/English revolution, 121,
    125–6, 134, 135–6, 138
classical/classicism, 61, 96–7, 133,
    166, 168, 194 n.52
clergy, see benefit of clergy
closure, 27–9, 50, 68, 70, 82–4,
    91, 115, 135, 139, 141, 213
Cockburn, J. S., 169 n.18, 170
Coleman, D. C., 177
commemoration, 39–42, 44–5, 47,
    49, 67, 91; see also mourning
commonwealth, 139–40
community, 94, 147, 149, 188 n.47
compromise/compromise forma-
    tion, 12–13, 30–1, 50, 57, 64,
    68–9, 82–5, 91, 213, 215, 231
condition/conditionality, ix, 5, 9,
    16, 24–5, 56, 79, 97–100,
    112, 144, 149, 209–10, 218–
    21, 223, 227, 233
consensus, 228
conservatism, viii, 8, 17, 30, 46–7,
    49, 51, 68, 70–1, 74, 79,

83–4, 90, 210 n.2
Constantine, Al, x
containment, 123, 141, 154, 162,
    196, 197 n.55, 200
context/contextualisation, 71, 125,
    134–5, 141, 216
continuum, the, 56, 100, 106, 112,
    217, 220
conversation, 158 n.10, 196 n.54
corporeality, 127, 130–1, 133, 145;
    see also body; incorporeality
crisis, 22, 24, 30, 32–3, 36, 38, 44,
    52, 56, 60–2, 70, 72–3, 77,
    84, 87, 90–1, 94–5, 99, 211,
    212, 214–15, 220, 231
    of representation, 22, 56, 80,
    100, 220
    see also representation
Cross, Gustav, 205 n.66
cultural anthropology, 151–2, 154,
    158, 165, 195, 197 n.55; see
    also anthropology
culturalism, ix, 22, 99, 141n., 160,
    163, 165, 196–8, 200–3, 205,
    209, 211, 230
culture, viii, 7, 23, 28, 32, 40, 76,
    144, 146–65, 182, 185, 191–3,
    196–200, 202–5, 212 n.6,
    214, 234
    high, 167 n.16, 212 n.6
    native, 196 n.54
    treasures of, 202
    see also poetics of culture; Ren-
    aissance culture

daily/everyday life, 10, 146
Danby, John, 152 n.6
dead, the, 39–41, 47, 62, 105–6,
    113, 144–5, 169, 192, 203–4,
    211 n.3, 214, 215–18, 225, 230
deconstruction, 38, 56, 80, 83, 102,
    123–5
deformation, 6, 13, 61

delirium, 95, 96, 97, 101, 113, 228
demography, 176–9
demonisation, 17, 53, 60, 63–7, 72, 76, 78, 81–2, 89, 91, 112, 124, 149
depredation, 7, 8, 16, 22, 30, 31, 38, 41, 46, 50, 52, 69–70, 72, 77, 81, 83, 88–9, 111, 212 n.6, 214
Derrida, Jacques, 125, 226 n.29
Descartes, René, 95–6, 130–1, 209, 218 n.15, 219
desire, 19, 22, 30, 55, 66, 75, 78, 88, 97, 101, 130, 136–7, 140–1
diacritic/diacritical, 105, 109–10, 114, 215, 217, 229, 231–2, 233
dialectic/dialectical, 15–16, 19, 22, 26, 31, 49–51, 64, 69, 70, 85, 103, 106–7, 109, 122, 163, 189, 211, 217, 218, 221 n.19, 223, 231
difference/*différance*, 54, 65, 86, 103, 107, 108, 112, 114, 125, 141–2, 220, 226–9, 231
dirt, 147, 193
discontinuity, 22, 40–1, 57, 63, 80, 217, 218 n.14
disidentity, 7, 15–16, 20, 23, 28, 34, 36, 44, 53–5, 57, 76, 78–80, 91, 93, 95–6
disorientation, 227 n.30, 229 n.31
displacement, 5, 9, 11–16, 19, 21, 29, 37–41, 56, 58, 75, 78–9, 85, 88, 91, 110, 114, 213, 215, 230; *see also* place
display, 184 n.40, 191–2, 195, 202–3; *see also* gaze, the; spectacle
dispossession, 5, 8, 16–17, 20–1, 23–4, 44, 78–85, 91, 214
Dollimore, Jonathan, 195 n.52
dominant, the, 11, 43, 46, 63, 64, 88–9, 94, 105, 109–12, 134, 139, 141
domination, viii, 3, 15, 29, 71, 86–7, 89, 90, 112–14, 124–5, 133, 135–8, 140–1, 197 n.56, 201 n.61, 212 n.5, 215, 231–2, 233
Douglas, Mary, 149 & n.5, 152, 193
Duvignaud, Jean, 152

emergence, 14, 17, 20–1, 24, 30, 55, 57, 68, 74, 109, 132, 138, 211, 231
emergency, state of, x, 108, 111, 204, 220, 231
Emmison, F. G., 170 n.18
enemy, the, ix, 113, 164, 201, 216–17, 229
Engels, Friedrich, 100
Englishness, 194 n.52
Enlightenment, viii, 216
epistemology, 36, 49, 53, 62, 100, 102, 113, 134, 141–2, 161–2, 196 n.53, 200–1, 202 n.63, 209, 218 n.15, 229, 232
erasure, 5, 15, 19, 21, 26, 80, 84, 100, 214, 216, 222 n.21, 223–4, 231
Essex Early Modern Research Group, x, 193 n.50, 221 n.19
ethics, 8, 64, 68, 94, 97, 226 n.29, 229
Ethiopia, 223
ethnography, 146, 149–50, 155–6, 159–60
event, the, 4, 9, 11, 13, 19, 29–31, 39, 50–3, 54, 60, 61, 70, 78, 80–2, 85–90, 108, 194 n.52, 214, 225, 231–2
exoticism, 191–2, 194, 205, 222

facticity, 51, 112, 225, 231
fascism, 66, 106, 230
Ferguson, Margaret, 202 n.63
fetishism, 146

figure/figuration, 18, 28, 52, 55, 75, 83, 106, 108–9, 114, 128–34, 138, 140, 142, 149, 162–5, 195, 200, 201, 212, 214, 218, 219–20, 229 n.31, 230–1

Ford, Henry, 97

forgetting, 48–9, 51, 78–9, 80, 86–8, 92, 104–6, 110–11, 205, 212, 214–15, 217–18, 225, 231–3; *see also* memory

formation, 3, 5, 12–13, 16, 22, 31, 33, 49, 67, 71, 75–6, 78, 82–3, 85–7, 89, 100, 108, 147, 212–13
    social, 74, 101, 213 n.7
    see also deformation; tragic formation

Foucault, Michel, 24, 110, 114, 125, 132, 137, 141, 165 n.14, 185, 197, 229 n.31, 233 n.34

Freud, Sigmund, 94, 96, 97, 113

Fukuyama, Francis, 210 n.2, 222 n.21, 232

functionalism, 196, 197 n.55

gallows, *see* scaffold

gaze, the, 48, 55–6, 100, 195, 196 n.54; *see also* display; spectacle

Geertz, Clifford, 152, 154–62, 195, 196 n.53 & n.54, 199 n.58, 200 n.59

gender/gendering, 54, 64, 81, 109, 129–31, 138; *see also* masculinity; sexuality

geometry, 137–8

ghosts, 32, 34–7, 45, 53, 75, 81, 106, 115, 214, 222 n.22, 225

globalisation, 210, 226, 227 n. 30

Goldberg, Jonathan, 152 n.7

Gramsci, Antonio, 109, 230

Greater London Council, 172 n.22

Greenblatt, Stephen, 152–4, 156–7, 159–64, 196–7, 198 n.57, 199 n.58, 200

ground/grounding, 8, 17, 24, 28, 31, 34, 46, 48, 75–6, 103, 107, 110, 126, 160–1, 195, 197, 214

Habermas, Jürgen, 220 n.17

hanging, 169–73, 176–81, 183–4, 186 n.44, 187, 189, 190, 192, 195, 201–2, 203 n.64; *see also* scaffold; benefit of belly

happiness, 93, 96, 98, 114

Hassan, Ihab, 230 n.32

haunting, 106, 112, 168, 209

Hegelianism, 107, 215

hegemony, 63, 76, 109, 201 n.61

heritage, 104, 231 n.33

Herr, Michael, 224–5

hierarchy, 18, 31, 57, 65, 77, 82–3, 122, 125, 134, 141, 183, 212 n.5

Hill, Tracey, x

historical materialism, 106, 204; *see also* materialism

historicisation, 141, 229, 232 n.34

historicism, viii–ix, 71, 73, 91–2, 102–15, 122–4, 126, 194 n.52, 204, 209n., 211, 217–18, 222 n.21, 228–30, 232, 233; *see also* New Historicism

historicity, viii–ix, 33, 39, 41, 46, 47, 51, 81, 85, 88, 91–2, 97, 100, 104, 106–7, 110–15, 122, 212 n.6, 214–15, 228–9, 231–3

historiography, 5, 9, 24, 30, 216 n.9

history, 7, 11–12, 22, 32–3, 40–1, 51, 64, 67, 76, 82, 85, 90–2, 99, 101–15, 210 n.2, 215, 217–20, 222 n.21, 223, 227–32, 233
    end of, ix, 93, 104, 109, 210–11,

212–14, 215, 217–18, 222
n.21, 223, 224 n.25, 230–2
popular, 151 n. 6
Hobbes, Thomas, 17, 121, 122, 134–
41; *see also* nature, the state
of; power
hollowing, 36, 45, 52, 62, 91, 108,
213, 214, 232
Hong Kong, 222
Howard, Jean E., 152 n.7
Hulme, Peter, 194 n.52, 201 n.61
humanism, viii, 16, 18, 21, 23, 25,
56, 79, 83, 94, 101, 219, 227,
229 n.31; *see also* anti-humanism; liberal humanism
Hutchings, Paula, x, 218 n.14

idealism, 3, 4
identity, 7–26, 34–8, 42, 50, 53–8,
61, 66, 69, 76–7, 79–82, 87,
94–6, 103, 114, 153, 198 n.57,
213, 219, 225 n.27
saving, 12, 29
see also disidentity; likeness;
place; saving; self, the; unlikeness
ideology, end of, 210
incorporeality, 21, 133; *see also*
body; corporeality
indeterminacy, 43, 141, 218 n.13,
221, 224
information, 211–13
institution, 164, 194
interim, 52, 70, 74
interpretation, 154, 156–62, 196
n.54, 198, 200, 203–4, 211
invasion, 6–7, 22, 27–30, 31–2, 46,
51, 58–9, 68, 70, 72–7, 84, 92
signs of, 59, 74, 87, 112, 222
n.21
see also land
Jameson, Fredric, 198 n.57, 215
n.9, 220 n.18

Jeaffreson, J. C., 170 n.18, 172–3
jetztzeit, 217
Joughin, John, x, 212 n.6
Justices of the Peace, 169–71, 173
n.24, 177–8, 180, 186, 188

Kantorowitz, E., 98
kingship, 18, 25–7, 52, 60, 63, 66,
90, 139; *see also* sovereignty

land, 3–7, 14–15, 17, 20–2, 29, 31–
2, 52, 61, 72–8, 87; *see also*
invasion; sovereign realm
legitimacy, 5, 17–18, 28, 29, 31–2,
38, 46, 49–50, 60, 66, 68,
73–5, 84, 87; *see also* legitimation
legitimation, 22, 30, 32, 46, 52, 56,
70, 76, 84, 86, 104, 107, 113,
124, 136, 139, 162, 202, 212
n.6, 220 n.18, 234; *see also*
legitimacy
Leninism, 228
Lévi–Strauss, Claude, 194 n.51
liberal humanism, 219; *see also* humanism; liberalism
liberalism, viii, 18, 65, 196, 210
n.2, 216, 227; *see also* humanism; liberal humanism
likeness, 9, 20, 23, 25–6, 32, 34–8,
54, 56; *see also* disidentity;
identity; unlikeness
literary criticism, 151 n.6, 156–7,
167
Long, Michael, 152 n.6
Los Angeles, 219, 221–2
Lyotard, Jean–François, 198 n.57,
209 n.1, 210 n.2, 218 n.15,
222 n.21, 232

Machiavelli, Niccolò, 18, 213 n.7
Mailer, Norman, 198 n.57
Makeba, Miriam, 224 n.24

marking/unmarking, 19–20, 46, 143–4, 149–51
martial law, 184
Marx, Karl, 97, 105–6, 109–11, 215–18, 220, 226, 232
Marxism, 105, 108–9, 213 n.7
masculinity, 42, 131; *see also* gender; sexuality
Masekela, Hugh, 224 n.24
master discourse, 21, 28, 45, 50, 57, 63, 67, 70, 78, 83, 194 n.52, 212 n.6, 213–14; *see also* meta–narratives; project, the
master-narrative, *see* meta-narrative
materialism, 20, 69, 106, 122; *see also* historical materialism
melancholy, 93, 211, 229
memory, 32–5, 38–51, 56–7, 78, 81, 85–7, 91–2, 104–7, 112, 212, 215–18, 230, 233; *see also* forgetting
messiah/messianic, 217, 232
meta–narrative/master–narrative, 50, 51, 93, 103–4, 109, 210; *see also* master discourse
metaphor, 5, 25, 31, 33, 37, 58, 71, 80, 114, 133, 155–6, 200, 204
metaphysics, 5, 7–8, 17, 26, 30, 46, 52, 58, 60, 73–5, 79, 89, 91, 101, 124, 146, 149–50, 174, 216, 228, 230
Michelis, Angelica, x
Milton, John, 121, 122, 125–35, 138–9, 141
miscegenation, 149
modernism, 63, 97, 100, 124, 220, 222, 224
modernity, viii, 17, 40, 85, 89, 94–8, 99, 132, 204, 214, 229, 233 n.34
early, 94, 99
Moema, Thele, 223 n.24
Montrose, Louis Adrian, 152 n.7

Moretti, Franco, 116, 213 n.7
mourning, 39, 46–9, 112; *see also* commemoration
Mullaney, Stephen, 152 n.7

National Interest, The, 210 n.2
nature, 6, 8, 12, 17–18, 25, 37, 131, 136, 140–1, 147, 198 n.57, 226 n.29
the state of, 135–6, 139
see also Hobbes, Thomas; wilderness
Nazism, 216
New Historicism, ix, 123–5, 152, 154–5, 158–60, 162–5, 191, 195–6, 199–201, 203, 211; *see also* historicism
New York, 221–22
Nietzsche, Friedrich, 93, 97, 101, 103, 105, 111, 215 n.9, 231
Norris, Christopher, 225 n.28
nostalgia, 12, 39, 47, 51, 58, 62, 68–70, 75–7, 81–2, 86, 89, 91, 104, 107, 108, 111, 112, 134, 200, 210 n.2, 213, 230, 232, 233

occlusion, viii, 7, 45, 49, 86, 88, 97, 111, 190–5, 202–3, 205–6
Olsen, Charles, 230 n.32
ontology, ix, 49, 53, 56, 62, 100, 161–3, 200, 203
organicism, 200
Orgel, Stephen, 152 n.7
ostentation, 190, 192
other, the/otherness, 13–14, 96, 148, 191 n.52, 194 n.52, 222–3, 225, 227
Ovid, 194 n.52
oyer and terminer, 169, 171, 183–4

paradise, 105, 113, 217, 222 n.21
parallax, ix, 51, 107, 122, 134, 142, 214

pastiche, 42, 104

pastoral, 3, 93, 98, 114

peace, 136, 140, 146

peine forte et dure, 173–4, 176–9, 190

phenomenology, 196

place, 11, 20–1, 27, 31, 63, 68, 75, 79, 213, 214; *see also* displacement; identity

play, 124–5, 141, 227

plenitude, 6–8, 12, 35, 52, 66, 75, 77, 91, 93, 97, 108, 114, 213; *see also* sovereign plenitude

poetics of culture, 204; *see also* power culture; power, poetics of

pollution, 75, 145, 149

polysemy, 82

population, *see* demography

positivity/positivism, ix, 52, 60, 75, 78, 81, 87, 106, 128, 146, 150

post–historical, 97, 230

postmodern condition, viii–ix, 98, 231; *see also* condition; postmodernism; postmodernity

postmodernism, ix, 16, 94–114, 124–5, 209–11, 212 n.5, 215, 216 n.11, 217–32; *see also* postmodern condition

postmodernity, viii, 98–101, 214, 220 n.18, 222

power, 3–6, 10, 17, 28–9, 31, 36, 39–40, 42, 47, 49–50, 63, 83–4, 86, 88–91, 114, 121, 124, 132, 160, 162–5, 185, 188, 195–203, 212–14, 233 n.34

cultural, 123, 153–4

early modern, 16, 169

Hobbesian, 136–41; *see also* Hobbes

poetics of, 124, 164–5, 201; *see also* poetics of culture; sovereign power

state, 48, 70–1, 101, 127, 184 n.40; *see also* state, the

practice, 18, 113, 159, 162–3, 184 n.40, 198 n.57, 228, 231, 233

pregnancy, *see* benefit of belly

present, the, vii, 29, 45, 51, 62–3, 76–7, 86, 93, 99–100, 103–4, 106–9, 204, 217, 220, 230–3

primitive, 140, 143–6, 149–51, 168

prison, 81, 169, 171–80, 188, 190

deaths, 173–9, 190

gaol fever (typhus), 175

project, the, 19, 24, 28–31, 38, 43, 46, 49–51, 55, 60, 62, 64–5, 68–71, 74–92, 113, 194 n.52, 214, 229, 231; *see also* master discourse; sovereign project

public/private, 39–41, 132

punishment, 140, 149, 165, 171, 179 n.34, 180, 183, 185, 187 n.44, 188 n.47, 189–90, 203 n.64

puritan, 96, 133

Rabinow, Paul, 152

Ravenscroft, Edward, 203 n.66

Reagan, Ronald, 198 n.57

real, the, 68, 71, 111, 114, 198 n.57, 202 n.63, 214

Renaissance, the, viii, 63, 94, 99, 153, 219–20

culture, 152; *see also* culture

studies, 122, 152, 194, 200, 211 n.3, 232 n.34

representation, 25, 34–8, 44, 48–57, 60, 69, 73–8, 80–2, 87, 101, 103, 137, 142, 191, 194, 212 n.5, 225

of power, 29, 47; *see also* crisis of representation

residual, the, 8, 30, 50, 54, 76–7, 82, 109, 132, 138, 231
resistance, 10–12, 78, 82–3, 106, 125, 134, 185, 188–90, 197, 212
Ricoeur, Paul, 157–8
rite/ritual, 39, 44, 144–7, 149, 163
Rome, 143–51, 168, 193, 220 n.21
Rosaldo, Renato, 196 n.53
Ryle, Gilbert, 156

sacred, the, 23, 25, 31, 51, 52, 59–60, 68, 69, 71, 73, 77, 86, 89–91, 139, 144–5, 213 n.7
sacrifice, 143, 145–6
savagery, 150–1, 168, 191, 193, 206
saving, 12–13, 19, 27, 29, 65, 72–4, 84, 212 n.6; see also identity
scaffold, 165, 189–90, 200; see also hanging
science, 130–1, 136–8, 195
self, the/selfhood, 9, 11, 13–16, 20, 22, 38, 47, 54–7, 76, 79–80, 93–8, 157, 229 n.31; see also identity
self–fashioning, 97, 153
semiosis, 26
semiotic, 155, 160
sense, 60, 65, 69, 126, 226, 233 n.34
sexuality, 17–19, 21; see also gender, masculinity
Shakespeare, 7, 18, 29, 37, 42, 45, 48, 56, 65–7, 70–1, 73, 75–80, 85–92, 139, 143n., 151, 162–4, 167 n.16, 190–1, 194–5, 197, 203, 205, 219
    as cultural formation, viii, 91, 167 n.16, 182, 192
    Hamlet, 31–57, 59–60, 69, 72, 75, 78, 84, 86–7, 89, 192, 209n., 229
    Henry V, 192
    history plays, 52, 72–4, 86
    King Lear, 3–32, 34–5, 37, 38–9, 44, 49–51, 52, 54, 57, 60, 69, 71, 72–3, 75, 78, 84, 87–8, 89, 192
    Macbeth, 51–70, 71–3, 75, 81, 84, 86–7, 89, 139
    The Tempest, 167 n.16, 201 n.61
    the Shakespearean text, 17, 22, 43, 52, 82, 90, 143n., 165, 195, 203, 205, 232
    Titus Andronicus, 143–51, 165–9, 190–5, 202–5
    tragedies, 6, 31, 35, 41, 52, 54, 61, 64, 68, 70–4, 83–8, 91–2, 194 n.52, 215; see also tragedy
Simon, Paul, 223 n.24
simulacra, 220, 222 n.21, 223, 225
situatedness, 220–1
slippage, 15, 19, 38, 43, 64, 123, 134–5, 139–41, 157, 196 n.54, 212 n.6
social democracy, 106, 228
sociology, 151 n.6, 155–6, 160–1, 176, 188, 197 n.55
Somalia, 223
South Africa, 224 n.24
sovereign, the, 6, 11, 41, 54–5, 57, 69, 74, 78, 80–2, 139–40
sovereign order, 10, 23, 46, 64
sovereign plenitude, 4–5, 38, 50, 70; see also plenitude
sovereign power, 3, 19, 23–5, 38, 41, 46, 55–6, 74, 82, 136, 138, 140, 200, 214; see also power
sovereign project, 16, 21, 27, 52, 59, 76; see also project
sovereign realm, 3–7, 10, 22, 29, 31–2, 35; see also land
sovereign representation, 23, 52
sovereignty, 7–8, 15–16, 21–36, 38–9, 46, 48–60, 63, 70–8,

81–4, 86–91, 136, 139–41, 212–14, 231; *see also* kingship
space, 4, 19, 26, 28, 224, 233
spatialisation, 224
spectacle, 24–5, 32, 48, 69, 72, 82, 100, 144, 163–6, 185 n.40, 191, 195, 200–1, 203, 206; *see also* display; gaze, the
Speed, Stephen, x
Star Chamber, 126–7, 189
state, the, 46, 121, 184 n.40, 201 n.62
state apparatuses, 201 n.62
strategy, viii–ix, 23, 77, 108, 125, 133, 134, 141, 159, 200, 205, 211, 212 n.6, 233 n.34
structure/structuration, 13, 31, 40, 46, 49–50, 71, 82, 100, 134, 138, 146–50, 161, 191, 193–4, 195 n.52, 206
subjection, 14, 23, 94, 134, 139, 233
subversion, 64, 82, 89, 123–4, 137, 141, 162, 196, 197 n.55, 200
succession, 46, 50, 52, 59, 67, 217
Sudan, 223
symbology, 17–18, 21, 23–5, 27, 29–30, 38, 50, 68, 70, 76–7, 80, 86, 215

taboo, 144, 149–50, 194 n.51
technology, 34, 94, 112, 224–5
  military, 224–5
teleology, 228–9
temporality, ix, 56, 62, 77, 93, 99, 106–10, 114, 215–16
Tennenhouse, Leonard, 163–5, 200
terror, 58, 124, 135, 141, 226
textuality, 116, 124–5, 128
theatre, 48, 83, 133, 162–4, 197, 200, 202
theatricality, 162, 164–6, 191–2, 195–7, 200–1, 203
thick description, 156–9

third world, 222
tigers, 193, 218, 233
time, 23, 36, 47, 55, 60–4, 66–9, 81, 91, 101, 105–10, 213, 216 n.11, 217–18, 219, 224, 225 n.27
torture, 174
totality/totalisation, 63, 70–1, 74, 83, 94, 100, 103, 107–8, 160, 165, 211, 224, 226–8
traces, 69, 78, 80, 83, 88, 91, 191, 195, 214
tradition, 7–8, 16, 45, 56, 73, 76–7, 83–4, 86, 89, 91–2, 104–5, 108, 148, 167 n.16, 203, 204–6, 216–17
'tradition of the oppressed, the', 105, 218 n.14, 220
  see also Benjamin, Walter
tragedy, ix, 22–3, 27, 41, 49, 50, 57, 65, 72, 78, 82, 84, 101, 106, 110–11, 115, 192, 194 n.51, 211, 212–15, 218, 220, 230–3; *see also* Shakespeare
tragic formation, 16, 29, 49, 54, 57, 62, 72, 77–8, 81, 90–2, 110, 212–15, 230, 232; *see also* formation
transformation, 15, 26, 64, 84, 90, 113, 220, 228–9
transgeneric logic, 163, 165, 200
transgression, 26, 60, 63, 66, 72, 81, 96, 126–7, 132
truth, 9–10, 42, 82, 107, 112, 122, 125–6, 128–35, 138–42
Turner, Victor, 152
unaccommodation, 15–17, 21–3
uncanny, the, 113, 168, 191–92
unlikeness, 23, 25–6, 34–8, 47, 90; *see also* identity; likeness
Vietnam, 224–5
violence, ix, 7, 10, 20, 41–2, 44, 51–3, 55–60, 62–6, 74–5, 77, 78,

85–9, 91, 110–12, 122, 126–31, 134, 138, 140–1, 148, 164–5, 167, 180, 182, 185, 189–91, 192, 194–5, 201–3, 205–6, 213, 220, 225, 226

virtual/virtual effect, viii, 83, 85

war, 5, 32, 58, 72, 74, 122, 125–6, 129, 135–6, 138–40, 142, 145, 213, 224–5, 233 n.34

Weber, Max, 155

West, the, 39–40, 94, 148, 151, 204, 219, 227

White, Jonathan, 192 n.49

wilderness, 147–8, 193

Williams, Raymond, 116

writing, 34, 55–7, 80, 85, 125, 128, 133–4, 155, 157

Wyatt, Thomas, 166 n.17